D1518327

THE PAPACY
IN THE
MODERN WORLD

The Papacy
in the
Modern World
A Political History

FRANK J. COPPA

REAKTION BOOKS

Dedicated to Father Robert Trisco, in appreciation of advice given, judicious critiques offered, and above all for his friendship over the years.

Published by
Reaktion Books Ltd
33 Great Sutton Street
London EC1V 0DX, UK

www.reaktionbooks.co.uk

First published 2014
Copyright © Frank J. Coppa 2014

Printed and bound in Great Britain
by TJ International, Padstow, Cornwall

A catalogue record for this book is available from the British Library

ISBN 978 1 78023 284 3

CONTENTS

Introduction: Harmony and Hostility between the Papacy and the Powers

Thou art Peter, and upon this rock I will build my Church, and the gates of hell shall not prevail against it. And I will give unto thee the keys of the Kingdom of Heaven: whatsoever thou shall bind on earth shall be bound also in heaven and whatsoever thou shalt loose on earth shall be loosed also in heaven.

The Petrine Doctrine, MATTHEW 16

IN EARLY NOVEMBER 2010, DURING A VISIT TO SPAIN,[1] POPE Benedict XVI (2005–13) spoke of his commitment to the theology of St Augustine, reiterating his often expressed convictions on the unity between faith and reason and the importance of both tradition and transformation in humanity's development. Recognizing the importance of both Church and state, and the contribution of each to the development of mankind, he regretted the clash between the two over the centuries and invoked the reconciliation of religion and reason, which he insisted ensured the well-being of humanity as a whole.[2]

Religion, Benedict stressed, had played an important role historically not only in Europe but also throughout much of the world. This was true for India, China and Japan in Asia; the Turco-Arabic, Muslim and Hebrew civilizations of the Middle East; the societies of sub-Saharan Africa and the cultures of the Americas, as well as the Christian civilizations in Europe and its colonies, under the leadership of the papacy, one of the world's oldest institutions. Over the centuries the Holy See has aroused intense interest along with vocal opposition both within and outside the Church.[3] From the age of the apostle Peter (*d. c.* AD 64) to that of Pope Benedict XVI, the papacy's legitimacy and performance has been defended and extolled by some, but denounced and denigrated by others. Nonetheless, developments such as Benedict XVI's unexpected resignation of the papal office at the end of February 2013 aroused the interest of friends and foes alike. Interest in the institution is not new, and has persisted during the course of its five chronological periods: the early age to 590; the medieval papacy; the Renaissance and early modern years; the modern period; and the contemporary one (1958–).[4] The present book focuses on the broad role of the papacy since the end of the eighteenth century, the reaction and response it has evoked over the years, and explores especially its relations with the modern world, marked by both confrontation and accommodation.[5]

For centuries there were those who questioned Rome's rule and challenged the nature, claims and basis of papal authority. Thus while some were grateful for the crucial role played by the Church and its leaders in the preservation – some have said salvation – of Western civilization, others were dissatisfied with the institution and those who directed it, and clamoured for change.[6] To understand the problems and promise of the modern and contemporary papacy, which includes the seventeen popes from Pius VI (1775–99) to Francis I (2013–),[7] something must be said about its long, and at times troubled past, as well as its accomplishments.

Over the centuries the papacy has confronted and survived a series of political, military, religious and ideological challenges, especially in Europe – leading some to describe it as Eurocentric. These problems were fostered by the emergence of state sovereignty and the recourse of some popes to Renaissance pleasures and less-than-pious lifestyles, which contributed to the Reformation, followed by the wars of religion. Later, the Enlightenment, which championed reason over faith, created a host of new problems for the modern papacy, from the American and French revolutions to the present. Although the papacy has a long history and important past, this cannot be explored and discussed in detail here, for it would require not one but several additional volumes – which reflects neither my interest nor my intention. On the other hand, this long papal past cannot be totally ignored, and is outlined briefly in the pages that follow.

From the first there was disagreement on the factors that contributed to the success of the Church and its leadership. There were those who attributed Christianity's rapid diffusion to outside forces, such as the Emperor Constantine's Edict of Milan (*Edictum Mediolanense*) issued AD 313, some 1,700 years ago, which proclaimed religious liberty in the empire. In the words of the historian Giovanni Vian, '[Constantine] made it possible for the Church to be what it is today.'[8] Others attribute its formation and expansion to the apostles Peter and Paul, followed by the bishops of Rome, who assumed the title of popes, asserting that they served as successors of St Peter. The latter were convinced that it was the papacy that enabled the Church to survive the collapse of the Roman Empire in the West after 476. Under the papacy's guidance, the Church was seen to serve as a bridge between classical culture and the organized administrative and political structure of the Roman Empire and the chaotic and feudal world that followed the fall of Rome. To deal with the ensuing confusion and disorder, which has been historiographically dubbed a 'dark age', the popes, who had imbibed Roman law and embraced and adopted the empire's organizational principles and practices, transcended the religious realm by assuming a wide range of educational, financial, economic, social, organizational and political responsibilities, alongside their religious role.[9]

The champions of the papacy perceived and praised its organizational expertise and cultural transmission as major factors in the development, preservation and eventual triumph of Western civilization. In fact, for many decades religious figures and secular leaders collaborated in re-establishing order in Europe, which was concretized in 962 when Pope John XII (955–64) crowned Otto I Holy Roman Emperor, which proved advantageous for both. On the other hand, support for the papacy proved far more elusive in the Eastern empire, whose political structure survived and did not need the papacy's massive intervention in civil society. Its clergy eventually rejected the Petrine Doctrine, which upheld and justified the claims of the bishops of Rome to direct the course of the universal Church. Disagreement over the papacy's proclamation of its

primacy and expanded role in Church, state and society led to dissension, and in 1054 contributed to the 'Great Schism' between the
Eastern and Western churches.

The papacy eventually faced problems not only in the East but
in the West as well, where competition between the popes and the
leaders of the reconstituted states led to conflict rather than cooperation. With the passage of time, the papal alliance with princes in
their struggle for absolute power backfired, as did the theological
justification for absolutism. Once political consolidation commenced
under monarchical leadership in the countries of the Continent, the
far-reaching educational, social and political practices and claims
put forward by the papacy were challenged and checked, along with
its unique and dominant role in the religious realm. Thus the
princes as well as the emperor rejected the *Unam sanctam* (1302) of
Boniface VIII (1294–1303), which insisted that all individuals,
including kings and other rulers, were subject to the temporal
authority of the pope. There were numerous reasons for the critique
and curtailment of temporal papal power, including the desire and
determination of political elements to establish their own churches
free from papal control or supervision. Marsilio of Padua (1270–
1303), in his *Defensor pacis* of 1324, presented the state as the sole
defender of the political order.

In turn, the charge was launched that a number of Catholic
powers sought to exploit the Curia, the College of Cardinals and
even the pope to attain control of the Church in their territory.[10]
The various rulers who championed political centralization loudly
rejected the papal contention that they were intermediaries between
God and king and cross and crown, insisting that they derived their
authority directly and solely from God. These figures therefore
refused to accept the claim that the tiara or triple crown that the
popes wore represented the authority of the pope as 'Father of
Kings', 'Ruler of the World' and 'Vicar of Christ on Earth'. They
found even more objectionable and unacceptable the contention
that the tiara represented 'papal power on earth, heaven and hell'. A
number of German principalities experienced this conflict between
pope and princes regarding their rights and responsibilities, along
with a series of religious, ideological, social and political differences

that troubled relations between Church and state in Central Europe.

While some rulers sought only autonomy from papal supervision, the more powerful aimed to choose and control the popes and relied on the cardinals they had recommended for inclusion in the College of Cardinals to prevent the selection of candidates they opposed for the office. They also called upon the French, German and Spanish cardinals to block the election of candidates they opposed, for their rulers claimed the *Jus exclusivae* or right to exclude a candidate from attaining the tiara. They were opposed by a second group of cardinals, usually named after the pope who had selected them and generally led by a papal nephew or other family member of that pope. Finally, a third group of cardinals emerged who determined to pursue an independent course and were popularly known as the Squadrone Volante, or 'Flying Squadron'. The members of this third group pledged to resist the influence and bribes of the centralized states, but also attempted to limit papal power.[11] Their task proved increasingly difficult. Problems also flowed from the Great Western Schism (1378–1417), in which three rival popes claimed the office, leading to the resignation of Gregory XII in 1415 – the last pope to resign before Benedict XVI in 2013.

In the West, the strongest opposition to papal power flowed from the development of state sovereignty and papal participation in the excesses of the Renaissance. The abuses of the 'Renaissance Papacy' contributed to the popular dissatisfaction that led to the outbreak of the Reformation in Germany in 1517. During the course of the ensuing conflict, Martin Luther – whose 95 critical theses sparked the conflict – called upon the princes of Germany to prevent the triumph of Rome. They responded positively, not primarily out of religious conviction but in order to wrest control of the Church in their states from the papacy, and out of the desire to establish churches under their sole direction. Their action contributed not only to the outbreak of the Reformation but also the critique of the Enlightenment.

The political and religious divisions that sparked the wars of the Reformation were only temporarily resolved by the provisions of the Diet of Augsburg (1555), which followed the religious conflict and gave the German rulers of even small states control of the Church within their territories. The attempt to undo this settlement contributed to the outbreak of the Thirty Years War (1618–48), which ended with the Treaty of Westphalia (1648). The terms of this agreement during the pontificate of Innocent X (1644–55) solidified and ensured the triumph of the sovereign states and their rulers, and the rejection of the over-arching claims of the trans-national papacy. The powers simply ignored Innocent's *Zelo domus Dei* (dated 1648 but published in 1650), which declared the treaty null and void. Nor did Rome's international standing improve as a result of the Peace of Utrecht (1713), which ended the War of the Spanish Succession (1701–14) for most of its combatants.

The papacy's earlier position in international affairs had to be redefined when many states were no longer Catholic, and those that were proved little inclined to follow papal directives. The setback to its international primacy was but one of the many problems that burdened the papacy in the centuries that witnessed the emergence of fully independent and sovereign states on the Continent. The new rulers even challenged the long-standing clerical role in society, education and charity – in all of which the papacy had earlier played a prominent part. Furthermore, once political unity no longer depended on religious uniformity, as it often had in the past, the need for papal support was not deemed essential. Consequently, the various powers proved far less inclined to make concessions to the Holy See in either internal political issues or international and diplomatic affairs.

The subordination of the papacy during the early modern age, wedged between the Renaissance and the modern period, was ideological as well as practical. In France, these manifestations were supported by Gallicanism, which took many forms between the fourteenth and eighteenth centuries. Royal Gallicanism consistently challenged the ultramontane assertions of Rome – which affirmed the authority of the pope over the kingdoms of the Continent – and upheld the temporalities of the Church and even the nomination of bishops in the hands of monarchs. The divisions regarding the status, rights and responsibilities of the papacy, along with the sale of indulgences and offices and the selection of a series of popes who wallowed in luxury and violated rather than observed most of the sacraments, created consternation in the Catholic camp and undermined its moral stance in international relations, giving rise to a broader range of critics.

Ecclesiastical Gallicanism in France exalted the status and rights of the bishops perceived as successors of the apostles, whose importance increased when they met in council. In fact, theological Gallicanism proclaimed that it was the councils rather than the pope who could not err in matters pertaining to faith and morals, asserting and seeking to ensure their supremacy. The movement insisted that all clerics, including popes, had to submit to the decisions of the councils. Finally, the Gallicanism of the *parlements* claimed that its courts were supreme in ecclesiastical matters and served as intermediaries between the French Church and the papacy.[12] Gallicanism also influenced the French clergy, whose Four Articles of 1682 – drafted by Jacques Bossuet, bishop of Meaux – noted that: 1) the popes, and the Church over which they preside, have dominion over things spiritual but not over things temporal and civil. Consequently, civil rulers cannot be deposed by ecclesiastical authorities; 2) the Holy See has no right to judge or reject the decrees of councils; 3) apostolic authority must be regulated in accordance with the canons established by the Holy Spirit throughout the centuries; and 4) while the pope plays a role in the resolution of questions of faith and morals, even here his decisions and determinations are subject to scrutiny and revision.

In addition to these four Gallican articles, there were more than 80 'Liberties of the Gallican Church', drawn in part from the pages of Pierre Pithou's *Les Libertés de l'église gallicane*. The most important of these reaffirmed the right of French monarchs to legislate on religious matters, established that papal legates could not enter France or bishops leave the realm without monarchical consent, and that papal bulls and letters could not be read in France without royal permission. To ensure non-interference in state matters, and preclude the use of spiritual means to achieve political ends, it was specified that royal officials could never be excommunicated for actions undertaken in the discharge of their official duties. The

Gallicanism of the crown insisted on the right of the king to nom-
inate all bishops as well as appoint those who held major benefices.[13]
In effect, Gallicanism was perceived not only as an attempt to marginalize the papacy but also an attempt to establish secular control
over the Church in France. Theological Gallicanism found support
among a segment of English Catholics as well as in the Jansenist
movement.

Within the Church, Jansenism, named after Cornelius Jansen,
the Flemish bishop of Ypres (1585–1638), brought forward ideas
and practices that clashed with traditional ones regarding free will,
predestination and the role of the papacy in the Church and society.
Like Gallicanism, this movement supported the supremacy of the
councils over the papacy. These ideas were elaborated in the three
volumes of Jansen's *Augustinus*, published posthumously in 1640.
They argued that God's redemptive love was the sole means of
salvation, expressed in the Five Propositions that were seen to focus
on grace, free will and salvation. The Inquisition condemned the
volumes in 1641, followed by a papal denunciation two years later.
More specifically, in 1653 Pope Innocent x (1644–55) condemned
the Five Propositions. Jansenism, however, survived a series of
Rome's condemnations and the repressive measures of the French
crown, both of which perceived it as a threat to their right to control
and administer the Church. The movement continued, but its
adherents preferred to call themselves 'disciples of St Augustine'
rather than 'Jansenists'.[14]

Many of these and other practices were synthesized in the book
produced by Pasquier Quesnel (1634–1719) in 1692 titled *Le
Nouveau Testament en Français, avec des réflexions morales*. Quesnel
argued that individual consciences could determine moral truths
without the intervention of priests, bishops or even the pope. He
further maintained that Jesus had not assigned supreme authority
in the Church to any one individual but to all the faithful followers
acting through representative councils. Upset by, and suspicious of,
any rival new testament, especially one that limited the role of the
papacy, Pope Clement xi (1700–1721), in his bull of 1713, *Unigenitus*,
denounced more than 100 propositions in Quesnel's work, condemning the theology of the book and the attempt to establish

secular control over the Catholic Church.[15] The Papacy, however, proved unable to eradicate Jansenist thought or prevent the formation of the Jansenist Church of the Netherlands in 1773. Jansenism also survived in Germany.

In the eighteenth century, a German version of Jansenism emerged from the writing of the auxiliary bishop of Trier, Johann Nikolaus von Hontheim (1701–1790), who published under the pseudonym Justinus Febronius. His main work, *De statu ecclesiae* . . . (*Concerning the State of the Church and the Legitimate Power of the Roman Pope*), was influenced by Jansenism, Gallicanism and Conciliarism, along with other critiques and movements of the Enlightenment. He denounced the restrictions and limitations imposed by Rome on the German bishops and invoked the restoration of their rights. He also hoped to bring about the unification of the divided Christian Churches by forging an episcopal and national Church structure, while positing that authority in the Church should be exercised only by the entire body of believers.[16]

Published in 1763, his book called for the restoration of the rights of the bishops which, he charged, the Holy See had 'usurped' over the centuries. At the same time it rejected the notion that the pope could, or should, function as an absolute monarch, since Febronius sought to facilitate the reconciliation of Protestantism with Catholicism by diminishing the power of the Holy See. Indeed, he asserted that power was entrusted by Christ to the whole body of the Church. He also rejected the notion of papal infallibility, asserting that a pope may not, on his own authority, without a council or the assent of the entire episcopate, make any decisions on matters of faith or morals. In fact, Febronius denied the pope any jurisdiction or control over the other bishops. Even in matters of discipline, he argued, the pope could not unilaterally issue any decree that would impact on the whole body of the faithful. Finally, Febronius claimed that a council, rather than the papacy, served as the final court of appeal in the Church. The chief role of the papacy, in his view, was to provide the universal Church with a centre of unity. Determined to limit papal power and authority in Germany, and conscious of the role the princes had played in defying Rome during the Reformation, he urged the princes to support his efforts

to limit the papacy further. In Catholic Austria Febronianism contributed to Josephism.

Understandably, the Febronian critique of papal practice was
not well received in Rome. Pope Clement XIII (1758–69) condemned his volume at the end of February 1764, and in May of that
year ordered the German episcopate to suppress the work. Since the
movement continued to attract disciples, in 1786 Pius VI (1775–99)
condemned the movement once again.[17] In response to the threat
such works posed, the popes resorted to denunciations and condemnations, along with various other means, to protect their rights
and those of the Church over which they presided. One of these
was the conclusion of concordats, formal agreements or mutual
contracts between the Holy See on the one hand and a state on the
other, for the broad ordering of Church–state relations.[18] Others
believed that the convocation of Church councils would strengthen
the position of the Church and its leader. In fact, both failed to do
so.[19] It was only at the earlier Council of Trent (1545–63) that the
spiritual jurisdiction of the popes over all Christians was recognized and reaffirmed, and the popes proclaimed the major authorities in matters of faith and morals. At Trent it was also decided that
the Church was a monarchy ruled by the pope as a right of apostolic
succession, rather than a community governed by councils. From
the papal perspective Trent proved to be of decisive importance.

Nonetheless, the papacy was compromised by the rational
climate of the eighteenth century, which created a host of problems
for the worldly, pleasure-seeking popes. Church leaders still found
themselves in competition with secular forces over the content and
control of education, which was increasingly seen to be a state
function rather than a religious one in the West. The *philosophes*,
encyclopaedists and other 'enlightened figures' recognized that initial hostility towards the Jews was based on religious considerations
– anti-Judaism – rather than racial considerations, later known as
anti-Semitism. They denounced the Church's failure to curb anti-
Judaism and claimed that this exposed its inability to educate.
These intellectual critics increasingly deemed the anti-Judaism that
prevailed in certain Church circles both irrational and immoral. It
was also seen to facilitate the segregation of Jews in ghettos, which

persisted. The glaring division between theory and practice regarding papal policy towards the Jews provided additional ammunition for critics of the Church and its papal leadership.[20]

The eighteenth-century Enlightenment, which championed reason over tradition, predictably proved critical of the practices of the Church and its leaders, and was supported by a number of monarchs, including Charles III of Naples and Spain (1716–1788), Leopold I, grand duke of Tuscany (1747–1792), and Józef Poniatowski of Poland (1763–1813), among others. The 'Enlightened Despots' included Catherine II, the Great, of Russia (1729–1796), Frederick II, the Great, of Prussia (1712–1786) and Joseph II of Austria (1741–1790). The spirit of the eighteenth century, one of reform and rejection of existing institutions, posed problems for the Catholic Church, which continued to wield considerable influence in society if not the state. Rulers such as Joseph II invoked a purified Catholic Christendom. On becoming co-regent of the empire with his mother Maria Theresa in 1765, this practising but far from subservient Catholic sought to reform the relationship between Church and state. Among other things, he perceived the need to curb the influence of the papacy and the Church in his state, along with the role of the Jesuits in education. He was restrained from doing so by the religious scruples of his mother. After she died in 1780, however, he became sole ruler, and immediately began his programme of 'liberating' Church, state and society, as well as education, from 'ecclesiastical bondage'. Without consulting Rome, he proclaimed religious toleration for non-Catholic Christians and subsequently provided a degree of toleration for his Jewish subjects as well.

Once more, acting on his own initiative without seeking Rome's consent, he abolished the Inquisition in his entire territory. Again acting unilaterally, forgoing even consultation with Rome's representative, he moved to dissolve the monasteries in the state, suppressing some 400 religious houses and 700 convents, and confiscating their properties. The monies obtained from the sale of their lands and buildings was used by the emperor to support the newly formed secular schools and charitable foundations, previously funded and staffed by the Church. He also issued orders that no one under the age of 24, or who had not finished his schooling, should be allowed to don the habit.[21] Pius VI protested to no avail, and early in 1783 Joseph issued a patent that eliminated the canonical role in marriage, while the concordat concluded in 1784 failed to curb Joseph's 'reformist' programme.[22]

In Tuscany, Joseph's younger brother Leopold instituted a reform programme that mirrored his own and likewise restricted the influence of the Church and the papacy in Florence. Furthermore, the powers simply ignored the papal protest against the partition of Catholic Poland in 1772 and its disappearance by 1795. Even the ruler of the Two Sicilies scorned Rome and in 1787 refused to continue to submit to the suzerainty of the pope, announcing that he would no longer send the yearly tribute of 7,000 gold pieces to the pope.[23]

Clearly, the marginalization of the papacy in internal and international affairs that prevailed during the early modern period continued during the age of the Enlightenment, since the popes from Clement XI (1700–19) to Pius VI (1775–99) were less than shining lights and were paid little heed by the princes and their 'enlightened' populations. Benedict XIV (1740–58), who sought to reach a settlement by concordat with the absolutist powers, was the least insignificant. Nonetheless, in his concordat with Spain of 1753, he was constrained to surrender almost all Church appointments to the Spanish monarchs, receiving precious little in return. The arrogance and hostility of the powers was expressed not only diplomatically but militarily as well. At the beginning of 1769 the Bourbon courts of France and Naples formed an alliance against papal Rome; subsequently the French occupied Avignon and the Venaissin, both of which were annexed by France in 1791, while the Neapolitans temporarily seized Benevento and Pontecorvo.[24]

Militarily, politically, diplomatically and ideologically assailed for centuries, the papacy clung tenaciously to its tradition of universalism, seeking to preserve its position as a supra-national organization in an age of national organization. By the end of the eighteenth century, however, this aim was more rhetorical than realistic. Only in the missionary effort was the papacy able to express its universalism, asserting in the first quarter of the seventeenth century that the administration of the foreign missions should be centralized in Rome under the direction of the Congregation for the Propagation of the Faith. Among other things, this entailed replacing the individual efforts of the different orders and eliminating the right of patronage hitherto enjoyed by Spain and Portugal. Despite the opposition of these powers, in 1640 Pope Urban VIII (1623–44) decreed that Propaganda Fide would have jurisdiction over all foreign missions, leading to another clash between the powers and Rome. Although Spain and Portugal resisted the changes, Pope Urban and a number of his successors persisted in their centralization efforts and control of the missions, insisting that the colonial powers desist from the Europeanization of the converts and calling for the training of an indigenous clergy. In its missionary efforts, Rome relied on the Society of Jesus (the Jesuits), devoted to the Papacy, both in Europe and abroad; this was one of the reasons the powers resented the order and sought to have it dissolved.

On the other hand, a number of popes pragmatically accepted the limitations imposed upon Rome and the Church by the sovereign states, and despite an occasional formal protest, seemed content to behave as Italian princes rather than as universal pastors, becoming embroiled in the alliances, diplomacy, wars and intrigues of the peninsula. They were often pressured to make concessions, such as submitting to the 'request' of the powers that the papacy cut the number of feast days and religious holidays; they did so for Spain in 1743, and for Naples, Tuscany and Austria in 1748.[25] This practice has continued to the present; in 2012 Portugal announced its intention of eliminating the feasts of Corpus Christi and the Assumption as national holidays.[26] Throughout most of the eighteenth century the powers and the *philosophes* resented the power and influence of the Jesuits, who were found in almost all the Catholic countries of Europe as well as in a number of non-Catholic states and the missionary territories. They numbered some 16,000 in 1650 and jumped to 22,000 in the next century, arousing the enmity of powerful forces in both Protestant and Catholic countries.

Papal critics especially opposed the Society of Jesus, formed by the Spanish nobleman Ignatius of Loyola (1491–1556) and six companions in 1534, and its fourth vow, which pledged the Jesuits' willingness to assume any assignment deemed necessary by the pope. Papal opponents also resented Jesuit control of education from the elementary level through to the universities; their intense missionary activity, with some 300 stations in the mid-eighteenth century; and their devotion to the papacy and determination to preserve its prerogatives. They also resented the competition that resulted from their participation in a wide variety of trading ventures. This led the powers to launch all sorts of accusations against the order – some real, others imaginary – and to call constantly for its dissolution. As soon as Clement xiv (1769–74) ascended the papal throne, Spain, Portugal, Naples and most notably France pressed him to dissolve the order. The new pope initially hesitated, finding various excuses for not complying with their 'request'. By 1773 the powers had run out of patience and the pope out of pretexts. Clement xiv felt constrained to suppress the Society of Jesus and did so by his brief *Dominus ac Redemptor*. Paradoxically, the order was dissolved in most countries on the Continent except non-Catholic Russia and Prussia, where Catherine ii and Frederick ii regarded the Jesuit schools as essential.[27]

Giovanni Angelo Braschi, who was elected pope in 1775 after a protracted conclave of some four months, due to the intrigues, interventions and contrasting interests of the powers, had to endure outside pressure from the start of his pontificate. Ascending the papal throne shortly after the Catholic powers of France, Portugal and Spain had constrained his predecessor to suppress the Jesuits, the new pope recognized the need to achieve some form of reconciliation with the states that were making additional demands. Although ambitious, handsome, aristocratic, diplomatically adroit, and vain, Pius vi proved unequal to the task, for the national rulers were unwilling to make any concession or take any step which would weaken their control over religion or the Church in their state.

Frustrated, the new pope pragmatically determined to shift his focus to developments within his own state, where he continued to exercise greater control. Adopting the attitude of an Italian prince, he enjoyed the prerogatives of power and shared the benefits – some said spoils – of his office with not only his nephews, but also

with other family members and friends. Responding to the impositions of the powers and their efforts to liberate themselves from
papal constraints, Pius chose to emphasize and enjoy his role as
ruler of the Papal States and focused much of his time and attention
on Rome.

Taking his name in honour of the saintly Pius V (1566–72),
the Braschi pope proved less than saintly during the first years of
his pontificate. His sumptuous lifestyle, ambitious construction
projects – such as the reconstruction of the Appian Way – and
generous gifts to family and friends bankrupted the papal treasury
and required increased taxation, which was resented by all classes
in the Papal States. Some complained that, rather than opposing
the irresponsible behaviour of the absolutist rulers, his conduct at
home tended to follow in their footsteps.

Pius VI's narrow vision, with its emphasis on the Papal States,
led him to virtually ignore the fighting at Lexington and Concord
the year he donned the tiara, and in part accounts for his scant
attention to the American Declaration of Independence in July
1776. Despite the recourse of the colonists' revolutionary leaders to
abstract principles and Enlightenment philosophy to justify their
actions, the new pope expressed no concern about the possible
consequences of the American Revolution for his state and
authority. He did not believe transatlantic events would, or could,
inspire revolution in the old world or fear that developments across
the Atlantic would stimulate nationalist sentiment in the Italian
peninsula to the detriment of his temporal power. He was mistaken,
and underestimated the power of ideas.

In fact, the events that erupted in the New World in the 1770s
clearly had European ramifications.[28] Opponents of the traditional European economic, social, political and religious order
were inspired by American developments, which they believed
were rooted in the Enlightenment.[29] Luigi Castiglioni, in his *Travels
in the United States of North America*, judged the American Revolution as 'one of the most memorable events of the century' and predicted it would have crucial consequences for Europe and the
world.[30] By and large, the Roman establishment responsible for
foreign affairs, including the Curia, the Secretariat of State and the

pope, did not agree. For them, events at home remained the over-riding priority. Nonetheless, Castiglioni's words and analysis proved prophetic.

Pope Pius VI shared neither the 'romantic optimism' of European reformers nor the trepidation of traditionalists in his assessment of transatlantic developments. Instead, he assumed the pragmatic position of assessing how American developments might benefit the Papal States. Increase in trade was one prospect, and this motivated the papacy to commence commercial relations with the newly formed American regime. It did so as early as 1784, following the Treaty of Paris, which confirmed the independence of the United States. Soon thereafter Pius appointed John Carroll provi-sional apostolic delegate to the newly formed republic, and in 1789 named him Bishop of Baltimore. In turn, the Americans commis-sioned the Italian Giovanni Sartori, the first of eleven consuls, to represent American interests in Rome. While Pius vehemently opposed the separation of Church and state at home, he did not protest or oppose the American adoption of separatism. America was an ocean apart, and largely Protestant, so its recourse to sep-aratism might prove a blessing more than a burden for its small Catholic minority. The separatism that he tolerated in an over-whelmingly Protestant state, however, was totally unacceptable in Catholic Italy, the seat of the papacy and the centre of Roman Catholicism.[31]

Dismissing and disregarding the warnings of those who feared for the future, the last pope of the eighteenth century did not realize, or simply refused to recognize, that Europe was on the verge of a revolutionary upheaval for which neither he nor the Curia was prepared. Not particularly interested in, or knowledgeable of, the intellectual climate of the age, nor the threat the Enlightenment posed for the social, political and religious establishments, for many years he continued to function like a worldly prince rather than a pious priest, seemingly oblivious to the dangers the new order pre-sented for the spiritual and temporal power of the papacy or its challenge to the Curia. Critics charged that Papa Braschi looked to the past, ignored the present and, as events soon proved, was not prepared to face the future. This position proved unfortunate, as did his failure to recognize and respond to the danger to Europe, Italy and Rome that would flow from developments in nearby France.

Despite the barrage of complaints and threats hurled against the papacy for years, and the criticism launched against the pontificate of Pius VI in particular, at the start of the nineteenth century the Church still occupied an important place in the social lives of many, if not most, Europeans. While the intellectuals and *philosophes* of the Enlightened classes proved unrelenting in their critique of the institution, and the rulers of many sovereign states sought to replace the Church's role in education and charity, for the bulk of the population, the Church remained a central part of daily life.[32] Steeped in this traditionalist environment, Pope Pius VI did not feel the winds of change. He was convinced that the Church would continue to play a central and crucial role in the lives of individuals from cradle to grave. His confidence stemmed from the fact that its liturgy was incorporated into the lives of the population, who accepted the Seven Sacraments from Baptism to Extreme Unction, went to confession, and received Communion at least once a year at Easter. This was acknowledged by the *philosophes*, who despite their call for change were convinced that a state could not exist without religion, and in large parts of Europe that meant Roman Catholicism.[33] They, however, rejected its traditionalism and invoked its transformation.

Unwilling to spend much time reading the critiques of the *philosophes*, Pius VI was unaware of the depth and bitterness of their criticism, the following they enjoyed among the educated middle classes in western Europe, particularly France, and the potential threat they posed to the aristocratic order that dominated both Church and state. His failure to accurately assess the depth and breadth of the dissatisfaction would have repercussions for the faith, the Church and the papacy. The danger multiplied following the outbreak of the French Revolution, for which neither the pope nor the Curia was prepared. Ideological considerations, class considerations in both Church and state, and the lack of availability of sources long rendered difficult an objective analysis of papal policy in the modern age opened by the Revolution.

When I began my study of the modern and contemporary papacy more than three decades ago, the *Bullarii romani continuatio* (*BullRomCon*), which published papal bulls and other important papal letters and documents in chronological order, proved useful – but only for the 22 years from 1835 to 1857. Furthermore, the central depository for the papers and correspondence of the Holy See, the Archivio Segreto Vaticano, conceived by Pius IV (1559–65) and established by Pope Paul V (1605–21) in 1612, was opened by Leo XIII (1878–1903) only in 1880. Access, however, to many of the papers therein was limited.[34]

Only in 1967 were the papers of the long pontificate of Pope Pius IX (1846–78) made available to scholars. The opening of this important archive made possible my biography of Pope Pius IX and my book on his secretary of state, Cardinal Giacomo Antonelli. The subsequent opening of this crucial source through the pontificate of Pius XI (1922–39) shed further light on the modern papacy, as did the selective opening and publication of the papers of Pius XII (1939–58).

Additional useful information has been provided by the *Acta Sanctae Sedis* (ASS) or the Compendium of Documents Produced by the Holy See from 1865 to 1908, followed and superseded by the publication of the *Acta Apostolicae Sedis* (AAS) or Acts of the Apostolic See from 1909 to the present. Sister Claudia Carlen has edited and published in five volumes *The Papal Encyclicals 1740 to 1981* (1981) and two volumes of *Papal Pronouncements* covering 1740 to 1978 (1990), both useful for an understanding of the modern papacy, as is *La Civiltà Cattolica*, the semi-official journal of the Vatican under the direction of the Society of Jesus. Equally helpful for understanding the papacy's stance on modern developments is *L'Osservatore Romano*, the daily newspaper of the Holy See founded by Pius XII's paternal grandfather Marcantonio Pacelli in 1861. The publication of many of the papers of John XXIII, who convoked the Second Vatican Council, and some of Paul VI, who bought it to completion, along with those of John Paul II, also provide important insights, as do the memoirs of their contemporaries.

The availability of a wide variety of sources allows the present book to probe the impact of more than 230 years of papal history

that includes seventeen popes from Pius VI (1775–99) to Francis I.
In doing so, it explores the development and transformation of the
papacy not only in the religious realm, but also in the political and
diplomatic world, as well as the social arena. It also examines the
papal response to the American and French revolutions, the ideologies of liberalism, nationalism, socialism and communism, along
with its recourse to impartiality during two world wars, its 'silence'
during the Holocaust and its active role during the Cold War.
Finally, it traces the loss of the temporal power in the decade from
1860 to 1870, which contributed to the transformation of the pope
from Italian prince to transnational religious leader. Some believe
that this is reflected in the fact that after more than 400 years of
Italian popes,[35] since 1978 there have been three non-Italian popes
in a row!

I

Revolution Turns the Papal World Upside Down

> The French Revolution was a great dividing-line in the political
> history of Europe, the sign of the downfall of the *ancien
> regime*, a sort of atomic bomb of which the fallout is still at work. It
> was a beginning as well as an end, the beginning of a still con-
> tinuing series of attempts to build new structures to take the place
> of the system that had collapsed.
> Alec R. Vidler, *The Church in an Age of Revolution* (1961)

THE CLASH IN FRANCE BETWEEN THE FRUSTRATED MIDDLE
classes and the intransigent aristocracy exploded in revolution in
1789. Initially, few appreciated the gravity of the situation for
France and the rest of Europe. This was true of Giovanni Angelo
Braschi, elected pope as Pius VI in 1775. He continued to live the
dolce vita in Rome, and initially did not understand, much less
confront, the political, social, economic, ideological and religious
earthquake unleashed by events in France. This explains why this
pope was no more disturbed by the news of the outbreak of revolution in France in 1789 than he had been by the eruption of the
earlier American uprising. To be sure, the French revolt was closer
to home, but both pontiff and Curia believed that the French were
chiefly concerned with domestic economic and political issues, and
represented no threat to those outside their realm.

As revolution erupted, Pius remained calm. He was convinced
that 'only a better organization of the political economy seemed to
be in question'.[1] Rome's clerical establishment shared the pope's
assessment. Indeed, they both believed that the disturbances in

Paris might prove beneficial for the Holy See because the harassed monarchy, seeking support and allies abroad, might be persuaded to end its Gallican campaign to restrict papal control of the Church in France.

This assessment of the disturbances in France was based on reports reaching Rome that domestic discontent was fuelled by the ostentatious lifestyle of the royal family and the wars of Louis XII, continued by his successors. To make matters worse, the bourgeoisie who bore the brunt of the cost of this fiscal extravagance, were politically and socially overshadowed by the first two Estates: the clergy and the nobility. The middle classes, who felt neglected and abused, were outraged by the prospect of additional taxes being thrust upon them.

France was rich but the government was poor, because the aristocracy fought to preserve its privileged tax position, and determined not to assume any further financial commitment. The ongoing fiscal crisis led Louis XVI in August 1788 to agree to convoke the Estates-General, which opened at Versailles on 5 May 1789. Prior to its opening, the aristocracy, supported by some members of the upper clergy, provoked a crisis by insisting that the Estates-General resume the form it had taken when it last met, in 1614 – more than 170 years earlier! This meant that the Estates would meet separately; each would exercise one vote, so that the upper clergy and aristocracy would be in a position to veto all the proposals advanced by the Third Estate. Immediately, the conflict over the nature of representation led to dissension, arousing the middle classes who resented and resisted their continued fiscal, social and political subordination.

The aristocratic faction's refusal to remedy the financial crisis by assuming their fair share of the tax burden unwittingly provided the middle classes with an opportunity to challenge the historical but increasingly unrealistic claims of the nobility. This was appreciated by the lower French clergy, who were subject to the upper clergy, and had a catalogue of their own complaints. From the first, therefore, the parish clergy proved more prone to sanction change and reform than the upper clergy, who identified with the aristocracy, from which they were drawn.

The insistence of the privileged classes on meeting and voting separately provoked an outburst of criticism, even after it was proposed that the dissatisfied Third Estate would be accorded double the membership of the first two bodies. The exasperated members of the Third Estate quickly deemed this 'compromise' absolutely unacceptable, for this would still leave them with one vote against the two wielded by the clergy and aristocracy. In June 1789 this led the Third Estate, with the support of part of the lower clergy, to proclaim itself the National Assembly, and after rumour spread that the military planned to shut it down, in mid-July the Parisians stormed the Bastille prison and the peasantry in the countryside went on a rampage. These actions in both capital and countryside precipitated the collapse of the royalist, aristocratic regime.[2] Thus the festering economic and political grievances of the middle classes and the peasantry's resentment of subservience and servitude worked in tandem to provoke a revolution of far-reaching consequences that would eventually transcend France. It would impact most aspects of life and institutions in France and western Europe – and the Catholic Church was not immune from the turmoil and transformation.

Even though the National Assembly and the Constituent Assembly that followed targeted royal absolutism and aristocratic dispensation, the Church, which enjoyed a privileged position in state and society, was bound to be affected. It was quickly constrained to relinquish its exemption from taxation and forced to witness the supervision of education transferred to the state. The Assembly's assertion 'that all men had a right' – in Catholic France – 'to think as they chose in matters of religion and express their opinions on the subject'[3] was denounced by Pius VI as 'indifferentism'. He also resented the Assembly's unilateral abrogation of the concordat of 1516, which for centuries had governed Church–state relations and guaranteed certain ecclesiastical rights.[4] The pope and Curia were further troubled by reports that the Assembly planned additional steps to regulate the Church and clergy. The Holy See regarded these 'reforms' as 'harassment'.

This 'persecution' of the Church led Catholics in France and Italy to look to the pope for legal and moral leadership to counter what they perceived as the anti-clericalism of the revolutionary regime. Pius hesitated in assuming opposition to the Assembly, fearing that it might make matters worse for the Church and its clergy. These and similar concerns were taken to explain the pope's early 'silence'. Some pointed to his advanced age as he approached seventy-three. Others were afraid that open opposition would lead the French to seize the papal territory of Avignon, while still others feared that public confrontation might provoke the French to undertake more punitive action against the Faith – and prove more of a burden than a blessing. The fact that the Catholic population of France was then the largest in the world, accounting for some one-third of the faithful, contributed to papal reluctance to antagonize their government.

There were those in Rome who initially discounted and disregarded the 'supposed' anti-Catholic bias of the National Assembly, noting that a majority of its members were Catholic, and one-fourth of these were priests – even though many were tinged with Gallicanism. In fact, on 4 May 1789, the day before the opening of the Assembly, a Mass of the Holy Spirit was celebrated with the intention that it would enlighten its deliberations.[5] This led some to assume that the body wished to reform and retain the Church rather than reject and replace it. This assessment was questioned and challenged when the Assembly sanctioned the seizure and sale of Church lands in 1789, and took a series of steps to outlaw the religious orders. Conservatives concluded that this was done to weaken the faith, the Church and its clergy, convinced that the confiscation of property was ideologically driven and part of a plot to undermine Catholicism in France.[6]

In fact, the seizure of land, supported by 568 members of the Assembly, was motivated first and foremost by fiscal rather than ideological considerations.[7] Nonetheless, it had far-reaching consequences, for without the land and other properties the clergy found it difficult to support the Church. This led the provisional government to intervene and pledge to pay the salaries of clerics. In doing so, however, it increasingly thought of the priests it supported as its employees, and treated them as such, and with a Gallican mentality believed that the state had the right to reorganize the Church. In Austria, Klemens von Metternich almost immediately understood the danger that this and other French developments posed for all of Europe.[8] By mid-September 1789, Pope Pius VI had fully recognized the danger confronting the Church in France and dispatched a confidential letter to Louis XVI, invoking his protection. The king, more pious than his two predecessors, esteemed the pope and sympathized with his plight, but his own freedom of action had been severely curtailed by the Assembly. It was questionable whether he could protect himself, let alone the papacy and the Church. At the end of March 1790, Pius VI finally condemned state intervention in the affairs and organization of the Church, but his condemnation was not made public and did little to restrain the Assembly's ambitious ecclesiastical 'reformism'.

In April 1790, the task of proposing change for the Church and clergy was assigned to a committee of the Assembly, presided over by a bishop. The episcopal minority of nine members resigned from the committee when they learned of the anti-clerical intentions of the majority, and were quickly replaced by fifteen new members who proved to be more amenable to the majority's outlook and proposals.[9] The Committee's subsequent report, presented to the body as a whole, was debated, amended and approved in July 1790. Towards the end of August the king signed the law and took the oath of allegiance.[10] Without papal input or consultation, this measure reduced the number of French bishops and archbishops, and ruled that parish priests were to be elected by all the residents of the parish – Catholic and non-Catholic alike. The higher clergy were also to be elected, and Rome was to have no role in their selection or dismissal. While it is true that the resulting Civil Constitution of the Clergy dealt exclusively with ecclesiastical organization and discipline and did not address dogma, it annoyed Pius VI. He was angered by the seizure of lands and the dissolution of religious orders not involved in education or the dispensation of charity, as well as the slamming shut of most monasteries in France.[11]

Pius also resented the fact that he was neither consulted nor advised during the drafting of the Civil Constitution of the Clergy. Among other things, he opposed the Gallican provision that stipulated that the papacy would no longer exercise authority over the Church in France. The French bishops shared his concern and opposed the Civil Constitution of the Clergy, finding it 'odious', 'intrusive' and 'unacceptable'. In October 1790 all the bishops in the National Assembly – save two – signed a petition expressing their vehement opposition to the provisions of the Civil Constitution and seeking its modification or withdrawal. Their complaints were ignored. At the end of November and in December 1790, 127 bishops resigned rather than having to accept the Civil Constitution.[12] Only five bishops and archbishops accorded their approval. The dissenting majority once again invoked the pope's assistance to help thwart additional measures which they feared would prove detrimental to the Church and its leadership.

At this juncture Pius VI, still anxious to avoid arousing the revolutionary regime and fearing the prospect of a schism, did not publicly reveal his opposition to it for some eight months: 'We have refrained from declaring the authors of the baleful civil constitution separated and cut off from the communion of the Catholic religion', he wrote, wondering what he should do.[13] He posed the same question to a commission of cardinals selected to evaluate the Civil Constitution. Not surprisingly, their report proved clearly critical, and called for a condemnation. Still the pope hesitated to make his opposition public. It was only after the French Assembly approved legislation that required all clergy in office to swear allegiance to, and assure their acceptance of, the Civil Constitution that Pius pondered action.[14] His resolve solidified at the end of 1790, when the National Assembly decreed that the oath of the Civil Constitution should be taken by the clergy at parish Masses on 2 January 1791 and those in the Assembly on 4 January.

This mandate provoked a split in the French clergy and led Pius VI in mid-April 1791 to finally break his silence and issue the papal encyclical *Charitas*,[15] which condemned the Civil Constitution and particularly criticized the Civil Oath, which he condemned as schismatic and heretical.[16] In fact, Pius denounced the priests who swore allegiance to it. The rift between Rome and the Revolution was now painfully public, as was the growing division between Church and state. As a consequence, diplomatic relations between Rome and Paris were broken during the summer of 1791. Conflicted and confused, the troubled king sought to flee the country on 20 June 1791, but his carriage was stopped at Varennes and the royal family was 'escorted' back to Paris by a force of 150,000 men and entered the capital on 25 June as virtual prisoners. Informed of the attempted royal flight, the National Assembly stripped the king of the limited executive authority he had retained under the new constitution. The restrictions imposed upon the pro-papal French monarch proved a further blow against the Church as well.

Pius VI now shared the king's concern, which transcended Rome's earlier fear of the French seizure of some unimportant papal enclave in France. Neither the French monarch nor the pope was reassured or comforted by the pledge made at Pillnitz in August 1791 by the king of Prussia and the Holy Roman emperor, Leopold II (brother of Marie Antoinette), that they would take action against revolutionary France if all the other powers joined them in the endeavour – an unlikely prospect. At this juncture, the roles of Louis XVI and Marie Antoinette as sovereigns were seriously compromised. Depressed by the 'radical regime' that deemed them suspect, the royal family looked abroad for liberation. Leopold's ambiguous declaration reflected his belief that he should take some steps to help his sister and her husband, the French king. He did not, however, wish to become embroiled in a costly war that would probably compromise his domestic programme, curtail his reformism and possibly endanger his crown.

Leopold resented the pressure of the French émigrés, particularly the higher clergy, who had fled France and invoked military intervention. It is not precisely known how many clerics swore allegiance to the Civil Constitution, but the best evidence suggests that about half did. Those who signed, however, came overwhelmingly from the lower clergy; the upper clergy, resenting the loss of their vast estates and plethora of privileges, preferred to leave the country rather than submit to subordination and humiliation. They had the means and mechanisms to do so, and were welcomed in the Papal States and especially Rome by Pope Pius VI, and less enthusiastically allowed entry into the empire by Leopold II. This angered the revolutionary regime in France, which could not then punish the pope and his bishops for their vocal opposition and plots against the revolution. They therefore struck out against the lower clergy, who could not escape easily and were constrained to remain in France. The persecution of the clergy and the radical changes introduced provoked a counter-revolutionary backlash in parts of France, where a virtual civil war erupted. This movement opposed the revolutionary reforms, which were perceived as an attack on the traditional faith, the organization of the Church and its clergy, and above all the obligation to swear allegiance to the Civil Constitution. In many regions of France, especially in the countryside, the opposition to the radical regime was often led by parish priests, who had been targeted by the revolutionaries.[17]

The clerical opposition to the Republic's 'reformism' and the majority Girondist party both advocated the opening of a war against the conservative powers of Europe – but for different reasons. The clerics hoped that a military defeat would lead to the collapse of the revolutionary regime, while the Girondists expected war to unite and strengthen it. The latter favoured the war: first, to secure and safeguard the Revolution from the conservative Continental powers; second, to end internal dissension by rallying all Frenchmen against the foreign foe; third, they believed they had a mission to spread liberty and equality to their fellow men; and finally, they believed that this would facilitate France's historic mission to expand. Like the clerics, the king and his Austrian queen Marie Antoinette, who found themselves prisoners of the regime, favoured war in the expectation that the foreign powers would march on Paris, 'liberate' the royal family and overturn the revolutionary regime. This led the queen to plead with her brother, Leopald II, to intervene.

War materialized in April 1792, when the newly elected French Assembly declared war on Austria. Protestant Prussia rather than Catholic Austria assumed the initiative in the military campaign that followed. Advocates of the conflict were soon disappointed that the war brought neither unity to France nor liberation to the royal family. On the contrary, both the king and the Girondists suffered setbacks as a consequence of the conflict. Louis XVI (1774–93) lost his crown, state and head, and subsequently so did his consort. Meanwhile, the radical Jacobins seized the reins of power from the more moderate Girondists.

While revolutionary France found herself embroiled in war from 1792–3, she had to confront a rising in the Vendée prompted by the peasantry's opposition to the government's religious policy and persecution of the Church. The peasantry in western France, devoted to their priests, questioned the appropriation and sale of Church property, the restrictions imposed by the Civil Constitution on the Church and clergy, and the imposition of an oath to accept these changes. They also opposed the arrest of the nonjuring clergy, who refused to swear allegiance to the new order, which forced the remaining 'good priests' into hiding or exile. At this juncture, Pope Pius VI recognized the danger confronting the Church and clergy, abandoned his frivolous behaviour and did his best to protect the faith. With this thought in mind, he summoned the clergy to leave France and join him in Rome. Clerical opposition to the regime contributed to a full-scale counter-revolutionary movement.[18] Pius hastened to assist those who fled the revolutionary violence.[19] Unable for the moment to 'punish the pope', an insurrection in Paris led to an attack on the royal palace of the Tuileries on 10 August 1792, and the suspension of the king. In September 1792 the newly elected National Convention abolished the monarchy, and 22 September 1792 was proclaimed the first day of year one of the French Republican Calendar.[20]

The king was put on trial before the Convention at the end of 1792, found guilty in mid-January 1793, and executed on 21 January. This, and other executions, aroused both internal and foreign opposition, and soon the newly formed republic confronted a coalition of powers that included Austria, Prussia, Spain, Great Britain, the Dutch Republic and Piedmont. They were determined to prevent the Revolution expanding beyond the Low Countries, which had earlier been occupied. Although the Papal States did not have the means to join in waging the war, they did not hide their moral support for the first coalition. Meanwhile, the counter-revolutionary movements that emerged within France, often led and inspired by the clergy, provoked resentment and retaliation against the Church and its leadership. The Roman clerical establishment hoped and prayed for the collapse of the Revolution, but their prayers were not answered.

Confronted with internal and international opposition, the radical Jacobins had recourse to extreme measures to 'save the Republic'. Internally, they formed a number of committees to suppress the 'disorders', the best known or the most notorious of which was the Committee of Public Safety, which made a series of demands upon the pope that he rejected.[21] It had greater success at home. Under the dictatorial leadership of Maximilien Robespierre (1758–1794) it initiated a 'Reign of Terror' that lasted from September 1793 to his own execution at the end of July 1794, and whose victims numbered some 20,000. Among these was Queen Marie Antoinette, who was decapitated on 16 October 1793. Robespierre sought religious sanction of sorts for his actions and rule, not from the Catholic Church, which he scorned, but from the Cult of the Supreme Being, which he himself devised, serving as its high priest and main voice. To promote its broad acceptance, he introduced this new cult in the cathedral of Notre-Dame in Paris. While Pius VI looked upon the Civil Constitution of the Clergy as a mistaken attempt to impose Gallicanism upon the Catholic Church, he perceived the essentially irreligious and 'malicious' Jacobin programme as one that promoted de-Christianization and was a virtual 'rebellion against the Cross'.

To deal with the foreign war, in August 1793 the revolutionary regime instituted a *levée en masse*, a levy of the entire male population that was capable of bearing arms. This led to the creation of fourteen armies that outnumbered the smaller professional forces of France's opponents, and together with the repression at home achieved a series of French victories. The French overran Belgium and the Dutch Republic and in 1795 Prussia withdrew from the war, as did Spain. It appeared only a matter of time before the Austrians would follow suit. This turn of events caused consternation in Rome, which had favoured and supported the allied campaign against revolutionary France. The distress of Pius VI increased exponentially as the French assumed the offensive and resented the moral, if not material, support that the papacy provided to their enemies. Pius, in turn, was scandalized by the 'illegal' and brutal execution of Marie Antoinette. The execution of Robespierre and his followers on 28 July 1794 (ninth of Thermidor) did little to console the pontiff. The Directory that assumed control continued to humiliate the head of the Church and challenged the legitimacy of the Papal States. Although the 'Reign of Terror' ended, the campaign against the Church and clergy continued.

Following the Peace of Basel (1795) and the withdrawal of Prussia and Spain from the conflict, the war turned in favour of France. The repression of the Terror was no longer deemed necessary, and in August 1795 the Jacobin regime was followed by that of the more moderate five-member Directory. Nonetheless, the war against the empire continued, and for pragmatic and ideological reasons the new government also continued its opposition to papal Rome. In their catalogue of complaints, the French resented the refuge that Rome provided for the enemies of the Revolution; its support of the anti-French coalition; the murder of one of their representatives on the street of the Corso in Rome; its condemnation of the beheading of Louis XVI as illegal and immoral; and the papacy's attempt to control the policies and practices of the French Church. The Directors, like the Jacobins, rebelled against the traditionalism of Pius VI, who argued that no aspect of religious life should be under state jurisdiction, insisting that the regular clergy be responsible to Rome alone and that the supervision of the secular clergy, as in the past, should remain under the direction of the bishops. This papal programme was as objectionable to the Directors as it was to the Jacobins, both of whom sought the complete collapse of the papacy.

The French desire for revenge against Rome was fulfilled in 1796, when the Directory appointed Napoleon Bonaparte, the youngest general in the army, commander of the French forces in Italy. After winning a series of battles in northern Italy between April and October 1797, Napoleon was instructed to initiate a political as well as a military offensive. He was not only to defeat the Austrian forces in northern Italy, but also told to encourage revolution there, to dis-credit the spiritual and temporal authority of the pope. Desirous of pleasing his superiors, he promised 'to free the Roman people from their long slavery' and to polish off the 'old fox' but, conscious of the continuing influence of Catholicism in Italy, he moved cautiously.

Napoleon approached his assignments methodically by first defeating the Austrian army in northern Italy, which allowed his forces to push southward into the peninsula and 'liberate' the papal provinces of Ravenna, Bologna and Ferrara. Rome was vulnerable; indeed, in May 1796 Bonaparte received orders to occupy the capital, but for political rather than military reasons he took only the Legations (the northern provinces of the Papal States governed by papal representatives or Legates), but threatened to march on Rome to get the pope to negotiate and accept his harsh terms of surrender. The pope, who still refused to recognize the revolutionary government of France, opened talks with Napoleon by means of the Spanish envoy to the Vatican.[22]

Without the prospect of Austrian assistance, in the winter of 1796 Pius VI felt constrained to accept the severe impositions outlined by Napoleon at the Armistice of Bologna. It required the papacy to surrender Bologna, Ferrara and Ancona to the French, pay a tribute of 21,000,000 *scudi* and hand over 100 works of art, including paintings and statues and some 500 manuscripts of their choice. Furthermore, the papacy was to make the ports of its state available to the French but closed to its enemies. Finally, the pope was told to disband his army and send an envoy to Paris to negotiate a final peace treaty – implying that the papacy would have to make a series of additional concessions to attain a permanent peace. Following directions and orders from Paris, Napoleon imposed harsh terms. He carefully resisted, however, the temptation to eliminate the Papal States or destroy their ecclesiastical nature, convinced that this would create more problems than it would resolve. It proved to be a perceptive and accurate assessment.

There was criticism from part of the clergy for Pius VI's acceptance of the humiliating French terms and for meeting Bonaparte's ultimatum. In response, the pope, who abandoned his former frivolity, carefully explained and openly defended his pragmatic decision to accept the harsh and vindictive French terms in order to avoid greater harm to Church and clergy:

> The fate of Italy is to all appearances in the hands of the French; new victories daily assure their conquests. If the well-appointed

armies of the Empire had to yield to the impetuosity of the conqueror, and if the strongest powers are in his hands, what resistance or defense can this capital make? What success can we expect from the courage of our subjects? We should but shed innocent blood were we to think of defending it. Of two evils we must choose the lesser . . . But if necessity compels us to submit to such hard conditions, duty requires us to fulfil them exactly.[23]

There were, however, limits to what Pius would sanction to preserve a small part of his state, revealing an adherence to principle tempered by a prudence he had not shown earlier. Thus he, along with the College of Cardinals, balked at the Directory's provocative demand that he revoke all papal bulls issued since 1789, including that against the Civil Constitution of the Clergy. While Napoleon shied from a frontal attack upon papal prerogatives, concerned by the possible consequences, the Directory did not hesitate to do so. Napoleon's assessment proved accurate: 'We find the martyr's crown more brilliant than that we bear on our head', Pius blurted out.[24] Fully aware of the threat the French posed, in September 1796 Pius declared the Armistice broken, suspended the shipment of booty to France and created a citizen's army to protect the capital. Napoleon was ordered by the Directory to respond by declaring war on what remained of the Papal States in January 1797, march on Rome and depose the pope.

This last command posed a dilemma for the general. A military man who adhered to the military code, he did not want to disobey orders. Nonetheless, he did not want to appear as persecutor of a Church that retained its hold over a good part of the population. Napoleon's solution was to force Pius VI to accept the harsher terms of the Treaty of Tolentino imposed on 19 February 1797. This required Rome to fulfil the terms of the Armistice of Bologna, to cede Avignon, the Venaissin county, Bologna and Ferrara along with the Romagna, as well as pay an additional 30 million lire, and provide the French with thousands of horses. To prevent the French from penetrating beyond the Legations, Pius compromised once more and reluctantly but prudently accepted these harsh terms.[25]

Following these territorial losses, the Papal States were restricted to one of the least productive parts of the peninsula, whose future was bleak at best. To deal with its fiscal crisis, in 1797 Pius authorized the sale of Church lands to raise desperately needed capital; but this failed to relieve the financial pressure confronting what remained of the Papal States. Rome was plagued by treaty obligations and massive debts, and printed large amounts of paper money. This contributed to a raging inflation that hindered the truncated state's economic recovery while undermining its political stability. Old and ill, the pope proved unable to protect and preserve what remained of his state.

Napoleon informed the Directory that the bankruptcy and losses sustained by the papacy at the Treaty of Tolentino would prove disastrous for the Papal States and soon lead to the collapse of its temporal power – just what the Directory sought. Meanwhile, in June 1797 much of the territory the papacy surrendered was united with Lombardy to create the Cisalpine Republic.[26] Subsequently, in October 1797 the Austrians agreed to accept the Treaty of Campo Formio, which affected both Italy and Germany. By its terms the Austrians recognized French claims to the left bank of the Rhine and agreed to accept the Ligurian Republic, which replaced Genoa and the Cisalpine Republic with its inclusion of the Legations and other former northern papal territories, but did not touch the pope in Rome. The Cisalpine Republic, created by the French, was encouraged by the Directory to assume an anti-clerical and anti-papal policy. It did so by confiscating Church lands, outlawing the monastic orders, imposing compulsory civil marriage and introducing a separation of Church and state – even in the former papal territories.

While the pope and the Curia hoped that the enormous sacrifices they made would safeguard small parts of the Papal States and help preserve the principles of the faith there, the Directory harboured other plans: 'This ancient idol will be destroyed. Freedom and philosophy demand it', wrote one Director to another. He concluded: 'It is the decision of the Directory that when the proper time comes, the Pope shall disappear from the scene and his religion with him.'[27] General Bonaparte, contemptuous of all religion, recognized the hold Catholicism exercised over the masses, which had been strengthened by persecution. Having political as well as military ambitions, he did not wish to alienate the Catholic populations of France, Italy and Spain by assuming the responsibility for removing Pius from the papal throne. Furthermore, he foresaw that the French military would have to sustain a French satellite in Rome, weakening its hold on the more strategic northern part of the peninsula – threatened by Austria – which still controlled a formidable military force.

However, the three generals the Directory dispatched to the Eternal City to coordinate the collection of art to be shipped to Paris agreed to precipitate a revolution in Rome that would depose the pope, provoke his expulsion and undermine the 'superstitious Faith'. Generals Arrighi, Duphot and Sherlock began their second and still secret mission by demanding that the papal authorities release all those imprisoned in Rome for political crimes and, once out of prison, they were funded to enlist recruits to help provoke a revolution against the papal regime and against Roman Catholicism. It proved a difficult assignment, for most of the Roman population resented the French confiscation of their art treasures and their mockery of the pope, their religion and the God they worshipped. Their anger was compounded by the rumours that were circulating of divine discontent at the French persecution of the faith. Stories circulated of tears being shed by a picture of the Virgin as it was ripped from the wall of a church and of the statue of an angel turning its head in disgust as French looters approached, along with dozens of similar stories. Undismayed, but determined to eradicate what they mocked as superstition, the French generals forged ahead with their campaign against the pope and the remnants of the Papal States.

The second phase of the campaign against the temporal power was opened by the outbreak of a series of disorders sponsored and supported by the French. It created consternation among those Romans who resented French intervention in their lives, and led to the murder of General Mathieu Duphot and the withdrawal of the French ambassador, Napoleon's brother, Joseph Bonaparte. On receiving word of the murder, an outraged Directory had its pretext for military intervention, and ordered General Louis-Alexandre Berthier, who succeeded Bonaparte as commander in Italy, to invade the remnants of the Papal States and he moved south to do so. Pius dispatched various representatives to his camp to negotiate a settlement, but Berthier, following instructions, was determined to enter Rome. Nor was he stopped by the prayers made to the Virgin at Santa Maria di Campitelli, who had supposedly saved the city from plague in 1656, or the numerous sacred relics that were paraded around the various quarters of the city.

As the French forces approached the gates of Rome, papal advisers urged the pontiff to flee the capital, but Pius, who was now over eighty years old, refused to do so. He did seek the assistance of Spain and Naples, but neither proved willing to antagonize the French by coming to his aid. At this point, Pius had no other option or means to prevent the French from entering Rome. Having only a small military force, and determined not to suffer the loss of lives in a useless struggle, Pius found himself at the mercy of Berthier, who lied by indicating that his march on Rome had no aim other than to punish those who had murdered Duphot.

The pope, according to the Spanish ambassador, prayed, vegetated and waited for the inevitable French demands. The terms of capitulation on 10 February 1798, demanded by Berthier, did not reflect his aims but those of the Directory. It insisted on the surrender of the Castel Sant'Angelo, the freeing of all political prisoners, the disarmament of papal forces and the erection of monuments to commemorate the two Frenchmen murdered in Rome, along with various financial contributions to be calculated and made to the Paris government. In return, Berthier promised that Pius would be allowed to retain his throne and preside over his religion, and his property would be respected by the French entering the Eternal City. These pledges were soon broken.

Once Berthier had entered Rome on 11 February 1798 and his troops occupied the Castel Sant'Angelo, he did not hesitate to violate the numerous promises he had earlier made to the pope's representatives. In mid-February he sponsored a series of noisy demonstrations of 'Roman' Jacobins, radicals and nationalists, who called for an immediate end to the papal regime. He 'answered' their pleas by proclaiming the formation of a Roman republic and moved against the pope and what remained of the papal state. The resulting republic was a French rather than a Roman creation. Its constitution was modelled on that of the Directory which then controlled France. Politically and diplomatically, it was entirely under French influence and remained a French protectorate until its collapse. As in France, all titles, except that of citizen, were abolished along with the remnants of feudalism. The French also inspired the republic's most important legislation, which granted Jews equality under the law, with full citizenship. These changes came at a cost, above all the need to fund the French forces that kept the republicans in power. Funds were plundered from the wealthy and especially the Church, whose land, buildings and artwork were systematically looted. Not even the pope's private library and jewellery were spared. The fisherman's ring, symbol of papal authority, was assessed as having no intrinsic value.[28]

The behaviour, or more appropriately misbehaviour, of the republican regime led even former critics of papal Rome to appreciate belatedly the Papal States' conduct and policies and explore the prospect of its restoration. To eliminate such speculation, the agents of France sought to persuade the pope to recognize the Roman Republic and renounce his temporal power, though he would be allowed to retain his spiritual authority. Pius made it clear that he would not, and could not, do so. This led the French to make other plans to remove the person and influence of the increasingly popular pope, who cast a shadow over the Roman Republic. Although the Roman Jacobins wanted to keep the pope in Rome, they had to submit to French determination to depose and deport him. On 17 February 1798, the old and ailing pope was commanded to leave Rome within three days. His desire to remain in Rome, followed by his wish to settle in Naples, were both rejected by the French, who on 20 February carried him off to Tuscany. Despite his mistreatment, the pope behaved with great dignity and this increased his popularity in Rome, Italy and even France.

Pius was placed in a monastery in Siena and was not allowed to proceed to Florence, where the Directory feared he would have greater contact with the outside world; for a time it even considered shipping him off to Brazil. Given his poor health, that would have been a death sentence. Rather miraculously, Pius survived the earthquake that struck the monastery in which he was imprisoned, rendering it uninhabitable. Concerned that his misfortunes would lead some Italians to intervene on his behalf, at the end of February 1798 the French dragged the half-paralysed pontiff across the Apennines to Parma, where he remained until 10 April 1799, when he was abruptly carted off to Turin. Here he found only temporary refuge before being dragged across the Alps and imprisoned in a fortress in Valence in southern France, where he died on 29 August 1799, ending the longest pontificate in history. His brave and persistent resistance to French demands had enhanced his reputation, along with that of the papacy.

A week before the pope died, Napoleon abandoned his military campaign and his army in Egypt and sailed secretly to France, claiming that the Directory had mismanaged its struggle with the Second Coalition and thus undermined the French position in Germany and Italy. With the help of one of the Directors, the Abbé Sieyès, the immensely popular general orchestrated a *coup d'état* against the Directory and replaced it with the Consulate – making himself first consul in the process. Although his term of office was initially for ten years, he intended it to be permanent. He succeeded and eventually exercised supreme power because he restored peace internally and re-established French primacy in Europe. He did so by means of his military genius, as well as his prudence in the political and diplomatic realm, which made him a formidable adversary. To the surprise of many, his quest for the re-establishment of order in France and much of Europe relied not only on his extraordinary military skills but also on his diplomatic ability. This led him to foresee the advantages of conciliating rather than combating the papacy.

The reputation of the papacy had dramatically improved following the death of Pius vi in August 1799. The only pope for centuries to die in captivity, his suffering and heroic behaviour in the face of French violence and abuse increased the popularity of the papacy and made possible the restoration of the Papal States. Owing to the turmoil that still prevailed in Rome, the conclave that would select a successor met in Venice under Austrian protection. It sought a candidate who not only possessed profound religious sentiments, but who was also politically and diplomatically astute and could resist political pressure. The long-lasting conclave in March 1800 elected Luigi Barnabà Chiaramonte, a moderate as well as an aristocrat, who willingly and diplomatically accepted the title Citizen Cardinal and recognized the need to compromise. He appealed to the moderate members of the College of Cardinals and pleased conservatives by taking the name of his predecessor. Once he donned the papal tiara as Pius VII, his responsibilities would be great. The task of his pontificate would not prove easy.

II

The Papacy between Transformation and Restoration

REGARDING HIS BELIEF IN THE SOCIAL UTILITY OF RELIGION, Napoleon wrote:

> I see in religion the whole mystery of society. I hold . . . that apart from the precepts and doctrines of the Gospel there is no society that can flourish, nor any real civilization.[1]

During the last years of the Directory, a certain discontent emerged in France, fuelled by social divisions, internal unrest, religious persecution and the threat of foreign intervention. This led to the call for a greater sense of order and a stronger executive authority, and contributed to the coup of 9–10 November 1799 that brought the Consulate to power. The popular General Bonaparte assumed the role of first consul and would dominate diplomatic and military developments for the next decade and a half. In fact, Napoleon (1769–1821), master of France at the young age of 35, would become one of the most influential figures in the political life of the modern world. In France he worked to consolidate the Revolution; in Italy he sparked the Risorgimento and Italian consolidation; while in Central Europe his destruction of the Holy Roman Empire prepared the path for Otto von Bismarck's unification of Germany.

Napoleon's impact transcended the Old World to reach across the Atlantic, where it played an important role in stimulating the desire for independence of most of Spain's colonies. François-Dominique Toussaint L'Ouverture (c. 1743–1803) and the Haitian revolution, along with the sale of Louisiana to the United States in 1801, would later bring about important changes in the international power structure. Despite the importance of Napoleon's policies in France, Europe and the world beyond, not all aspects of Napoleon's life have been studied. The role of religion in his career has been somewhat neglected, if not totally ignored, especially the part played by Catholicism and its papal leadership in his rise and fall.

Napoleon's coup of 9 November 1799 overturned the anti-clerical Directory, establishing the more pragmatic Consulate.[2] Almost immediately, Bonaparte, suspicious of ideologues,[3] revealed a more accommodating attitude towards the Church. Born and baptized a Catholic, he had been a non-practising one since child-hood, but appreciated the role Catholicism played in inculcating a sense of order and respect for authority. Convinced that the consoli-dation of his power would only follow reconciliation with the Holy See and the restoration of the Church, one of his first decrees was to prescribe belated funeral honours for Pius VI. Shortly thereafter, he reopened Catholic churches in France while allowing émigré priests to return home. As Napoleon laboured to consolidate his power in Paris, at the end of November 1799 the cardinals of the Church jour-neyed to Habsburg-controlled Venice, where the bishop of Imola (Luigi Chiaramonti) was elected pope on 14 March 1800,[4] choosing the name Pius VII.

The newly elected pope, the son of Count Scipio Chiaramonti and the Marchessa Giovanna Chini, descended from a noble but politically moderate family, which led him to proclaim early on that liberty, equality and fraternity were not incompatible with Christianity, but in fact sprang from it. His pronouncement that revolutionary ideas were not necessarily in conflict with the Church delighted Napoleon,[5] as did his selection of the pragmatic and diplomatically astute Ercole Consalvi as his secretary of state. The two were well suited to reconcile Rome and the Revolution. In turn, Napoleon fully appreciated the role religion played in the consoli-dation and preservation of power. Pragmatic to the core, he was pre-pared to rely on religious reconciliation as well as military means to promote the peace and internal order desired by a majority of the French. In the spring of 1800 he organized another Italian cam-paign. He rapidly defeated the Austrians and imposed the Peace of Lunéville in February 1801, which gave him control of the Italian peninsula. In 1802 he signed the Peace of Amiens with Britain. These victories brought a temporary lull in the foreign war, allowing him to turn his attention to domestic matters and above all ending the bitter conflict between the Roman Church and the French state, which he deemed counterproductive for both. It was a pragmatic belief and accurate assessment upon which he was prepared to act.

Napoleon admitted that his attitude towards the Church and papacy was fashioned by practical rather than religious considerations, frankly acknowledging that he placed little belief in religious principles or practices.[6] An agnostic without any set religious beliefs, Napoleon appreciated the social utility of religion and admired the Catholic Church's top-down organization and sought its aid in his own consolidation of power. Unlike many of his ideologically driven predecessors, from the first he recognized that Catholicism still held sway over the peasant populations of France, Italy and Spain. He also understood that much of the resistance to the revolutionary regime at home and abroad stemmed from religious convictions. Consequently, his motivation for an agreement with the Church was largely political, a crucial part in his policy of pacification.

After he had prescribed belated funeral honours for Pius VI, he revealed his intention of reopening churches in France and restoring the faith to its 'ancient splendour', allowing émigré priests to return. 'When I talk directly to the new Pope', Napoleon remarked, 'I hope to have the good fortune of removing all obstacles blocking a complete reconciliation between France and the head of the Church.'[7] The general found a ready and willing partner for a settlement in the recently elected Luigi Barnabà Chiaramonti, a member of the Benedictine Order, and his brilliant secretary of state, Cardinal Ercole Consalvi, known in Rome as 'the Siren'. As bishop of Tivoli and Imola, and later as cardinal, Chiaramonti had favoured some form of agreement between the Church and the Revolutionaries, a sentiment he continued to harbour once elected pope. He was essentially, although not totally, moved by religious considerations and concern for the Church.

In his first encyclical issued on 15 May 1800 he implored peace for the Church.[8] His words were not lost on the victor of Marengo

(14 June 1800), who likewise sought a settlement, recognizing that a reconciliation with Rome was essential for the stability of his regime. Sensing that the French had wearied of religious conflict, Napoleon favoured negotiations with the pope, and Pius immediately seconded the idea.[9] Napoleon was convinced that the earlier concessions to the Church, and the restoration of the faith in the provinces, had been crucial in terminating the war in the Vendée. Furthermore, he deemed organized religion necessary for tranquillity, considering Catholicism, with its dogma and hierarchy, conducive to the preservation of order.

Both the general and the pope met with opposition in their quest for reconciliation. Some Republicans perceived the first consul's actions as a betrayal of the Revolution and a restoration of the old order. Meanwhile, a number of conservative clergy believed that the general would impose dangerous and destructive demands on the Church, undermining its status and threatening its future. Suspicion on both sides explains why the negotiations proved protracted and difficult, and why nine drafts of the projected accord were rejected before the tenth was finally accepted. On 15 July 1801 an agreement of two declarations and seventeen articles was approved.[10] Even the name of the settlement was disputed, and the term 'concordat' rejected in favour of 'Convention between the French Government and His Holiness Pius VII'.[11]

Although Pius suspected, and soon learned, that Napoleon was unwilling to make many major concessions, the pragmatic pope felt that an agreement would help restore the Church in France and papal rule in Rome.[12] These objectives were attained, but the price was high, for the general's demands were many and his concessions few. Among other things, Napoleon insisted that Rome accept the earlier seizure of Church land and property. Furthermore, he insisted that all the bishops resign and be replaced by a new hierarchy nominated by the first consul and consecrated by the pope. Finally, the agreement provided papal recognition of the legitimacy of Napoleon's regime. These were the three major concessions Pius VII made to Napoleon. In return, as a compensation of sorts, the French state would financially support the clergy and the papacy would be accorded the authority to demand the resignation of bishops.[13]

On 15 August 1801, Pius VII ratified the concordat and issued two encyclicals, *La Chiesa di Gesù* and *Tam Multa*. In the first he related the rationale for the agreement, outlining its principal clauses. In the latter he required the resignation of the entire hierarchy in the French lands, so that new appointments might be made in accordance with article five of the agreement.[14] This extraordinary exercise of papal authority represented a death blow to Gallicanism, which attempted to restrict papal influence over the Catholic Church in France. Skirting the issue of the temporal dominions, the accord secured for the pope not only the right to invest bishops, which he had possessed previously, but also under certain conditions to depose them, which in France represented an innovation.

Neither Paris nor Rome was totally satisfied with the settlement, although both drew substantial benefits from it. Pius appreciated the re-establishment of the hierarchy in France, the restoration of Catholic worship there and the end to the schism, while witnessing the virtual dismemberment of the remains of the constitutional Church. The centralization it sanctioned in the French Church reinforced the position of the papacy.[15] Napoleon, for his part, inherited the prerogatives of the monarchy vis-à-vis the Church and the clergy. He also attained the laicization of sovereign power while depriving the royalist opposition of the most potent weapon in their arsenal. The cardinals feared that Napoleon would exploit the agreement to render Rome a virtual French satellite, and later the general admitted as much. They compared Pius VII's conciliation unfavourably to the intransigence of his predecessor; they recited: 'Pius VI sacrificed his throne to save the faith: Pius VII surrendered the faith to save his throne.'[16]

Ignoring conservative criticism on the one side and the remnants of radicalism on the other, the pope and Napoleon remained convinced that their accord, with all its faults, was better than continuing without any understanding. Despite the critique of Napoleonic arrogance and the outrage of some in the Curia who deplored the concessions Pius VII made, the concordat survived and lasted for more than a century.[17] It brought some advantages, recognizing Catholicism as the faith of the great majority of French citizens. Furthermore, article one of the agreement provided that

Catholicism would 'be freely exercised in France; its worship shall
be public, conforming itself with police regulations'. Article twelve,
in turn, promised that 'All Churches, metropolitan, cathedral,
parish and others not secularized, necessary for worship shall be
placed at the disposal of the bishops.' In addition, article fourteen
provided that 'the government shall guarantee an adequate salary
for the bishops and clergy'.[18] Following the concordat, the Church
emerged more centralized than before the Revolution. At the same
time, the French left the pope in control of what remained of the
Papal States after the loss of the Legations and other territory ceded
at Tolentino. To placate the first consul, the pope created three new
French cardinals, including the archbishop of Lyon, Joseph Fesch,
who happened to be one of Napoleon's uncles.[19] Early in 1802, the
rapprochement in Church–state relations was also reflected in
Napoleon's granting of permission for the remains of Pius VI to be
returned to Rome.

It soon became clear that Napoleon sought more from the
Church than had been conceded in the accord. He really wanted a
Church that was submissive to the pope and a pope who was submissive to him – a notion that both Pius and Consalvi absolutely
rejected. Determined to extract more from Rome than it was
willing to concede, once the terms of the concordat had been agreed
in 1801, Napoleon unilaterally issued a series of Organic Articles or
administrative regulations in 1802 which further diminished papal
power over the French Church and increased and enhanced his own.
These articles provided regulations governing the calling and conduct of synods; required government permission for the nuncios to
exercise their authority; insisted on governmental consultation in
diocesan changes and liturgical reform; and forbade bishops from
leaving their dioceses – even to venture to Rome – without the
permission of the first consul. The 77 Organic Articles served as a
long addendum to the seventeen articles of the concordat. In his
allocution of 24 May 1802, announcing the implementation of
the concordat, Pius praised Napoleon for achieving the religious
rapprochement, even though he deplored the Organic Articles
and called for their modification.[20] He protested against their
implementation to no avail.[21]

Although Pius did not intend the French accord to serve as a model for subsequent agreements, its impact loomed large. A reluctant pope had to sign a concordat regulating Italian affairs. After bitter haggling, an understanding was reached in September 1803. Declaring Catholicism the religion of the state, it stipulated that the laws of the Republic would prevail in all matters not enumerated in the concordat. Napoleon's policies also influenced the status of the Church in Germany. By the Peace of Lunéville (9 February 1801) the German empire ceded all the ecclesiastical possessions on the left bank of the Rhine to France. Paradoxically, Napoleon's secularization of the ecclesiastical principalities of Germany, deplored by Pius at the time, worked to Rome's advantage by impoverishing the anti-Roman bishops of the Rhineland, and constraining them to look to the pope for support and protection.

Napoleon fared even better than the Church as a result of the concordat. His peace with the papacy and the resulting quiet in internal and international affairs proved useful and won him broad support. This contributed to his decision to hold a national referendum in August 1802, which confirmed him 'First Consul for Life'. This gave Napoleon the power exercised by absolute monarchs, except the right to transmit the 'throne' to his heir. This followed on 18 May 1804, when the French Senate – prompted by the first consul – approved a bill creating a French Empire with Napoleon as hereditary emperor. Pope Pius VII was invited to take part in the coronation in Paris in early December 1804, presumably to anoint and crown him. Perceiving himself the heir of Charlemagne, and appreciating the influence the Church still wielded in France and much of Europe, Napoleon invited papal participation to legitimize his coronation. His uncle in Rome, Cardinal Fesch, who served as the French ambassador, pressed Pius to accede to his nephew's request, citing it as an opportunity for Rome to engender goodwill. The pope, anxious for the emperor's support against hostile decrees, favoured accepting the invitation, but sought the consent of the cardinals. Only when a majority approved did Pius forward a positive response to Paris. On the eve of his departure, the pope frankly hoped that the visit would prove advantageous to the Church.[22]

By accepting the invitation to the coronation, Pius hoped to wring a number of concessions for the Church in France from the new emperor, imploring his assistance in early August 1804:

> We beseech and conjure you in the Lord, now that by God's providence you have reached the high degree of power and honor to protect the things of God, to defend His Church which is *one and holy*, and to use all your zeal to remove therefrom what ever may injure the purity, preservation, beauty, and liberty of the Catholic Church. You have already made us conceive great hopes; we confidently expect that you will realize it as Emperor of the French. We grant with our whole heart to your majesty, your august spouse, and all your family, our apostolic benediction.[23]

On 2 November 1804 Pius left for Paris accompanied by six cardinals and more than a hundred secretaries. The caravan of carriages attracted widespread interest and was warmly received by the people of France, and initially by their future emperor. Some believed that Napoleon displayed a certain insensitivity in presenting the pope with a tiara that sported as its central jewel the emerald that Pius VI had been forced to relinquish as part of the Treaty of Tolentino.[24] Others perceived it as a tribute to the power still exercised by Rome. Much more serious was the warning that Napoleon might try to keep him there. To counter that prospect, the pope issued a statement letting it be known that should he be detained against his will, his formal abdication would come into effect.[25]

In fact, the emperor did not intend to detain the pope at this juncture, but he did have a surprise for the pope upon his arrival in Paris. It was widely assumed that when Pius left Rome for Paris in November for Napoleon's coronation, he would be called upon to crown the emperor. During the coronation ceremony of 2 December, however, the pope was called upon only to bless the crown. Napoleon crowned himself, and then his empress. Those who knew Napoleon found his action predictable, expressing his conviction that he owned his crown and was responsible to no man.

Indeed, he was convinced that the papacy was responsible to him, and resented the adulation the crowds showered upon the pope as they sought his blessing. Pius lingered in Paris until the following spring, but all his attempts to modify the Organic Articles or obtain additional concessions proved unsuccessful. In March, Napoleon transformed the Italian Republic into the Kingdom of Italy, and assumed the Iron Crown of Lombardy. A medal commemorating the coronation, proclaiming Napoleon king of all of Italy, distressed the pope. Even worse, Pius learned that the French civil code, with its provision for divorce, would be introduced in the Italian kingdom, which included parts of the former Papal States. Both pope and cardinals realized that the peace established between Church and state remained as precarious as that between the powers.

Napoleon, accustomed to giving orders, did not hesitate to do so to the pope. Thus, when his younger brother Jérôme married an American, Elizabeth, from the Patterson family of Baltimore, Napoleon directed the pope to annul the marriage. Napoleon was upset not because the bride was a Protestant but primarily because he had not been consulted. Pius proved sympathetic, but explained that he could not satisfy the request because the marriage was valid according to canon law. The emperor, who felt doubly disrespected, was outraged. His anger increased in 1805 when the Third Co-alition against France was formed and the war resumed. Although victorious in the land campaign, he found it difficult to defeat the British, whose naval superiority protected the island nation. He therefore resorted to economic warfare by issuing the decrees of Berlin (1806) and Milan (1807), which prohibited all trade and financial intercourse with Great Britain. For this measure to suc-ceed, the emperor believed that it had to be observed by all the states on the Continent – including the Papal States. This created difficulties with Rome and the papacy.

Most of the European powers complied, deeming it politically prudent to not contest the Napoleonic dictate, nor arouse the volatile emperor, especially after he had invaded Portugal after it refused to adhere to the Continental System. The small and vulner-able papal state, however, determined to preserve its freedom of action, refused to follow suit and resisted French pressure for entering an alliance, opting instead for neutrality – which future popes deemed impartiality.[26] Pius sought to explain that God willed that the papacy pursue a peaceful policy towards all, 'even towards those from whom evil may be expected'.[27] Napoleon found the papal refusal to adhere to the Continental System intolerable, indeed treasonous. He made clear his conviction that in temporal matters Pius had to submit to his decision that 'no agent of the King of Sardinia, no Englishman, Russian or Swede can be permitted to reside at Rome or in any of the papal states; that no ship belonging to these powers shall enter the papal ports'. He reminded the pope that he was the emperor and this meant 'All my enemies must be yours'.[28] The papal refusal to accept Napoleon's mandate led the enraged emperor to take additional steps to pressure the pope into submission, and in May 1806 he ordered his brother Joseph to occupy the papal port of Civitavecchia.

Despite this hostile action and a series of other threats emanating from Paris, Pius VII refused to declare war on Britain or submit to the closures of the Continental System, informing Napoleon he recognized no power above his own in Rome. The emperor responded at the end of 1807 by ordering the French forces led by General de Miollis in Italy to occupy Rome. This prompted the invasion of 6,000 men into what remained of the Papal States early in 1808, and their entry into the Eternal City on 2 February. The French occupation of the capital and Castel Sant'Angelo did not budge Pius from his neutrality, or alter his refusal to bow to the emperor's demands. In retaliation, Napoleon issued a decree on 2 April 1808 that provided for the incorporation of the pontifical provinces of Urbino, Ancona, Macerata and Camerino into the Italian state he had created. Perceiving himself the logical successor to Charlemagne, he withdrew the donations of Pepin and the confirmation of Charlemagne, which had granted these territories to the papacy.[29] Pius VII ignored the decree.

Accustomed to obedience, Napoleon was determined to demonstrate to the pope and others, who might be inspired by his resistance, that it was dangerous to cross the emperor. In mid-May 1809 he issued a decree uniting the Papal States to the French empire and proclaiming Rome a free, imperial city. To win papal compliance and quiet the expected outcry, the Napoleonic decree assigned the pope an annual subsidy of 2 million lire and assured him control of his private palaces. Pius VII was not prepared to sanction the loss of the greater part of his state. Consequently, Napoleon's seizure of the papal state, and his termination of the temporal power, did not end the conflict between the pope and emperor. On the contrary, the battle of wills between the two was intensified.

Pius dismissed the decree of union, which he felt undermined his spiritual mission as much as his temporal power, and declined the French subsidy. In June, when the Imperial Decree was published in Rome, he issued a bull of excommunication.[30] The emperor responded on the night of 5 July 1809, when French forces broke into the Quirinal Palace, then the papal residence, disarmed the Swiss Guards and invaded the pope's apartments. Ordered by the French to renounce temporal power, Pius VII refused, which prompted the French to arrest him. The pope was forcibly moved out of Rome, dragged to southern France and later Savona. This second seizure of a pope in just over a decade would have far-reaching consequences for Napoleon as well as the Church, even though the impact at first appeared to affect Catholicism adversely rather than the emperor, who apparently had forgotten his own warning that one should treat the pope as if he had 200,000 men.[31]

The imprisoned pope did not cooperate with his captor, refusing to confirm the bishops named by Napoleon, so that within two years some 30 dioceses had become vacant. Napoleon, finally realizing the potential difficulties this impasse created, sought to resolve the dilemma. In mid-November 1809 he created an ecclesiastical commission to propose solutions to the increasing number of vacant dioceses and the difficulties this engendered. His efforts were torpedoed by Pius, who in December clearly denounced as invalid any mechanism designed to diminish or replace papal investiture. In 1810, Napoleon thought that if he transferred the pope to France he might prove more compliant, and as a first step dragged most of the cardinals to Paris along with the heads of the various religious orders and the officers of the congregations and tribunals. His efforts proved less than successful, for the greater part of the clergy remained loyal to Pius and refused to play any part in events sponsored by Napoleon. Thus they boycotted the emperor's civil matrimony of 1 April 1810 to the daughter of the Austrian emperor, Marie-Louise, as well as the religious one of 2 April.

The crisis continued, and the emperor found, to his dismay, that it was a campaign that could not be won by the force of arms alone. Therefore, in January 1811 Napoleon reconvened the Ecclesiastical Commission, reinforced by new members, to which he posed a number of questions. If the pope persisted in withholding the confirmation to bishops appointed by the emperor under the terms of the concordat, what legal redress existed? Regarding the pope's failure to provide canonical institution, the Commission proposed an addenda to the concordat, stipulating that if papal institution were not granted within a specified period, this privilege would be transferred to a provincial council. Should the pope refuse to accept the addenda, the concordat would be suspended, and a national council convoked to confront the crisis. The Commission urged the emperor to negotiate with Pius to avoid a confrontation that would prove detrimental to both Church and state.

Napoleon, distressed by the prospect of a protracted conflict with the Church, when he faced an increasingly hostile diplomatic situation, followed the Commission's advice, and early in May 1811 sent a deputation of three bishops to Savona, where the pope was confined, warning of the convocation of a national council if Pius persisted in his position. He did, and on 17 June 1811 the council opened in Notre-Dame in Paris.[32] Napoleon, who pushed the council to immediately approve a decree providing for an alternative to the papal institution of bishops, was furious with the 'quibbling' of the council, which he suspended 11 July. Following its closure, Napoleon began a campaign of intimidation against members of the council, which was reconvened at the end of July.

On 5 August 1811, the browbeaten members ratified a decree prescribing that if papal institution were not accorded within six months, the metropolitan, or the oldest bishop of the province, was authorized to do so. The decree was to be submitted to His Holiness for approval, and Napoleon dispatched another clerical deputation to Savona. Pius reluctantly endorsed the decree, hoping that his concessions would satisfy the emperor. Napoleon responded that he considered the concordat terminated, and would not permit any papal interference in the installation of bishops. Shortly there-after, he summarily closed the National Council.[33] Meanwhile, Tsar Alexander, motivated by internal considerations but also inspired by the resistance of Pius VII to French pressure, abandoned the Continental System, rendering a future war with Napoleonic France inevitable.

On 9 June 1812, with his Grande Armée poised for an attack on Russia, Napoleon, recognizing the centrality of the papacy in war as well as peace, transferred the pope from Savona, allegedly to prevent his capture by the British.[34] He arrived at the château of Fontainebleau on 19 June. Five days later Napoleon, at the head of the largest army ever assembled – 420,000 initially but over half a million including allied reinforcements – led these forces across the Niemen River, confronting little opposition.[35] It was only at Borodino (7 September 1812) that the Russians turned to fight, inflicting heavy casualties on the enemy, but withdrawing under the cover of darkness. A week later Napoleon entered Moscow un-opposed, but found the city in flames. Expecting the Russians to surrender, Napoleon was surprised by the resolve of Alexander to continue the conflict.[36]

Despite the series of French victories that culminated with the occupation of Moscow in September, Alexander refused to sur-render. This campaign proved to be the beginning of the end for Napoleon. After waiting in vain for Alexander's submission, on 17 October the French made preparations for withdrawal. In Paris, Cardinal Fesch, learning that the Grand Army had vanished in the retreat home, commented that while his nephew was lost, the Church was saved.[37] His words proved prophetic, for the emperor hastened back to Paris in December to silence his critics and rebuild his forces, while mending his relations with the opposition, including the pope. On 1 January 1813 he dispatched his good wishes to Pius, proposing a new concordat, recognizing its import-ance for the survival of his regime. The pope in turn, anxious to preserve the Church in France and the areas still occupied by Napoleon, proved amenable.

Napoleon descended on Fontainebleau, where Pius was confined, on 19 January 1813, even as the coalition of Austria, Prussia, Great Britain and Russia planned for the formation of a quadruple alliance to combat Napoleon. Hoping to quieten the home front, in five days Napoleon and Pius hammered out the basis for a new accord. The document, signed on 25 January, contained eleven articles. Among other things, it provided that the pope would be assured the exercise of the pontificate, and the dominions not yet alienated would be administered by papal agents and not subject to taxation, while the pope promised to provide canonical installation to bishops nominated by the emperor within six months. Pius almost immediately reconsidered his stance, fearing that it prejudiced the rights of the papacy. His reservations were reinforced by the cardinals, who were now allowed to meet with him. Cardinals Consalvi, Pacca and Di Pietro advised the pope to write to the emperor, rescinding the articles because they contained unacceptable provisions and because Napoleon had presented them to the Senate as a final agreement, rather than a draft. On 24 March 1813 Pius wrote to Napoleon, retracting the transactions concluded at Fontainebleau.[38]

Ignoring the papal disclaimer, Napoleon recalled the French cardinals from Fontainebleau. Only the war in Germany restrained him from resorting to harsher measures, and at the end of April the emperor left to take command of his reconstituted forces. In July 1813 Pius appealed for the return of his entire state. He was not satisfied by the allied stipulations of Teplitz, which promised to restore to the pontiff territories not ceded in the Treaty of Tolentino.[39] Following the 'Battle of the Nations' in October, Napoleon had to withdraw to the west, and on 1 January 1814 General von Blücher crossed the Rhine. Shortly thereafter, Napoleon, fearing that the pope would be freed by the advancing allies and used as a propaganda ploy, released him and restored his sovereignty. On 11 April 1814 Napoleon abdicated unconditionally at Fontainebleau, and on 24 May Pius entered Rome. September witnessed the opening of the Congress of Vienna and the Restoration, which prevailed despite Napoleon's brief return during the 100 days, from March–June 1815. Following Waterloo, Napoleon was exiled to Saint Helena while Pius once again returned to Rome from Fontainebleau. For the faithful, this papal restoration, while Napoleon was permanently exiled, represented the triumph of the spirit over the sword.

Napoleon's final defeat came when he lost the two advantages he had earlier possessed: reconciliation with the Church and papacy, and his military edge. The first he lost by his elimination of the temporal power and the imprisonment of Pius VII; the second by the Treaty of Chaumont of March 1814 signed by Britain, Austria, Prussia and Russia, which formed the Quadruple Alliance. By its terms, each of the Allied Powers agreed to retain 150,000 men under arms, promised not to sign a separate peace as they had in the past, and agreed to continue the alliance for two decades to ensure the preservation of the peace.[40] In fact, two agreements were concluded in the quest for peace: the Treaty of Fontainebleau, with Napoleon, and the Treaty of Paris of May 1814, with the French state.

Fontainebleau proved an extremely generous agreement, as did the Treaty of Paris. By the terms of the first, the emperor was allowed to keep his title and was made sovereign ruler of the island of Elba, dangerously close to the coast of Italy. He was also granted a subsidy of some 2 million francs, while his family members were granted pensions. The Treaty of Paris provided that France would keep the borders she had in 1792, which included Avignon and Venaissin. France paid no indemnity, while Britain returned most of the colonies she had seized during more than a decade of warfare. Following Napoleon's return and defeat in the 100 days, he was exiled on Saint Helena, where he remained until he died of cancer in 1821. The second Treaty of Paris, while not as generous as the first, was not particularly harsh.

Following the collapse of the Napoleonic empire at the hands of the Quadruple Alliance of Great Britain, Austria, Prussia and Russia, the allies pledged to preserve the settlement reached in Vienna in 1814–15, which included the restoration and return of the Papal States. Despite this common commitment, dissension soon arose over a number of issues, especially regarding the scope and implementation of the alliance. Disagreement emerged over the questions of why and when the powers should intervene.

Should there be intervention against ideas and ideologies that the allies opposed or only against aggressive actions? Should they intervene against dangerous internal developments or only when such movements threatened other states or the international order? Were they to pursue restoration or reaction? These and other issues were discussed at the Congress of Vienna (1814–15), attended by most of the rulers of Europe – but not by the pope.

Pius did not participate for a number of reasons: first and foremost, he had been away from Rome for half a decade and did not want to leave again so soon. Furthermore, in his absence a series of problems had emerged in the Church that required his attention in the nine years between his restoration in 1814 and his death in 1823. These included: diocesan reconstruction, reorganization of the religious orders, restoration of the Jesuits worldwide and revitalization of the missions, which had been neglected during the Napoleonic era. The French invasion and occupation had created problems for the Church, not only in Spain but also in much of Latin America, which had declared its independence. Pius was particularly distressed by the wretched condition of the missions, caused in part by the decline of Spain and Portugal; the disestablishment of the Society of Jesus; the revolutionary upheaval in Latin America following the French takeover of Spain; and xenophobic outbursts in the Far East.

The restored Pope was upset by the news from Catholic Latin America, where revolutionary movements assumed an anti-Catholic stance and struck out against the Church hierarchy. Divisions within the clergy continued, with its aristocratic members supportive of Spain, while a good part of the lower clergy supported the reformist and revolutionary movements. At the same time, the pope sympathized with the French clergy who had been reduced to poverty. These preoccupations with the religious needs of the Church worldwide led Pius to neglect the political situation in Rome and the provinces of the Papal States, which witnessed the emergence of an ultra-conservative group known as the Zelanti or 'zealous ones', who opposed all reform and most change in both Church and state. In effect, they opposed the papal programme, which favoured a balance between reform and restoration and moderate changes which would address the problems that prevailed in the post-revolutionary world.

The Papal States, indeed all Italy, were troubled by the political, diplomatic, economic, fiscal and social problems that burdened most of Europe at the war's end. The pope's course of moderate reforms was brilliantly defended at the Congress of Vienna and executed outside by Ercole Consalvi, the papal Secretary of State, who in Vienna managed to regain the reconstituted Papal States along with the northern Legations. His call for a religious restoration alongside the political one proved persuasive and successful. Consalvi recognized that the return of the state necessitated a strategy to retain it and proposed a programme of moderate reforms. His position was strikingly similar to that of Metternich, who shunned constitutionalism in Italy, but from the beginning of the Restoration saw the need for administrative reform in the peninsula, and particularly the Papal States.[41]

Pope Pius VII concurred with Consalvi on the need for a moderate reformism to make papal control acceptable to the population at large. To quiet conservative concerns, Consalvi patiently explained that this entailed humanizing the state's administration and government, not liberalizing it. He believed and confessed to the nuncio at Vienna that the constitutional principle was incompatible with pontifical government.[42] If applied to the government of the Church, the fundamental principle of constitutional government, Consalvi argued, might quickly lead to heresy. He worried that once constitutionalism was introduced in the governance of the Papal States, its subjects would soon desire that it be extended to the government of the Church itself.[43] Thus he deemed the first unwise, for it would lead to the second, which he considered heretical and therefore impermissible. In light of the administrative changes and modest, limited reforms introduced by Consalvi, he was taken aback by the opposition his cautious changes encountered. He was further scandalized, upon his return from Vienna, to witness the influence that the ultra-conservative faction of the Zelanti had gained in Rome.

The pope and his chief minister and adviser continued to believe that timely reform was far better than repression to preserve order, and relied on a reformist programme to avert revolution. In July 1816 they introduced a series of additional administrative improvements and modest reforms, in their effort to reconcile the Church and papacy to the modern world. Although these contributed to the tranquillity of papal Rome in 1820, a year of tumult and revolution elsewhere in the peninsula, conservatives denounced them as dangerous and charged that they would undermine the papal state. The old pope was confused by the conflicting advice he received on how to govern the state and the Church. There was also dissension on how best to preserve order, and with whom – if anyone – the papacy should ally itself. Pius continued to receive very different solutions from Consalvi, Metternich, Tsar Alexander and the Zelanti. It was the Zelanti that persuaded the pope in September 1821 to condemn freemasonry and other secret societies. They were also Consalvi's most formidable opponents and sabotaged many of his reforms. Their conservative course ended Rome's reformist programme and inaugurated a time of trouble for the papacy and the Papal States.

III

The Papacy in an Age of Liberalism and Nationalism, 1820–1846

IN HIS ENCYCLICAL *MIRARI VOS* OF 15 AUGUST 1832, POPE Gregory XVI (1831–46) denounced many developments of the age and the difficult times confronting the Church:

> The divine authority of the Church is opposed and her rights shorn off. She is subjected to human reason and with the greatest injustice exposed to the hatred of the people and reduced to vile servitude. The obedience due bishops is denied and their rights are trampled underfoot. Furthermore, academies and schools resound with new, monstrous opinions, which openly attack the Catholic faith; this horrible and nefarious war is openly and even publicly waged. Thus, by institutions and by the example of teachers, the minds of the youth are corrupted and a tremendous blow is dealt to religion and the perversion of morals is spread. So the restraints of religion are thrown off, by which alone kingdoms stand.[1]

The nineteenth century was a paradoxical age for the papacy, which witnessed revival and restoration, criticism and praise, and the clash of Gallicanism and Ultramontanism. Following the restoration of 1814, Rome, along with the powers, pondered how best to preserve the peace. At war's end, Britain, which had forged the alliance to defeat Napoleon, proposed a limited alliance for the preservation of peace and tranquillity. The eastern powers of Austria, Prussia and Russia, on the other hand, sought to pursue a more interventionist stance in the post-war period by supporting Tsar Alexander's 'Holy Alliance'.

Moderate voices in Rome called for the papacy to remain impartial in territorial disputes – a stance that would prevail in both the nineteenth and twentieth centuries and influence the papal position in the First World War as well as the Second World War. Nonetheless, the papacy remained determined to retain the Papal States. Both Pope Pius VII and his brilliant secretary of state Cardinal Ercole Consalvi, who had managed to regain almost all the Papal States at the Congress of Vienna, deemed the state necessary to ensure papal independence. This was virtually a unanimous conviction in both the Church and Curia. Debate and dissension centred on the best means to preserve and retain temporal power, which was deemed essential for the freedom of the papacy.

While some recognized the need for reform of the Papal States, and others called for reform of the Church, the Zelanti opposed both. These conservatives, really reactionaries, profoundly distrusted the laity and called for a complete return to clerical control in the state as well as the Church. At the same time, they also demanded an overall restoration of the pre-revolutionary conditions in society and the prompt elimination of all French innovations – some of which Consalvi found reasonable and useful and sought to retain. The Zelanti strongly disagreed. Their programme was both rigid and unenlightened. When confronted with the need to preserve the state in an age of transformation, virtually none in this reactionary circle thought of winning support by making concessions. Instead, some of the Zelanti called for stronger military measures by papal allies in the peninsula; others counted on the military intervention of Metternich's Austria, while still others looked to Tsar Alexander's Holy Alliance, which aimed to preserve the religious principles of the established order. Introduced by the tsar in 1815, it insisted that sovereigns conduct themselves as Christians – and threatened intervention if they did not!

Consalvi had preferred the more straightforward Quadruple Alliance, even though three of its four powers were non-Catholic. Formed in 1815, it was envisioned and championed by Lord Castlereagh, the British Secretary of State. Castlereagh's alliance called for the four powers – Britain, Austria, Prussia and Russia – to defend the settlements made in Chaumont, Vienna and Paris, but only after due consultation and deliberation. Although Rome deemed it preferable to the Holy Alliance, the papacy, which had neither the means nor the convictions to sanction military action, did not openly endorse it. Furthermore, to have joined or openly supported even a favourable alliance would have violated its adherence to impartiality. To Consalvi's relief, Pius VII understood this and was one of the few rulers in Europe who rejected Alexander's alliance, and favoured reform over repression.[2] Consalvi encouraged the formulation of a decree that streamlined the administration of the seventeen districts into which their state was now divided. He and Pius VII also sanctioned and subsidized the drafting and implementation of a new civil and penal code that incorporated many of the French innovations, eliminating torture and arbitrary arrest, while separating criminal tribunals from ecclesiastical courts.

These and the other Consalvi reforms were designed to satisfy needs and bring a degree of quiet and stability to the Papal States and papacy, whose diplomatic outreach was extended by the heroic stance assumed by Pius VI and Pius VII during their captivity at the hands of the French. Both were widely perceived as martyrs, strengthening their case for the return of their state. The papal position was also enhanced by the concordats concluded by a series of European powers: Catholic Sardinia and Bavaria in 1817, Catholic Naples in 1818 and Protestant Prussia in 1821. This strategy appeared effective, for when revolutions erupted in Spain, Naples and Piedmont in 1820–21, the Papal States remained quiet.[3] For some it seemed a clear confirmation of the efficacy of Consalvi's reformism.

Following the outbreak of the Carbonari-inspired revolution in Naples in early July 1820, Consalvi opted for pragmatism rather than ideological concerns and accorded the constitutional regime in Naples de facto recognition. He did so to protect the Catholic faith, which in the age of restoration remained the largest religious group in Europe – some 100 million to 40 million Protestants and another 40 million Orthodox Christians.[4]

The Zelanti, entrenched within the Curia and the College of Cardinals, were not convinced, and deemed Consalvi's innovations not only unwise but also dangerous. They charged that his liberal policy had made it possible for a revolutionary spirit to emerge in Rome and its provinces and had allowed Carbonarism, which had originated in Naples, to penetrate the papal state. Furthermore, the conservatives claimed that the concessions Consalvi granted did not reflect the aims of a religious state, but those of a secular power. Among other things, they sought to highlight the primacy of the papacy in international relations; restore Catholicism as the religion of state in traditional Catholic countries; outlaw or subordinate other sects; marginalize non-Catholic countries; and limit state sovereignty, liberalism and nationalism in Italy and beyond.

They urged collaboration with conservative Catholic powers to achieve these goals. Upset by Consalvi's refusal to abandon his moderate programme, they used their increasing influence to sabotage his plans for all future innovations. The pope supported Consalvi's reformism, but his preoccupation with Church matters, such as erecting dioceses in Boston, New York, Philadelphia, Richmond, Charleston and Cincinnati, left much of the political burden on the shoulders of his secretary of state.

Consalvi was frustrated by the antics of the Zelanti, who were convinced that repression rather than reform was needed to preserve the temporal power of the papacy, and whose sustained attacks led to the derailment of a number of his reforms. Consalvi proved more successful in preserving his moderate course in international relations, resisting the Zelanti's desire to join the conservative, illiberal and anti-nationalist bloc. Thus he refused to sanction the Austrian suppression of the Neapolitan revolution of 1820, and protested against their movement through papal territory to do so. Subsequently, he showed his independence by preventing the Papal States from joining the conservative bloc at the Congress of Verona in October 1822. It was one of his last victories. The death of Pius VII in August 1823 pleased most of the Zelanti, and their pleasure was doubled when Consalvi followed him to the grave six months later, in 1824. The Zelanti, who disparaged the political realism and reformism of Consalvi and Pius VII, believed that they could finally select one of their own to don the tiara.

This prospect alarmed Metternich, who feared the consequences of the election of the intransigent Cardinal Antonio Gabriele

Severoli. It prompted the Austrian chancellor, who favoured a moderate papal administration, to authorize Cardinal Giuseppe Albani, representing Austrian interests in the conclave, to exercise the Austrian veto. This blocked Severoli's election. The frustrated conservative cardinals, having been denied their first choice, lined up behind another Zelanti, securing the election of Cardinal Annibale della Genga on 28 September 1823. The 63-year-old cardinal, who took the name Leo XII and was crowned on 5 October, fell gravely ill: 'You are electing a corpse', he told his supporters.[5] Shortly thereafter, however, he 'miraculously' recovered and his pontificate lasted from 1823 to 1829, to the delight of the conservative bloc who had elected him. In return, the Zelanti demanded an end to the 'liberal' and 'diplomatic' errors of Consalvi in exchange for a more 'reasonable' and 'religious' orientation in Church, state and society.[6]

Leo XII initially satisfied them by imposing strict censorship and assuming an intransigent stance against most of the innovations introduced by Consalvi – who had earlier fired him from the diplomatic service for his poor performance in the negotiations with France for the return of Avignon. In 1824 Leo pleased the conservative bloc by issuing the encyclical *Ubi primum*. This forerunner of the *Mirari vos* (1832) of Gregory XVI and the *Quanta cura* (1864) of Pius IX, denounced contemporary errors, especially liberalism, nationalism, indifferentism, toleration and the de-Christianization of society, which Leo XII found reprehensible and held responsible for the problems of the present. He warned Catholics at home and abroad to be aware of the dangerous messages, especially that of indifferentism described as freedom of religion, spread by the sects. In March 1826 he targeted the masons and the groups calling for the reorganization and unification of the Italian peninsula.

At home he was appalled and haunted by the emergence of the Italian unification movement, or Risorgimento, which he believed sought to 'steal' the papal state. He openly condemned freemasonry and a number of other secret societies that he believed plotted against the pope and his state. He not only opposed Italian nationalism but also those who championed it, as well as the broader unification movement. In opposition, he forged the counter-Risorgimento. He

did not hesitate to employ spiritual weapons in challenging opponents, relying on the Index and the Holy Office, because he deemed
the liberal and nationalist programme to be an attack on the
Church and religion. Continuing his combative campaign, he
restored the privileges of the aristocracy and the old ecclesiastical
courts. His anti-Judaism led him to restrict Jews to the ghetto once
again, obliging hundreds of them to listen to a weekly Christian
sermon, while prohibiting them from owning real property in
Rome. He also halted the laicization of the administration initiated
by Consalvi, while returning education to clerical control.

In addition, he displayed a certain puritan mentality that
annoyed the Romans, who sought to enjoy life. By his ordinance of
24 March 1824, most activities on Sundays were restricted, while
others such as the playing of games were prohibited. The sale and
use of alcohol was closely supervised and sharply restricted all
week long.[7] Restaurants as well as bars were shut down and visits to
cafés forbidden. Jail sentences were imposed on those who violated
these rules. Leo even found the waltz obscene and provided punishment for those who played or danced to it. Among the most
unpopular innovations he introduced was the stipulation that any
male who followed a young female too closely would be imprisoned
and would be released only if, and when, he married her.[8] He
established a special force of spies and informants to enforce his
restrictive rules and regulations, and increased jail space for those
who violated his laws.

Critics judged his pontificate of five and a half years as disastrous, charging that Leo XII sought to bind the Church, the papacy
and its state to a perpetual medieval past and a puritanical future.
Consequently, many were less than sad to see him die, but complained that even in death he created problems. He died during the
height of the carnival – which brought all festivities to an end. The
Romans complained that he had played three dirty tricks on them:
'You accepted the papacy, you lived too long, and you died during
the carnival and must be mourned.'[9]

Although ultra-conservative – some said reactionary – in
domestic affairs and Church matters, he was more moderate in his
diplomatic relations and in the realm of foreign affairs, returning to

the *via media* and limited reformism of Consalvi. This was very likely the case because he relied on the advice of the moderate Tommaso, Cardinal Bernetti, whom he made secretary of state in June 1828. Resisting the pressure of a number of conservative groups, he and Bernetti, following Consalvi's course, refused to align Rome with the Holy Alliance or any other conservative bloc. Guided by Bernetti, Leo xii played a crucial role in negotiating with the Ottoman sultan, Mahmud ii, for the emancipation of Armenian Catholics. For this reason, among others, Giovanni Maria Mastai-Ferretti, the archbishop of Spoleto and a future pope, praised Leo's policies at the time of his death in February 1829, at the age of 69.[10] He was one of the few moderates to do so. In fact, the more widespread dissatisfaction with the policies of Leo made possible the election of a more moderate pope. This was supported by the Austrian ambassador, who also sought the election of a moderate figure to guide both Church and state.[11] This would relieve Austria of the need for another costly and unpopular intervention in the peninsula.

Leo's successsor, the 68-year-old Cardinal Francesco Saverio Castiglione, elected at the end of March 1829, took the name Pius viii. From the start of his short pontificate of twenty months (1829–30), he made it clear that he did not share the reactionary political agenda of the Zelanti, which he felt provoked opposition and therefore hurt, rather than helped, the papacy retain the state that most clerics regarded as essential.

A firm admirer of Pius vii and his policies, Castiglione assumed the name Pius viii in his honour. Although he was a traditionalist in religious matters, as can be seen in his first and only encyclical, *Traditi humilitati nostrae*, which attacked indifferentism and hostility to Church dogma, he proposed a number of enlightened social and economic changes in his state, and favoured a relatively liberal foreign policy. The brevity of his pontificate, however, prevented the realization of many of his projected reforms. He was appreciated by the Romans for having repealed his predecessor's annoying edict on the sale and consumption of wine and other alcoholic beverages, along with many other of his bothersome and intrusive regulations.

Pius VIII did more to please the moderates. Among other things, he survived long enough to have to respond to the July Revolution of 1830 in France, which had international implications and a European-wide impact. Revolutions erupted in Belgium, Poland and Saxony, Hesse-Cassel and Brunswick in Germany, as well as in Modena, Parma and the Papal States in Italy. Conservatives were convinced that it formed part of a subversive international plot to undermine and replace the existing traditional Christian order with the radical one the revolutionaries envisioned. They blamed moderates such as Pius VII and Pius VIII for their vacillation and appeasement, but above all for their failure to respond energetically and crush the monster at birth. In a sense they sought to hold the reformers responsible for the revolutionary upheaval in France.

Pius absolutely refused to accept responsibility, noting that French conservatives had encouraged Charles X, who in September 1824 had followed his brother to the French throne to pursue the unpopular conservative course. Charles complied, increasing censorship and restoring clerical control of education, provoking demonstrations that alarmed the king and the ultra-conservatives who called for an end to the public protests and the immediate restoration of order.

Desirous of pleasing his ultra-conservative allies, the French king issued five ordinances on 25 July 1830. Together they suspended liberty of the press, dissolved the newly elected chamber, rejected the new electoral law in favour of the former and more narrow one of 1817, restricted the electorate to the top 25 per cent of voters and forced liberals and moderates out of their posts, replacing them with confirmed ultra-conservatives. In response, that night a revolution erupted in Paris, which culminated in pushing Charles off the throne and replacing him with Louis Philippe. Pius VIII pragmatically and quickly recognized the regime of Louis Philippe and urged the French clergy to swear allegiance to the new sovereign. Refusing to bind the fortune of the Church to Charles X and the legitimate Bourbon branch, he revealed that Rome could be flexible and preserve its independence vis-à-vis the secular regimes. He was also successful in completing negotiations for Catholic emancipation in Britain.

The unexpected death of Pius VIII at the age of 69, along with his abandonment of the conservative course, led to speculation that he had been poisoned by angry Zelanti. This provided a credible motive for some – but beyond the motive there was no evidence to suggest foul play. Nonetheless, sufficient suspicion had been aroused to prompt the cardinals to sanction a secret autopsy to determine the cause of his death. No evidence of murder was detected, and the autopsy found that asthma was the culprit.[12] Despite some substantial achievements in a short pontificate, the Zelanti were glad to see him go. The conservative opponents of this moderate pope sought to blame him for the widespread revolutionary turmoil that erupted in Europe in 1830–31, including the Belgian revolution against their 'union' with the Dutch, the revolution in Poland against Russian control, and disturbances in Italy inspired by the Carbonari and in Germany by the Burschenschaften. Revolution also erupted in the Papal Legations. In the eyes of his conservative critics, Pius VIII had sown the wind, and his successor would have to reap the whirlwind. They encouraged derision of this pope and encouraged the Romans to sing 'the eighth Pius was pope, lived and died and no one took note'.[13]

The conclave of 1830–31 resulted in the selection of the most conservative pope of the nineteenth century to date, the Camaldolese monk Cardinal Bartolomeo Alberto Cappellari, who took the name Gregory XVI. Following his election in early February 1831, the revolution feared by both moderates and conservatives erupted in the Papal States, overrunning the Romagna and spilling into the Marches and Emilia. The secretary of state, Cardinal Tommaso Bernetti, hoping to avoid identification with counter-revolutionary Austria, invoked the support of Naples and France, but both refused assistance, facing problems of their own at home. Bernetti's attempt to create a popular counter-revolutionary force or civic guard, known as the Centurions, from the loyal peasantry likewise failed, proving unruly and disruptive and 'a cure worse than the disease'. Following the proclamation of a provisional government in Bologna, which announced the end of the temporal power, the danger escalated. The revolutionaries marched southwards, threatening Rome itself. Indeed, the young prince Louis-Napoléon, nephew of the general and French emperor, who helped plan the rebellion, brazenly warned Gregory that the forces advancing towards the capital were invincible.[14] At this juncture Bernetti, at the behest of Pope Gregory, was constrained to call upon Metternich's Austria to quell the revolt, and it did.

Austrian intervention proved decisive in the suppression of the Italian revolution, but aggravated rather than mitigated nationalist resentment, as Bernetti had feared. Moreover, her military intervention, followed by an occupation, humiliated France, which reacted by sending an expedition to Ancona to protect Gallic interests in Italy and preserve the 'balance of power' in the peninsula. The French did more, insisting that a conference of the major powers (France, Austria, Britain, Russia and Prussia) be called in Rome to propose reforms in order to avoid future disruption in the Papal States.[15] Gregory disliked the idea, but was indebted to the powers and therefore had to submit to what both he and his secretary of state considered a humiliation.

Even Metternich's Austria, which had crushed the revolution and saved the Papal States, supported the call for change, pressing Rome for administrative reforms. Indeed, the Austrian minister, deploring the intransigent stance of the Zelanti, noted that his government had long proposed improvement of its provincial administration. Metternich considered such changes indispensable for the future tranquillity of the Papal States and Italy, proposing that the *motu proprio* of Pius VII and Cardinal Consalvi serve as the basis for these necessary revisions. From Spoleto, Archbishop Mastai-Ferretti also invoked reformism as the best means of avoiding either revolution or reaction.[16] In May 1831 the Conference of Ambassadors drafted a memorandum to Gregory XVI, cataloguing the changes needed to satisfy the population, insisting among other things that the pope treat all his provinces equally and admit laypeople to most administrative and judicial functions. The memorandum also sought greater independence for the municipalities and the establishment of a national assembly.[17] A consultative organ for the administration of the Papal States had been mentioned before, but the first concrete proposal appeared in the Memorandum of the Powers.

This modest programme was not welcomed in Rome, especially the call for a consultative assembly. Cardinal Bernetti rejected such a body, insisting that the principles inspiring it violated the special nature of the pontifical regime. Pope Gregory concurred, finding most of the innovations inopportune and fearing that such reform in the state would inevitably provoke the call for similar changes in the governance of the Church. He accepted a number of other recommendations, however, to avoid an open confrontation with the powers, and in July 1831 issued an edict promising to introduce gradually the requested reforms and granting an amnesty to the rebels. He proved unwilling to do much more. In reality, this attempt to modernize the papal regime found scant support in Rome, since Gregory threatened to go into exile rather than submit to humiliating conditions.[18] His sentiments were reflected in the *Catechism on Revolution* of 1832, which emphasized the incompatibility of revolution and Catholicism. 'Does the Holy law of God permit rebellion against the legitimate temporal sovereign?', the catechism asked, and responded: 'No never, because the temporal power comes from God'.[19] Following this mandate, in June 1832, in a letter to the bishops of Poland, Gregory urged Catholic Poles to be submissive to legitimate authority in the form of Russian domination, avoiding revolutionary agitation.[20]

At home, Gregory excommunicated those who incited rebellion against his government in Ancona, using spiritual weapons to protect temporal interests.[21] Fearful of contact with, and possible contamination by, the outside world, he opposed the introduction of railways in his realm because this would facilitate the infiltration of liberal ideas and subversive doctrines. He likewise resisted the illumination of streets in urban areas, perhaps because he feared that this would serve to encourage nocturnal gatherings and the concoction of plots. This reclusive pontiff was alarmed by the disturbing depictions of 'liberal licence' and 'criminal charges' drawn by Zelanti clerical circles. To make matters worse, Gregory was distressed to learn that some within the bosom of the Church advocated the right of revolution, freedom of religion and the separation of Church and state, as had been established in France and Belgium following the revolutions of 1830.

Gregory disagreed with those who sought to align the Church with liberal action or national liberation in Europe, scorning the attempt to 'Christianize the revolution' by building a bridge between Catholicism and liberalism. The introduction of a separation of Church and state in Belgium as well as France distressed Gregory, but inspired Félicité de Lamennais, who with a group of friends founded the daily *L'Avenir* ('The Future'), whose motto was 'God and Liberty', and recognized the material-economic basis for social and political change. His programme scandalized conservative Catholics who deemed these ideas heretical, since part of the Catholic press proclaimed that one could not be Catholic and liberal.[22] At the end of 1831 Félicité de Lamennais, accompanied by his collaborators on the newspaper Henri Lacordaire and the comte de Montalembert, decided personally to answer the conservative charges in the Eternal City, even though the Camoldolese monk who sat as pope had long opposed revolutionary ideas and believed in hierarchy, order and the virtue of obedience.[23]

Liberal Catholics who favoured the separation of Church and state proved unrealistic in assuming that the pope, who had invoked Austrian intervention against the insurrection in his state, while denouncing revolutionary movements in Poland, Belgium and even Ireland, would miraculously bless democracy and the 'liberal' and 'revolutionary' ideals it championed. They soon learned otherwise. The editors of *L'Avenir* received a frosty reception in Rome, where they were all but ignored. Lamennais, seeking vindication, waited in Rome for more than two months before their audience with the pontiff. When Gregory finally received them, Lamennais was dismayed that the pope did not discuss his work or the controversy it engendered, graciously dismissing him and his colleagues. Nonetheless, a congregation was appointed to examine the movement and the newspaper that popularized its position.[24]

Their work was reflected in Gregory's encyclical, *Mirari vos* of 15 August 1832, which implicitly condemned both the ideas of *L'Avenir* and the General Agency for the Defense of Religious Liberty, the international organization that Lamennais had founded.[25] In the encyclical, Gregory censured the spirit of a false enlightenment and the blind worship of innovation, returning to the themes he had expressed in *The Triumph of the Holy See and the Church against the Assaults of Innovators* (1799). Without mincing words he condemned the separation of Church and state, advocated by the *Avenir* movement. Shortly thereafter, in October 1832, Gregory denounced the false idols worshipped by 'modern civilization', criticizing those who used the cover of religion to defy their princes, and plunge their country into misfortune.[26]

Lamennais initially submitted to the papal critique, and on his return to France closed *L'Avenir* permanently. Inwardly, however, he resented the papal critique and Gregory's attitude. His opposition was made public with the publication in 1834 of *Paroles d'un croyant* or 'Words of a Believer'. This provoked a second condemnation in Gregory XVI's encyclical of 1834, *Singulari nos*, but it did not silence or persuade Lamennais to recant. Instead, he left the Church.

Meanwhile, Gregory had to confront not only liberal Catholicism in France, which called for a complete separation of Church and state, and nationalism in Italy, which sought a united peninsula that incorporated the Papal States, but also an outburst of anti-clericalism in Catholic Spain. The latter emerged when the various factions in the struggle for power sought papal support. When it was not forthcoming they resorted to retaliation against the Church. The difficulties Gregory confronted were compounded in 1834 when Madrid was stricken by an outbreak of cholera and the radical groups hinted that the epidemic was spread by the religious orders, unleashing a gullible public to launch a series of brutal attacks on religious houses. These not only led to murder and mayhem but also to the seizure and confiscation of clerical property. Gregory's protest fell on deaf ears.

On 4 July 1835 the Jesuit order was suppressed in Spain, to the pope's dismay. More heartache was in store for Gregory when in 1836 a decree was issued that stipulated that only clergy approved by the regime could enter or remain in the country. Although difficult to enforce, the intent was painful for the pope. In early March 1841, Gregory issued an allocution listing the wrongs and abuses imposed on the Church in Spain – again to no avail. Even Gregory's encyclical of 22 February 1842, which implored Christians to pray for Spain, was not allowed to be read in that country. Those who predicted that things could not be worse were quickly proven wrong. During the greater part of the last decade of Gregory's pontificate, from October 1836 to January 1845, all official relations between Spain and the Holy See were ended.[27] The Holy See's relations with Portugal were little better than those with Spain. Finally, Gregory also had problems with Catholic Austria, where Joseph II had virtually transformed the Catholic Church into a national one. This situation continued during the 43-year reign of the Emperor Francis II, which ran from 1792 to 1835.

Small wonder, then, that Pope Gregory found much in the European situation to be deplorable. Convinced that modernization, liberalism and nationalism in Europe besieged the Church and that the prevailing historical relativism destroyed traditional dogma, Gregory saw the need for the Church to transcend the old continent by asserting its universal nature and seeking consolation abroad. For this and related reasons, he believed that the future of the Church depended on the work of the missions that carried Catholicism beyond the old world, where secular ideologies attempted to undermine the traditional faith. As a consequence, Gregory sent missionaries to China, North and South America, India, Ethiopia and Polynesia, both to make converts and win supporters. He immediately made it clear, however, that the faith was to be transmitted to free men, and in an apostolic letter at the end of 1839 he condemned the slave trade as unworthy of Christians.[28] He also opposed the revival of colonialism, with its racist undercurrent, that the European powers utilized to justify their aggression and expansion.

In a secret consistory he praised the martyrs in China (1835–40) who surrendered their lives so that the faith might live, especially praising the fortitude of Chinese women, citing their perseverance in the profession of the Gospel despite grievous afflictions.[29] Gregory returned to these themes in *Probe nostis*, his encyclical of 18 September 1840 on the propagation of the faith. In it he catalogued the trials of the Church, as well as the omnipresent, deceitful attempts of 'modern civilization' to pervert the minds of the faithful. As political and social upheaval disrupted Europe, Gregory was 'thankful for the success of the apostolic missions in America, the Indies, and other faith-less lands.'[30] In his crusade against the errors of the modern age, and the revolutionary agitation he believed they spawned, Gregory made some concessions in diplomacy and some minor compromises in the political arena, if not the religious sphere.

In his relations with the powers, Gregory revealed a degree of political pragmatism by following the precedent established by Pope Leo XII, which had allowed the Holy See to make appointments in Latin America and India. He indicated that where there were changes of government, the Roman pontiff would enter into diplomatic relations with those who exercised de facto power. He made it clear, however, that the Holy See did not intend to legitimize such regimes. This distinction between *de facto* and *de jure* governments enabled Rome to condemn the revolutions yet accept some of their consequences. No such flexibility was displayed by the Church in its own state, where Gregory's siege mentality prevailed.

He found the Neo-Guelph programme, which looked to the papacy to foster national unification in Italy, little better and perhaps more unrealistic than Giuseppe Mazzini's revolutionary organization 'Young Italy'. His intransigent anti-national stance contributed to the unrest in the Italian peninsula and particularly in his own state. While Gregory revealed a degree of pragmatism in foreign affairs, such was not the case at home or in Church matters, where his intransigence prevailed, provoking incessant disturbances and revolts.[31] He feared that revolutionary agitation lurked everywhere. Both liberals and conservatives continued to fear the outbreak of revolution at home and abroad, which could not be checked by Gregory's recourse to prayer – although they continued to propose different solutions to the problem. Thus when Gregory XVI died in the sixteenth year of his pontificate,[32] the moderates called for reform and the conservatives invoked the forceful restoration of order.

Since Gregory's pontificate had pursued a conservative course and resolved few problems, there were those in the Curia and the College of Cardinals who called for change and a more conciliatory policy that was better attuned to the modern world. They complained that the last pope idolized the Middle Ages, and sought to mire the Church and papacy in its old-fashioned mentality. His devotion to understanding the past and preserving the artefacts and manuscripts which shed light on historical developments was little appreciated. Pope Gregory was accused of being more concerned with manuscripts than people, the dead rather than the living, the past rather than the present. The majority of cardinals in the conclave desired a candidate who was neither intransigent nor permissive on reformism, while enjoying the support of the powers. This reversion to reformism played a part in the election of Cardinal Giovanni Maria Mastai-Ferretti as Pope Pius IX in June 1846.

IV

Pio Nono's Transition from Reform to Reaction

FOLLOWING THE ITALIAN SEIZURE OF HIS STATE, A GROUP OF visiting Romans enquired about the prospect of a reconciliation between the papacy and the Italian kingdom, but Pius proved pessimistic, asserting:

> No, no sort of conciliation is ever possible between Christ and Belial, between light and darkness, between truth and lies, between justice and usurpation.[1]

Giovanni Maria Mastai-Ferretti, who assumed the chair of Peter in June 1846 and served as the longest-reigning pope (1846–78), remains one of the most important. He helped shape the modern papacy, the modern Catholic Church and the course of Italian unification. During his pontificate he proclaimed the dogma of the Immaculate Conception, issued the Syllabus of Errors and was responsible for the declaration of papal infallibility, among other things. Nonetheless, for many he remains an enigma. Heralded at his accession as the 'liberal' pope who would reconcile liberty and religion, the Church and modernity, and Catholicism and Italian unification, he was seen at the end of his reign as the high priest of reaction, as well as the chief protagonist of the counter-Risorgimento.

When he was elected in 1846, Italy and the Papal States teetered on the brink of revolution. Precious little had been done in Rome to eliminate the general discontent since the upheaval of 1830–31, when Gregory XVI had been named pope and Mastai-Ferretti, then archbishop of Spoleto, had been constrained to abandon his post due to the spreading revolution. Order had been restored only

following Austrian military intervention. For many this pointed to
the need for change, which the major powers – Britain, France,
Austria, Russia and Prussia – noted in a memorandum calling for
administrative, fiscal and political reforms, including the creation
of a consultative assembly to advise the pope on governmental matters.[2] Most of their suggestions, although moderate and reasonable,
were ignored by Pope Gregory, which Mastai-Ferretti privately felt
was a mistake.

At this juncture Mastai-Ferretti, unlike many other clerics, did
not fear change. In fact, he was convinced that some reform in
Rome was both necessary and long overdue. During his years as
bishop of Imola (1832–46), he had maintained contact with liberals
such as Count Giuseppe Pasolini of Ravenna and sought some
conciliation between past and present, religion and progress, liberalism and Catholicism.[3] Although not a revolutionary, and strictly
speaking not even a liberal, he was critical of the outdated, slow
and ponderous Roman administration. He believed it provoked
rather than prevented the constant round of revolt and repression
in the papal state. He was convinced that a little common sense and
Christian justice on the part of the government would improve
matters.[4] Since repression had not brought peace he suggested that
a limited reformism might prove better, and did not comprehend
the government's unwillingness to alter its conservative and ineffective political course. Nor did he understand its opposition to the
introduction of railways, the illumination of major roads, gas
installations and the construction of suspension bridges. Theology,
Mastai-Ferretti observed, was opposed to neither science nor technol-
ogy.[5] Concerned about the disturbances in Rome and its provinces,
he saw the need for the papal state to achieve a reconciliation with
the modern world.

Elected pope in 1846, he took the name Pius in honour of Pius
VII, whose moderate reformism he favoured. His own reformist
attitude was perceived as a welcome change from the outlook of
his conservative predecessor, Gregory XVI. In truth, neither the
personality nor the performance of the new pope was objectively
assessed, but viewed through the prism of liberal and national
aspirations in the peninsula. Finally, there was a tendency to confuse

his role as pope and prince. It was in the latter capacity that Pius
invoked reform. While earlier his had been a lonely voice in the
wilderness, the call for reform in the Papal States now emerged
almost everywhere – in the provinces and cities as well as from
the Roman establishment – as Pius IX was petitioned to initiate a
new course.[6]

The recently elected pope wished to do so, but insisted that all
innovations should be compatible with the special nature of the
ecclesiastical government.[7] To assure himself of the orthodoxy of
the various proposals circulating and under consideration, he
created a commission of cardinals to screen and evaluate his
projected innovations. This body approved his general amnesty,
which demonstrated the goodwill of the new government.[8] When
the amnesty was proclaimed in July 1846,[9] it aroused the enthu-
siasm of the masses throughout Italy, and Pius was soon perceived
as 'father of his people' and 'saviour of the peninsula'. Overnight he
was transformed into a national figure, and praised by massive
demonstrations before the papal palace. The adoring crowds not
only sought the apostolic benediction but also implored Pius to
continue – indeed extend – his reformist programme to include
political as well as administrative changes.[10] The turn of events
alarmed the Austrians. In Vienna, Metternich realized that this
pope's reformism transcended what he had originally intended,
and worried that a continuation along this path would provoke
unfortunate consequences.[11]

In fact, this pope, following in the footsteps of Consalvi and
Pius VII, sought reform, not revolution. Furthermore, he envisioned
technical, administrative and economic reforms in his state rather
than changes in the Church. In Church matters he was a traditionalist, as was made clear in his first encyclical, the *Qui pluribus* of 9
November 1846. In it he revealed that while he saw the need to
reform the state, he would not sanction or tolerate criticism of the
Church or attempts to get it to accept the 'monstrous errors' of the
age. Among these 'errors' he cited rationalism and indifferentism
and praised his predecessor, Pope Gregory, for his campaign against
them.[12] He felt, however, that the state could be criticized, changed
and improved for the good of its citizens as well as the Church.

He had earlier explored and discussed the changes needed, and outlined a programme in his *Thoughts on the Public Administration of the Papal States* (1845).[13] In it he referred to and seconded the proposals put forward by the long-ignored Memorandum of the Powers of 1831, carefully considering and reviving the suggestions shelved by Gregory XVI. Others suggested that this was 'too little, too late'. Most approved his selection of the liberal Pasquale Gizzi as his secretary of state, along with his general amnesty, which released hundreds of inmates while allowing scores of exiles to return to Rome. These measures won Pius a liberal image at home and abroad, and widespread popular support.[14] Critics complained that Pius had not formulated fixed limits to his goals, and allowed himself to be pressured by the numerous and increasingly massive demonstrations motivated by a political agenda, which weakened the state and threatened the Church.

Pius ignored most of the early criticism and determined to use the power of the papacy to remedy the problems he believed prevailed in his state. He created a commission of cardinals to co-ordinate his general reform programme, and another to propose changes in the state's judicial system. Initially, things went well and citizens were delighted that the price of salt was decreased and extraordinary tribunals abolished, while six railway lines were projected and telegraph companies charted.[15] Pius examined the management of hospitals, prisons and religious institutions, finances, and the collection of public revenue. At the same time he opened a number of public offices to laypeople, leading some to suspect that he intended to secularize the administration. This clearly was not his intent, but he did use his position to reduce unemployment by calling upon the heads of the various provinces to provide jobs and reduce crime. His reforms were widely known and appreciated as a result of a new press law that tolerated the expression of liberal and nationalist, as well as reformist, sentiments, which had formerly been prohibited.

The pope's reforms were enthusiastically received and produced more and larger 'demonstrations of gratitude', which pleased him but frightened a number of others. Metternich in Vienna deplored the course of events, warning that if the pope continued to pander to the radicals he would be forced out of Rome. This view was shared by Pius IX's secretary of state Cardinal Gizzi, who continued to stress the difference between progress and constitutionalism – accepting the first but rejecting the latter. It was he who convinced the pope to speak out against the increasingly loud and large demonstrations that threatened stability and order. Only at the end of the first year of his pontificate did Pius denounce those who habitually disturbed the peace of his state.[16] This proclamation, deemed the work of the conservatives in the Curia, did not undermine the pope's popularity. Indeed, Pius was seen to ignore the warnings and, encouraged by the mass gatherings and public marches, proceeded along his reformist course, ignoring the concerns of conservatives at home and abroad.

Eventually, as the demands of the demonstrators increased, Pius began to realize that his initial modest goals were being subverted. He particularly deplored the attempts to influence spiritual matters, and was scandalized by the popular pressure to expel the Jesuits from Rome.[17] Meanwhile, the public, or those who allegedly spoke on its behalf, demanded more than administrative changes, and as early as January 1847 a committee was formed to introduce a series of broad political innovations.[18] To quieten the outcry, early in the spring of 1847 provision was made for a national consultative assembly in Rome, and in June a measure approved for the creation of a council of ministers. Cardinal Gizzi, a member of the moderate camp, revealed the government's determination to continue its administrative reforms, adding that there were limits to what could be conceded politically, given the special nature of the pontifical regime.[19] The negative reaction to his words alarmed Gizzi, who saw the need to curtail the policy of making concessions to keep the crowds quiet. He confided to the Sardinian representative that if things got any further out of hand, he would have to appeal for Austrian intervention. Shortly thereafter, he alerted Vienna to the possible need for its assistance.[20]

Pio Nono's reformism raised national expectations that could not be fulfilled easily, just as the publication of Karl Marx's *Communist Manifesto* in February 1848 promised a new social order that could not soon emerge. Metternich worried about the impact of Mastai-Ferretti's actions not only in Rome but throughout Italy and beyond.[21] Although he had long favoured a limited reformism in Rome, the Austrian chancellor believed that the new pope had granted more than was necessary or prudent. Above all, he feared the consequences of the amnesty in the Legations.[22] Metternich remained suspicious of both the orchestrated ovations made to the pope and the incompetence and indecisiveness of the papal authorities, who allowed control of public order to slip through their feeble hands. He again warned that this misguided course would eventually force Pius to flee Rome.[23] Having long sided with the reformers against the reactionaries in the Curia, Mastai-Ferretti continued to invoke reform to forestall revolution.[24]

In 1848, the year that brought revolution to Palermo, Paris and a good part of Central Europe, the pope created a special committee of ecclesiastics to coordinate existing institutions, and to determine whether he could grant his people the constitution, or *statuto*, they sought. Frightened by the paroxysm of revolution, which would soon storm the gates of Vienna, the committee reported that granting a *statuto* was preferable to the other two alternatives for dealing with the volatile situation: revolution or foreign intervention.[25] The pope concurred, but made it clear that the constitution must in no way restrict the rights of the Church or go counter to the convictions of the faith. This helps to explain article 25 of the constitution, which specified that the profession of the Catholic faith was a prerequisite for citizenship.[26] Privately, Pius had reservations about granting the constitution, but hoped that making such a concession would help preserve the authority of the papal regime during this time of trouble.[27] He would grant everything compatible with his position as pope, who united both temporal and spiritual power, trusting that this would suffice to restrain the revolutionary impulse. The course of events would soon put the papal decision to the test.

After the anti-Austrian insurrection in Venice on 17 March 1848, followed by the uprising in Milan of 18–22 March (the 'Five Days of Milan') and the Piedmontese decision of 23 March to help their brethren across the Ticino River, there followed a call for a national crusade to expel the foreigner, and the pope was pressed to participate. As an Italian, Pius indicated that he welcomed the events of 1848, but as head of the universal Church he could not forget his primary responsibility to preserve its integrity, independence and impartiality.[28] Thus while he allowed papal military forces to march northward, he issued instructions that their mission was purely defensive, prohibiting them from assuming an aggressive stance. In March, and even more so in April, while Pius was moved by the national struggle, his first preoccupation remained the welfare of the Church and he was haunted by the fear of a possible schism on the part of German Catholics.

The emotional pope was stunned by reports that the people of Austria held the Holy Father responsible for the war that was being waged against them.[29] 'Italian nationalism is overrunning the whole of Italy, and it is a natural sentiment', Pius wrote, 'but my position is such that I cannot declare war against anyone.'[30] Days later he revealed his intention to make his position public.[31] He did so in a controversial allocution of 29 April 1848, which asserted that as common father of all Catholics, he was not prepared to wage war against Catholic Austria, although he could not prevent his subjects from entering the conflict as volunteers. The reaction to the pope's statement was immediate and negative, provoking a revolution in Rome and forcing Pius to flee his capital at the end of November 1848, after the assassination of his minister Pellegrino Rossi.[32] Subsequently, an assembly proclaimed the end of the Papal States, replacing it with a second Roman Republic (1849). From his exile in the Kingdom of Naples, Pius condemned the republic and its constitution, and excommunicated the radicals and revolutionaries responsible for both.

Ably assisted by Cardinal Giacomo Antonelli, the pope argued that Rome had become 'a den of wild beasts', 'apostates' and 'heretics', which he could not tolerate and which justified his flight.[33] In exile he came to regret his earlier concessions, which he concluded in retrospect had contributed to the revolution and weakened his spiritual sovereignty. From his bitter exile in the Kingdom of Naples, Pius branded the Roman Republic 'an iniquity', deeming the temporal power not only legitimate but also absolutely essential,[34] and demanded its return. He called upon the Catholic powers of France, Austria, Naples and Spain to overturn the Roman Republic and restore his sovereignty. Their intervention did not quieten the fears of the pope, who was haunted by the revolutionary outburst. In exile, he abandoned the last vestiges of his earlier reformism.

Mastai-Ferretti was now convinced that a war was being waged upon religion and considered the revolutionary upheaval nothing less than a part of that satanic scheme.[35] For this among other reasons, he belatedly concurred with Consalvi that constitutionalism was incompatible with the governance of the papal state.[36] Consequently, much that he had tolerated earlier he now deemed suspect and inadmissible, including freedom of the press and liberty of association.[37] He increasingly seconded Donoso Cortés's rejection of modern civilization, rationalism and progress. 'In regard to parliamentarianism, to liberalism, and to rationalism', Cortés had quipped, 'I believe of the first that it is the negation of government; of the second, that it is the negation of liberty; and of the third, that it is the affirmation of madness.'[38] Thus the turbulent events of 1848–9, which Pius perceived as an attack on the temporal power as well as the faith, firmed his resolve to wage a counter-offensive. This determination was reinforced by social and religious developments that flowed from the Industrial Revolution, and Rome's condemnation of the excesses of economic liberalism and communism. His reaction against the schemes of Italian nationalism and the unification of the peninsula is known as the counter-Risorgimento.

Chagrined that his concessions to constitutionalism had led to revolution and the loss of the temporal power he deemed essential for the Church and papacy, Pius now pursued a conservative and cautious course and shunned even moderate reformism. When questioned why he abandoned the reasonable changes he had earlier favoured, he replied honestly that those who had been scalded by hot water feared even the cold.[39] Having been burnt in the governance of his state and in his role as ruler, following his return to Rome in 1850 he abandoned his reformism. Although he drafted the general outline of the new political policy in the *motu proprio* of 12 September 1849, he left the day-to-day course of action in the capable hands of his chief minister, Cardinal Giacomo Antonelli.

Pius, in turn, focused on his role as priest and pope, along with Church matters including a number of beatifications, the re-establishment of the hierarchy in England and Wales in 1850, and the elevation of the sees of New York, New Orleans, Saint Louis and Cincinnati to the rank of archbishoprics. In 1853 he effected the restoration of the Catholic hierarchy in the Netherlands. He shared and continued Gregory's interest in the missions and during his pontificate established thirty-three vicariates, fifteen prefectures and three delegations for the mission territories. Working closely with the prefect of Propaganda Fide, Pius created a number of new missionary institutes especially in Italy, to compensate for those the republicans had closed or curtailed. These included the Pontifical Missionary Institute of Milan, the Silesians of John Bosco, the Missionary Institute for Africa and the Association of the Sacred Heart of Jesus.[40]

Among his other religious concerns was his desire to recognize the special role of the Virgin Mary, the mother of Jesus, in the Church, to whom he had been devoted from childhood. He did so by the proclamation of the dogma of the Immaculate Conception (1854), which stipulated that she was born without the stain of original sin. Critics charged that he had done so unilaterally, indeed arbitrarily, and this was a step towards his later proclamation of papal infallibility. It was an inaccurate assessment, for Pius did in fact consult the bishops and a series of theologians on the issue, and out of the 600 who responded, 540 favoured the projected defin-ition. It was with broad support that he issued *Ineffabilis Deus*, which proclaimed the dogma of the Immaculate Conception on 8 December 1854. It is true that this pope favoured protecting and enhancing the position of the papacy in the Church, and supported centralization by imposing the Roman liturgy on the bishops of the eastern Churches united with Rome, calling upon all bishops to make periodic or *ad limina* visits to Rome.

While he achieved considerable success in the religious realm and was loved and admired by the broad masses, Pius IX confronted a series of challenges in the political arena. Many of his political problems stemmed from his anti-nationalist stance in an age of nationalism and his determination to preserve the temporal power while Cavour's Piedmont sought to unify the peninsula. Cavour's newspaper *Il Risorgimento* reported early on that the pope's failure to support the 'national crusade' was crucial and would inevitably lead Italians to conclude that the national movement and the temporal power were incompatible.[41] In fact, Cavour and his allies took steps to retaliate against Rome. The actions of the Piedmontese led Pius to suspect that they coveted the Papal States, and this explains the papal decision to exclude them from the Catholic coalition of France, Spain, Austria and Naples to overturn the Second Roman Republic and restore the papal state to Pius.

Partly in retaliation, and partly flowing from their reform programme, in 1850 Cavour and his political allies passed the Siccardi Laws, which terminated the various forms of ecclesiastical jurisdiction hitherto enjoyed by the clergy in their state. This legislation also eliminated the Church's ancient right of asylum in Piedmont and limited public observance of Catholic holidays to six, while it provided for the suppression of mortmain – which ensured the Church the inalienable possession of its land. Finally, the legislation indicated the Turin government's intention of introducing legislation making marriage a civil contract, a measure Pius was known to oppose vehemently.[42]

To make matters worse from the papal perspective, it soon became clear that Cavour was contemplating other measures against the Church. In the mid-1850s he supported the Law of Convents, which not only provided for their suppression but also imposed taxes upon episcopal and Church property. In January 1855 Pius denounced the legislation as 'impolitic and illegal', which moved Victor Emmanuel to seek a compromise – which led Cavour to resign. The king, who needed Cavour's diplomatic skills to deal with the peacemaking at the Congress of Paris of 1856, put aside his objections to the Law of Convents and allowed it to pass in May 1855. Cavour returned to office and hired his 'cousin', the voluptuous Contessa di Castiglione, to seduce Napoleon III and convince him to support the Italian cause. She claimed to have achieved both objectives and later deemed herself the 'Forgotten Figure of the Risorgimento'.[43]

The Crimean War, and the Peace of Paris which ended it, brought a shift in the diplomatic balance of power that proved favourable for Piedmont but less than favourable for the papacy. Russia, the leading conservative power, was defeated and no longer supported Austria's conservative course and the status quo. Instead, she turned her attention to domestic matters and internal reform because she resented the fact that Austria had done virtually nothing to assist her during the Crimean conflict. The fracture of the Austrian-Russian 'alliance' worked to the advantage of revisionist France and Cavour, who sought to reorganize Italy and encouraged them both to do so. In July 1858 Cavour ventured to Plombières, where he and Napoleon III plotted provoking Austria into war with the intent of pushing her out of Lombardy and Venetia and allowing Piedmont to create a kingdom of Northern Italy. In return for French assistance in the creation of the North Italian kingdom, Cavour promised to turn over Nice and Savoy to France.

In April 1859 war erupted between Austria on the one side, and Piedmont and France on the other. Franco-Piedmontese forces pushed the Austrians out of Lombardy while Cavour secretly encouraged and supported revolutions in Parma, Tuscany and the Romagna. Pius IX, the temporal ruler of the Romagna, was distressed by its revolt and rightly suspected Piedmontese complicity there and in Bologna. Neither he nor his chief minister Cardinal Antonelli found credible the Piedmontese king's assertion that he had intervened there only to prevent anarchy by restoring law and order. Both suspected that the Piedmontese sought more, to the dismay of the pope, who cried out: 'First they only spoke of the Legations, now they also want the Marches and Umbria.' He concluded by asking rhetorically: 'how can I concede such things?'[44] Cavour did indeed want more. Under the pretext of preventing Giuseppe Garibaldi, who had captured Sicily and Naples, from marching on to Rome, Cavour attained the approval of Napoleon III to have the Piedmontese military forces march south towards the border with Naples. In the process, Piedmont absorbed most of the pope's territory, leaving only a small area surrounding Rome, protected by French forces, under papal control. To make matters even worse from the papal perspective, in announcing the formation of the Kingdom of Italy in 1860, Cavour proclaimed that Rome, too, would eventually have to be surrendered by the papacy to become the capital of united Italy.[45]

These events, which delighted Italian nationalists, depressed Pope Pius IX, who refused to accept or in any manner sanction the spoliation of his state. Already in his allocution of June 1859, *Ad gravissimum*, he declared the rebellions in Bologna, Ravenna and Perugia null and void and invoked the intervention of the powers. None was forthcoming, however, because Russia and Austria had suffered military setbacks, while France had collaborated with Cavour and helped create the present situation. Pius IX's recourse to a general excommunication of those responsible for the seizure of the papal state was all but ignored, while Cavour, for his part, used the conflict with the pope and Church to obtain political advantages at home and abroad, and proved able to attract an increasing number of radicals to his banner. The Piedmontese chief minister understood the papal anger but hoped that Pius would eventually be reconciled to the loss of his state, and its incorporation into the Kingdom of Italy, proclaimed in 1861. Pius was not reconciled to this when Cavour died in 1861, and in fact his address of June 1862, which cited his need for the state, was signed by 21 cardinals, 4 patriarchs, 53 archbishops and 187 bishops. Publicly, Pius insisted on the need for the temporal power.

Meanwhile, Giuseppe Garibaldi, earlier responsible for overturning the Kingdom of Naples, in 1862 determined to add Rome to his conquests. His attempt to seize Rome and bring it into the newly formed Kingdom of Italy was helped rather than hindered by the Italian authorities. As thousands of volunteers joined the general in shouting 'Either Rome or Death!', the Italian authorities sought to convince Napoleon III that only an Italian incursion and occupation of the Eternal City could stop the *Garibaldini*.

Napoleon, unwilling to alienate French Catholics any further, did not accept this conclusion. Threatening retaliation, he constrained the Italians to block the volunteers at Aspromonte. The military attempt having failed, the Italians had recourse to diplomacy to acquire Rome. In September 1864 an agreement was reached between Paris and Turin whereby the French promised to withdraw their military from Rome within two years, in return for an Italian pledge not to undertake any incursion into Rome, while assuring that no one else did so from their soil. To convince the French that they no longer sought to make Rome their capital, the Italians promised to move the capital from Turin, always perceived as a temporary capital, to Florence, presumably their permanent centre of government. Pius, having decried the duplicity first of the Kingdom of Piedmont, followed by that of the Italian state, suspected the Italian commitment to abandon their claim to Rome. His assessment proved accurate.

The terms of this September Convention disturbed Antonelli, and even more so the pope. Pius perceived it as part of the liberal-nationalist conspiracy against the Church and papacy, and responded in December 1864 in the encyclical *Quanta cura*, to which was attached a long list of erroneous propositions of the age, soon dubbed the 'Syllabus of Errors'. It included a denunciation of religious liberalism along with the growing secularism and materialism of the time. It also condemned absolute rationalism, naturalism and latitudinarianism, creating consternation in liberal circles, which resented Rome's condemnations. They found even more disturbing the papal denunciations of political developments, especially those catalogued under 'Errors of Civil Society' and 'Errors of Modern Liberalism'. These included the separation of Church and state, freedom to choose any religion, liberalism, nationalism and democracy. In the eyes of critics, the papal inability to reconcile itself with 'progress, liberalism and civilization as lately introduced' pointed to the failure of the papacy and the papal state.[46] The French protested against the papal bull, which considered excommunicated all those who constrained clerics to appear before secular tribunals.

The Italians disliked the syllabus and understood, as most others did not, that it was largely directed against them. They were not intimidated, however, and continued their campaign against the Church and papacy. As before, they insisted that newly named bishops swear allegiance to the Italian government and in 1866 approved a civil marriage law by which the state no longer recognized a Church marriage as sufficient, and required a civil marriage as well. That same year the state suppressed and refused to recognize all the religious orders and congregations in the kingdom.[47] While Pio Nono was worried about actions directed against the Church and the faith, his secretary of state expressed concern about the future of Rome in 1866, as word spread of a likely Italian involvement in the impending conflict between Prussia and Austria. Antonelli feared that during the war the Italians would attempt to complete their unification by moving against either Rome or Venice. Luckily for the papacy, they sought to obtain Venice in 1866, and succeeded. The cardinal, like the pope, however, suspected that they still lusted for Rome, after hearing reports that the Italian king complained that while Italy was made, it was still not complete. The Vatican's fears were compounded when the French left Rome in 1866 under the terms of the September Convention and Garibaldi attempted to seize the city in 1867. This prompted the return of a French military force, which defeated the Garibaldi 'volunteers' at Mentana. The French thus ensured that Rome would remain papal for the moment, though Antonelli and the pope worried about the future. Their fears were far from groundless.

Despite a series of losses and other ordeals, Pius ix kept his faith and his lively sense of humour. Thus when a lady approached him, gushing that she had obtained one of his socks and that her sick leg was miraculously cured after donning it, the pope shot back: 'Ah nice, by using only one of my socks you are cured, while I who use two am unable to rid myself of my leg problems.'[48] When the French withdrew from Rome, a member of their ministry sought to reassure the pope that all would be well, telling him that he should not worry because the emperor would be there. 'And I am here', Pius replied, 'and everyone knows that Paris is quite far from Rome.'[49]

Once Austria was defeated and concentrating on internal reforms rather than developments in Italy, Antonelli recognized that papal control of Rome was largely, if not completely, dependent upon French support. Consequently, the secretary of state asserted clearly that the papacy and Church should not – indeed must not – anger or alienate Napoleon iii. For this and other reasons, Antonelli was reluctant to reject the emperor's suggestion that a conference of the powers be convoked to propose a solution to the Roman question. Largely at Antonelli's suggestion, Pius did not reject Napoleon's proposal outright, but his insistence that at the conference the principle of legitimate rights must prevail and guide the solution, effectively torpedoed the emperor's proposal. In point of fact, the pope continued to emphasize religious issues and the conference he envisioned would focus on them.

It is difficult to know precisely when Pius ix decided to convoke a Church Council, but he had reportedly considered doing so as far back as his exile in Gaeta. However, he revealed his intention of doing so only on 6 December 1864, two days before he issued *Quanta cura* and the attached Syllabus of Errors. The timing sheds some light on the pope's concerns and the matters he found troubling when he asked the cardinals of the Curia to consider his proposal, which a majority of the cardinals obediently approved. In March 1865, a commission of five cardinals was appointed to catalogue the matters to be considered, and the following month, 36 bishops of the Latin rite were asked to provide additional input. It was only on 29 June 1868, with the bull *Aeterni patris*, that the pope fixed the date of the first Council in some 300 years, on 8 December 1869, the Feast of the Immaculate Conception. It was expected that the Council would last some two years and conclude with the festivities of 1871, to celebrate the 25th anniversary of Pius ix's pontificate.

In April 1869, before the opening of the Council, a number of important events in the life of Pope Pius were celebrated: the golden jubilee of his priesthood, the fiftieth anniversary of his first Mass, the fourteenth anniversary of his miraculous escape from death following the collapse of the floor at Sant'Agnese, and the nineteenth anniversary of his return to Rome. During the course of these celebrations Pius was showered with gifts and praised, but the pope was looking forward to the events of the Council on which his attention was increasingly focused. Despite the contention of some that Pius did not play a crucial role in shaping the agenda and outcome of the Council, the opposite is the case. The papal bull convoking the Council expressed Pio Nono's objective of securing and safeguarding the Church and society from the calamities of the modern age, and aimed to correct, if not extirpate, these threatening errors. Furthermore, it was he who opposed inviting secular princes to participate in the Council, as they had in the past. Finally, Pius was largely responsible for focusing the Council on the need to strengthen the papacy, including the need to proclaim papal infallibility, to protect the Church, the faith and Rome from the errors, ideologies and policies unleashed by the present age.

The prospect of the Vatican Council proclaiming papal infallibility was brought to public attention by an article on 6 February 1869 in the Jesuit-run journal *La Civiltà Cattolica*. From the first, the notion provoked controversy both inside and outside the Church, with some ardently supporting the proclamation and others vehemently opposing it. One of the chief opponents of the proclamation was Johann Josef Ignatius von Döllinger, the dominant Catholic theologian of the University of Munich. Writing under the pseudonym Janus, he produced a series of articles which sought to show that no such thing as an infallible pope had ever existed in the long history of the institution. Not surprisingly, most Protestants and Orthodox opposed the proclamation and some in these two camps now regretted having rejected the invitation to attend the Council to voice their opposition therein.

A number of states, including Catholic Bavaria, feared the political as well as religious consequences flowing from papal infallibility, and sought to initiate and orchestrate joint action on the part of the powers to prevent its proclamation. The Italian government, however, was one of the few that favoured and seconded the Bavarian proposal. Most of the other powers, including Protestant Prussia, opted for non-intervention. Some, such as Cardinal Henri-Marie-Gaston de Bonnechose of France, sought to dissuade Pius privately from forging ahead on infallibility, but this only aroused the pope, who reportedly responded that the cardinal made a habit of opposing things: 'I remember that on a former occasion you were opposed to raising the doctrine of the Immaculate Conception to a dogma', he blurted out. He went on to say: 'thank God we willed that it should be so, and it was so; and we will that the infallibility of the Pope shall be made a dogma, and it shall become one though the influence of the Council of 1869'.[50] To expedite its approval, Pius decided to give it precedence by taking it out of its assigned order, despite the vocal opposition of the minority. When the cardinal archbishop of Bologna, Filippo Maria Guidi, supposedly suggested changes in the proclamation, in keeping with tradition, the angry pope allegedly retorted: 'I am tradition.'[51]

Although the pace of progress on infallibility was steady, the pope was impatient because he was supporting more than half the Council members, and in light of the Piedmontese and Italian seizure of most of his lands and assets, he had a limited income and for a time faced financial ruin. It was Antonelli who saved Pius and the papacy by reorganizing Peter's Pence, the contributions of the faithful worldwide.[52] In fact, the pope was still dependent upon this charity and therefore could not support long delays. Nonetheless, he kept his sense of humour, noting that by the time he was proclaimed infallible he would have failed financially.[53] Partly to satisfy Pius, at the end of June 1870 the debate on infallibility was closed, and on 13 July a preliminary vote was taken. It was accepted by 451 members and rejected by 88 members, with 62 withholding approval pending modification, while 76 members boycotted the session.

A small delegation of five members of the opposition met Pius and promised unanimous support for the proclamation, if it were modified to read that the pope had first to meet with the bishops. Pius refused to accept this modification, which he believed undermined it. When the final vote was taken on 18 July 1870, many of the bishops opposing the measure chose to leave Rome rather than vote against the measure. Only two members of the Council voted against the proclamation on 18 July: Edward Fitzgerald, bishop of Little Rock, and Luigi Riccio, bishop of Caizzo. The dogma read:

> We teach and define that it is a dogma divinely revealed: that the Roman Pontiff, when he speaks *ex cathedra*, that is when in discharge of the Office of Pastor and Doctor of all Christians by virtue of his supreme Apostolic authority, he defines a doctrine regarding faith or morals to be held by the Universal Church, by the divine assistance promised to him in blessed Peter, is possessed of that infallibility with which the divine Redeemer willed that his Church should be endowed for defining doctrine regarding faith or morals; and that therefore such definitions of

the Roman Pontiff are 'irreformable' of themselves, and not from the consent of the Church. But if any one – which may God avert – presume to contradict this our definition; let him be anathema.[54]

Pius did not have much time to celebrate his victory in having infallibility proclaimed on 18 July 1870. The very next day, 19 July, the Franco-Prussian War erupted, with far-reaching consequences not only for France and Germany but also for Italy and the papacy. Once the war started to go badly for the French, in August they felt constrained to withdraw their forces from Rome, leaving the Eternal City vulnerable to an Italian invasion. It did not take long in coming, for in mid-September an Italian army of 60,000 men marched towards Rome – ostensibly to preserve order there but actually to capture it and make it their capital. Bombardment of its gates followed by the Italian entry and occupation on 20 September 1870 led Pius to protest against the Italian invasion, but no one came to his assistance. The Italian army orchestrated a plebiscite in October 1870, in which the Romans allegedly voted in favour of union with the Kingdom of Italy. In turn, Pius suspended the Vatican Council, excommunicated all those responsible for planning and executing the invasion and annexation, and locked himself in the Vatican, proclaiming himself a prisoner therein.

In an attempt to calm the pope and reassure the powers, particularly the Catholic ones, that Pius was not being mistreated, the Italian government approved the Law of Papal Guarantees on 13 May 1871. This legislation at once respected the inviolability of the pope and recognized in him all the attributes of sovereignty. In compensation for the losses he sustained at the hands of the Italians, the law provided for an annual payment of 3,225,000 lire in perpetuity – and not subject to taxation. Both the pope and Antonelli recognized that their acceptance of this law would legitimize the Italian action and therefore rejected it and the subsidy. Pius denounced it in his encyclical *Ubi nos arcano* of 15 May 1871, as well as his allocution to the College of Cardinals towards the end of October 1871. The pope's refusal to recognize the fait accompli did not prevent the Italian government from leaving Florence and moving to Rome. Nor did it prevent the states of Europe from recognizing Rome as the Italian capital. These actions led Pius to believe that the European powers had abandoned him.

His self-imposed imprisonment in the Vatican upset the formerly sociable pope, who received reports – often exaggerated – of Italian outrages in the holy city. In 1872 he was furious when he learned that the Italians had passed legislation suppressing Roman monasteries and selling their property. He resented the restrictions imposed on religious processions and the secularization of education in Rome. In light of these and other Italian 'crimes', Pius did not see how the Holy See could come to terms with such a regime. 'It is useless to talk of conciliation', he told a group of visiting Romans and foreigners at the end of November 1871, 'for the Church can never conciliate itself with error and the Pope cannot separate himself from the Church.'[55]

The 'intransigent' attitude of Pius ix disturbed Bismarck, the Prussian chancellor of newly united Germany, who found him difficult to deal with and resented his disapproval of Germany's annexation of Alsace-Lorraine. The papal refusal to accept Cardinal Hohenlohe as the German representative to the Holy See, and unwillingness to curb the opposition of the Catholic Centre Party to the Iron Chancellor's policies, led him to join with the German liberals in the *Kulturkampf* against the pope and the Church. While the liberals considered the pope who condemned liberalism an ideological opponent, Bismarck's aims were political rather than ideological. Nonetheless, Bismarck went along with the liberal laws of May 1873, which required Catholic clergy to receive part of their education in German schools, placed Catholic seminaries under state inspection and forbade Catholics from appealing to ecclesiastical courts outside Germany. Pius perceived these and other measures as part of the war being waged against the Church, but did not despair. He trusted that eventually divine intervention would protect the Church, its flock and its leadership. He died in 1878, adhering to that expectation.

V

Leo XIII: Conciliation with Modernity, Conflict with Italy

ARTICLE 131 OF LEO XIII'S ENCYCLICAL *RERUM NOVARUM* OF 15 May 1891 stipulated:

> Among the most important duties of employers the principal one is to give every worker what is justly due him. Assuredly, to establish a rule of pay in accord with justice, many factors must be taken into account. But, in general, the rich and employers should remember that no laws, either human or divine, permit them for their own profit to oppress the needy and the wretched or to seek gain from another's want. To defraud anyone of the wage due him is a great crime that calls down avenging wrath from heaven.[1]

Following the long, turbulent and troubled pontificate of Pio Nono (1846–78), preparation was made for the election of a successor to confront the problems facing the faith. Recognizing the importance of their decision, and seeking guidance, a solemn Mass to the Holy Spirit was celebrated on the morning of 19 February 1878, and afterwards the cardinals entered the conclave to select a successor. The task of the fathers assembled in the Vatican to elect the new pope was at once crucial and difficult. It was crucial because Catholicism confronted a host of serious problems and appeared to be at a turning point, requiring sound and strong leadership. It proved difficult to decide who could best guide the Church during this period of prevailing trials and tribulations. Disagreement ensued on whether the new pope should follow the path and policies of the pope who had made most of them cardinals, or pursue a less confrontational course to resolve the problems the Church faced.

The picture was complicated by the fact that assessments of the past pontificate varied widely, even though 60 of the 61 cardinals in the conclave had been named by Pius IX. Furthermore, the conflict between intransigents and moderates in the College of Cardinals continued, dividing those who favoured confronting the errors of the age from those who sought conciliation with the modern world. While some praised Pius IX for his adherence to principle, others pointed to his failure to use diplomacy to achieve papal goals; some deemed his self-imposed imprisonment courageous, but others pointed to the unfortunate consequences that flowed from the papal isolation. Clearly, Pius IX had reasserted Rome's traditionalism vis-à-vis 'modern civilization', but his critics cited the great cost to the Church, the clergy and the faithful.

During the longest pontificate to date, the Church had not only lost its state but the papacy also appeared to be isolated, and abandoned and disregarded by all nations.[2] It had become embroiled in a bitter conflict with the Kingdom of Italy over the Roman Question, and with Bismarck's Germany in the *Kulturkampf*. Pio Nono's decision to call for a monarchical restoration in France proved counter-productive, arousing the republicans, who retaliated by restricting the influence of the Church in state and society. While Pius IX's admirers applauded his conclusion of a concordat with Russia, critics complained that it had never been implemented, and persecution of the Catholic Poles continued unabated.[3] Relations with Austria and Switzerland were not good, and in much of Europe and the world beyond, the issue of papal infallibility provoked controversy and aroused opposition. In fact, at the death of the intransigent Pius, fewer than half a dozen states sent representatives to the Holy See, and the position of the papacy in the eyes of many reached a low point.

Despite these deep divisions in the conclave, within two days, on the third ballot on 20 February 1878, the cardinals selected the 68-year-old urbane, aristocratic and cultured Gioacchino Vincenzo Raffaele Pecci. He received 44 votes out of the 61 cast, more than the two-thirds needed for election.[4] Some were surprised, because Pius had named him papal chamberlain, and usually the *Camerlengo* is not considered for the papal position. Speculation spread that the choice and the haste of the conclave reflected the fear of possible Italian intervention in the election, or the attempt to exercise the veto power still claimed by Austria, France and Spain. Others believed that the dire situation required immediate leadership and hoped that the new pope would pursue a more flexible and diplomatic policy than his predecessor.

Those who did not want another long pontificate voted for Pecci because of his advanced age and poor health. He was judged a safe interim candidate by almost all. Conservatives were won over by his hard line on the Roman Question and strong support of the papacy's temporal power, while liberals supported him for his diplomacy, social consciousness and concern for workers. Apparently, many settled on Pecci because he was neither an extreme reactionary nor a radical reformer. In fact, his selection of the moderate cardinal Alessandro Franchi as his secretary of state pleased both liberals and conservatives. In Italy, the rest of Europe and most of the world beyond there was a muted response to his election, for Pecci was little known outside Perugia.

Pecci was born on 2 March 1810 into the aristocratic Siennese and profoundly religious family of Count Luigi Domenico Pecci in Carpineto (Frosinone), in the diocese of Anagni, north of Rome. His brother Giuseppe became a priest and cardinal, while his deeply devout mother was a member of the Third Order of St Francis. The sixth child and fourth son of the Pecci family attended the Jesuit College of Viterbo (1818–24), and then the Roman College (1824–32), restored to the Jesuits the year he entered – and he excelled in both schools. In 1825 he headed a student deputation to Pope Leo XII (1823–9), and was impressed by his person and presence.

In 1830 he began theological studies at the Gregorian University in Rome. After he received a degree in Sacred Theology in 1832, he entered the Pontifical Academy of Noble Ecclesiastics, preparing for a future in the Vatican diplomatic service. The intellectually inclined Pecci studied theology and civil and canon law at the Sapienza (1832–7). Ordained a priest on 31 December 1837 and named one of Pope Gregory's domestic prelates, he was given the title of monsignor. At the end of 1837 he was selected to serve as apostolic delegate or governor in the principality of Benevento, surrounded by the Kingdom of Naples, where he fell suddenly and seriously ill. Following his recovery, in 1841 he was dispatched to Spoleto and Perugia, a centre of nationalist agitation, secret societies and widespread anti-papal sentiment. His diplomatic skills were attested to by his ability to garner the backing and support of conservatives, moderates and liberals alike.

He was moved once again by Pope Gregory, who in January 1843 consecrated him as a bishop and in February sent him to Belgium as nuncio (1843–6), where he remained for three years and expanded his social and diplomatic horizons. Pecci's years there were extremely important in his economic and social formation, for Belgium was highly industrialized in comparison to central Italy. In Belgium he witnessed first-hand the advantages and problems created by the emerging industrial society, especially the plight of factory workers, all too often treated as commodities rather than Christian souls. It is believed that it was not his critique of Belgian capitalism but his opposition to the government's secularization of education that led to his recall.

Reportedly, Monsignor Pecci was highly valued by King Leopold I of Belgium, who was the uncle of the young Queen Victoria. When she visited Brussels, the king introduced him to the queen and her consort, Albert. This encounter initiated Pecci's life-long belief in the importance of Anglo-Vatican relations. Furthermore, his recall resulted from the petition of the people and magistrate of Perugia, who asked at the beginning of 1846 that Pecci be appointed archbishop of their city and return to reside in it.[5] He did, but on his way back spent a month in London, and two months in Paris, renewing old contacts, making new ones and further broadening his background and outlook. King Leopold's request that Pecci be given a cardinal's hat was delayed until 1853 due to the death of Pope Gregory XVI in 1846, and Pio Nono's numerous and more pressing preoccupations during the restoration.

Although Pecci was named to the College of Cardinals in 1853, he remained in Perugia for some thirty years. All sorts of explanations were concocted for his 'exile' from Rome, including the rivalry and jealousy of Giacomo Cardinal Antonelli, or his reservations about the proclamation of the dogma of the Immaculate Conception, which Pius strongly supported. Some believed Pecci made matters worse, once the dogma was proclaimed, by pleading that those who believed otherwise should not be condemned. Finally, it was claimed that the pope allegedly resented his less than enthusiastic support of the 'Syllabus of Errors'. Much of this is conjecture, contradicted by his stance at the Vatican Council, where he supported the pope and the majority favouring infallibility, and joined them in denouncing contemporary errors. Furthermore, he did not believe that the condemnations anathematized the modern world or denounced all progress. In Perugia, Pecci faced a host of problems which increased dramatically after 1860, when the city was annexed into the new state. Pecci opposed civil marriage, the secularization of education and the confiscation of property belonging to the religious orders, as well as other anti-clerical measures. The rumours that he welcomed the Italian king to Perugia were simply not true. While Pecci could not stop Victor Emmanuel II from entering the city, he did not welcome, greet or meet him.

In addition to his diplomatic skills, Pecci was familiar with the broad social currents of the age, and particularly sympathetic to the needs of an industrial society and the working classes it produced. He took a special interest in the international meetings of social Catholics at Fribourg, under the leadership of Monsignor Mermillod. Basing his social concerns and thought on the Gospels and the long-standing concern of the Church for the poor, the new pope embraced Catholic social doctrine as part of his mandate to defend humanity. He perceived the social question linked to the Church's magisterial mission. Although Pecci favoured a moderate reformism, he did not come into conflict nor contradict Pius IX's policies, and was elected by a conclave almost entirely selected by the previous pope. Indeed, following his coronation in early March 1878, he issued his first consistorial allocution to the sacred college, in which he echoed much of his predecessor's critique of contemporary developments and cited the evils that assailed humanity from every side. Like Pius, Leo related his 'deep anxiety by the very sad state, in our days, of civil society almost everywhere and especially of this Apostolic See, which violently stripped of its temporal sovereignty, is reduced to a condition in which it [no longer enjoyed] the full, free, and unimpeded use of its power'.[6]

This pessimistic assessment of contemporary life and developments was repeated in Leo's first encyclical, *Inscrutabili dei consilio* (28 April 1878), which followed the critiques of Gregory XVI and Pius IX. Like his two predecessors, he outlined the evils of the world that tormented society in Christian countries and endangered its very existence. Among the evils he cited were the subversion of truth, opposition to authority, dissension within and between nations, contempt for law, materialism, and treason in high places. He listed the remedies provided by the Church, but all too often rejected by state and society.[7] This led to unfortunate consequences. In fact, he traced the cause of many of the contemporary evils to mankind's rejection of the 'holy and august' authority of the Church.[8] Leo, however, unlike his predecessors, focused on finding positive, Christian solutions to the problems of the present age.

Following his election, all sorts of rumours about Leo were bandied about – most of them untrue. Word spread that the new pontiff had considered blessing the faithful from the outside loggia of St Peter's but was discouraged from doing so by influential intransigents, a story never confirmed. Likewise unsubstantiated were the reports that Leo's initial liberal inclinations were thwarted by a conservative clique who restrained him. Finally, the notion that Leo had no fixed programme was likewise inaccurate. The new pope had two major objectives: one pastoral and the second political – and the two were related. His pastoral aim was to address the needs of his flock and provide for their social as well as religious needs in an age of industrial transformation, which he clearly perceived. In finding and fashioning solutions to the social ills troubling mankind, Leo believed that Catholicism would once again assume importance in state and society. His political objective was to improve the diplomatic position of the papacy so that it could once more play an important role in international relations and an influential one at home.

Leo XIII (1878–1903) proved more diplomatic than his predecessors, and from the first made a concerted effort to heal the rift between Rome and a series of governments without criticizing the course pursued by Pio Nono. In doing so, Leo was the first pope to recognize the extreme importance of the press, and used it to achieve his religious, social and diplomatic objectives. On the other hand, Pope Leo, like Gregory XVI and Pius IX, opposed a number of the new forces shaping post-1848 Europe, and appreciated the firm stand Pius had taken against the errors of the age and especially against the Piedmontese/Italian seizure of the papal state. He deplored, however, the papacy's isolation and its decreasing role in state, society and international relations that resulted. He therefore walked a fine line, unwilling to join the revolutionary forces yet reluctant to support the reactionary tendencies in the Curia and the papal court.

A strong supporter of the temporal power of the papacy, he resisted the attempt to regain it by condemning all manifestations of the modern world or withdrawal behind the walls of the Vatican. The new pope recognized the need for a more diplomatic, less intransigent papal approach in the realm of international affairs. Consequently, Leo determined to improve relations with the other powers while refusing to recognize the Kingdom of Italy – no easy task.[9]

From the first days of his pontificate, Leo XIII sought to stop, or better yet, reverse the negative developments of the past decades. Unlike Pio Nono, Leo had a broader perspective than that offered by mid-nineteenth-century Italy, having been exposed to industrial Europe and made aware of its political, social and economic problems, along with its religious ones which were troubling humanity. Like Pius IX, he rejected socialism and praised his predecessor for battling it as a cure worse than the disease. Leo issued a similar condemnation in his encyclical *Quod Apostolici muneris* of 28 December 1878, which condemned socialism, communism and nihilism. All three, he wrote, denied authority, attacked marriage and the family, and challenged the right to own private property.[10] He believed, however, that condemnations alone were insufficient to resolve the present problems of humanity, or restore the role of the Church.

To combat the errors of the age, Leo felt that the Church had to offer something positive in their place.[11] He therefore perceived a broader role for the papacy than simply protesting against the seizure of the Papal States in the hope of its restoration or denouncing socialism for its violations of Catholic beliefs and practices. New problems had arisen which Leo believed neither the Church nor its leaders could or should ignore; they would have to transcend a simplistic negativism by suggesting Catholic solutions to the problems plaguing the masses. In his encyclical *Aeterni patris* (1879) he called for the restoration of Christian philosophy in general, and the reinvigoration and study of Thomism in particular.[12] Pecci was familiar with the broad social currents of the age, and was sympathetic to the needs of the working classes. Basing his thought on the Gospels and the long-standing and continuous concern of the Church for the poor, the new pope perceived Catholic social doctrine as part of his mandate to defend humanity. In his mind, the social question was linked to the Church's pastoral and magisterial mission and could not and should not be ignored.

This conviction was confirmed by the development of the Catholic movements he witnessed in Belgium, and further broadened by his travels to London, Paris and the Rhineland, where he witnessed both the positive and negative features of industrialization. Thus when he returned to Italy as bishop of Perugia, Leo was a social reformer interested not only in the religious life and development of his flock, but in their economic and physical well-being as well. In a letter of 1877 he decried the 'colossal abuses perpetrated against the poor and the weak', invoking legislation to correct the 'inhuman traffic' of children in factories. Examining his speeches at Perugia and during the Vatican Council, reformers accurately assessed that Leo would be more attuned to the problems of the modern world. Indeed, some hoped that he would abandon the role of 'prisoner in the Vatican', seek reconciliation with Italy and address the looming social injustices, which had given rise to the radical proposals of socialism and communism.

In fact, Leo's pontificate marks the start of the official effort to restate the traditional social teachings of the Catholic Church to confront the problems of a transformed world and have the papacy play a leading role in this effort. In doing so, Leo had recourse to the encyclical, or circulating letter, which he prepared and wrote himself. During his pontificate he issued 86 encyclicals – more than any other Pope to date. By means of these encyclicals and discourses, Pope Leo sought a rapprochement of sorts with the modern world by bringing the saving force of Christianity to bear on the host of problems raised by the economic and social revolutions.[13] Rejecting the notion of liberal economists that labour was simply another commodity whose price was determined by supply and demand, he displayed a Christian concern for the poor, insisting on the need to alleviate their suffering. The human dignity of the worker mandated a just wage as the first step towards distributive and social justice. For this among other reasons, he proved more conciliatory and understanding of labour's plight than the archbishop of Quebec, who had condemned the Knights of Labor, an American union under the presidency of Terence Powderly. Pope Leo, appreciative of the conditions that led to its formation, did not follow suit. Instead, he proposed an alternative, Christian solution.

Leo's *Rerum novarum* of 1891, his 27th encyclical and one of his longest – more than 11,000 words – revealed his sensitivity to the problems of labour. It catalogued the trials and tribulations of the working classes in the new industrial society, and the need for the Church to address them. In it, Leo noted the moral failure of laissez-faire social indifferentism on the one hand while condemning Marxism on the other. Nonetheless, he recognized the need for a solution and believed that the Church could, and should, provide the answer. Translated into all the major languages of the world, it was without question the most important and influential document Pope Leo released. It focused on the rights and duties of capital and labour, as well as the role of the Church and the various states in ensuring justice for the workers – issues that no previous pope had seriously tackled or even addressed.

Not surprisingly, *Rerum novarum* quickly became the best known and most often quoted of Leo's encyclicals. It at once condemned socialism and the civilization that produced it, and proposed a Catholic solution to the social ills of the age. Tracing the changed relations between workers and employers, the pope stressed the need for an opportune remedy for the misery unjustly pressing on the greater part of the working class. The solution Leo proposed required the cooperation of Church and state, employer and employee, each doing its part and cooperating for the common good.

Rejecting class conflict, *Rerum novarum* proclaimed the worker's right to protection against economic exploitation and social injustice, indicating that when workers could not defend their own rights, the state had the responsibility and the right to intervene on their behalf. The encyclical broke new ground in invoking government intervention in the economy to protect the rights of the working class, and was the Church's first specific pronouncement on behalf of labour. It was based on Thomistic social theology – close to the heart of Leo XIII – which held public authority responsible for promoting the public good. It reflected not only the pope's personal concerns, but also the thinking of a select group of Catholic thinkers and reformers, led by the economist Giuseppe Toniolo.

While Leo recognized the workers' need and right to organize, he did not favour combative labour groups, and recommended societies for mutual help, various benevolent foundations to provide aid and assistance for the working man and his family, as well as institutions for the welfare of the young and the aged. Leo also referred to working men's leagues, preferring the guilds of the past to modern industrial unions. Still, his recognition that these working men's associations should be organized to improve the worker's material as well as spiritual well-being had a tremendous impact. Publication of this 'social Magna Carta of Catholicism' earned Leo the title of the 'working man's pope', inspiring Catholic social action in Europe and abroad. Among other things, it legitimized Catholic activity and participation in organized labour movements, especially in western Europe and the United States.[14]

Throughout his unexpectedly long pontificate, Leo remained preoccupied with the social problems that threatened domestic tranquillity. In 1895, in his encyclical *Permoti nos*, he addressed this problem in Belgium, insisting that while the social question involved external goods, it was pre-eminently concerned with religion and morals. Since God had created different classes, the pope invoked cooperation, with the workers trusting their employers and the latter treating their workers with 'just kindness and prudent care', both aiming for the common good. The workers' plight, the pope counselled, required a Catholic rather than a socialist or communist solution. The social question persisted, as did the fear and controversy it aroused, prompting the pope to dwell on it at the opening of the twentieth century.

Inspired by Leo's *Rerum novarum*, some Catholics called for political action to protect the rights of the masses, and Christian Democracy emerged in various European countries, including northern Italy, in the late nineteenth century. The pope preferred the title Christian Democracy over Social Democracy, but disagreed with the Catholic effort to resort to political action to protect their rights, condemning the efforts in a strongly worded encyclical, *Graves de communi* (18 January 1901). Workers were reminded that Catholics should defer to the Church in all matters of 'social charity and Christian justice'.

Leo expressed his position on Christian Democracy, emphasizing its moral rather than its political role. He called for cooperation instead of conflict between classes, indicating that he had enumerated the rights of those who control capital and those who contribute labour in *Rerum novarum*, wherein he had indicated that a just solution to the social question could be found only in the precepts of the Gospel. Thus, the pope viewed Christian Democracy not as a political movement but as beneficent Christian action on behalf of the people, without favouring or introducing one type of government over another. Furthermore, while safeguarding the needs of the working classes, the movement embraced all groups – irrespective of rank or position – as members of the same family, redeemed by the same Saviour. Leo sought to eliminate suspicion of Christian Democracy so that the movement might flourish, insisting that such an elevation of the masses conformed with the Church's mission. Although sensitive to social needs, Leo firmly rejected the efforts to create political parties that linked Christian principles to secular doctrines, and the Church to any form of political organization.[15] He invoked impartiality for the Church and papacy in internal as well as international affairs.

By seeking a Christian solution to the social question, and reconciliation with the democracies, Leo's pontificate was perceived by some as a movement away from the intransigence of Gregory XVI and Pius IX, marking the first attempt of the papacy to reach an accommodation with the modern world. In a letter to the College of Cardinals, the pope noted the benefits that would accrue to world peace if the Holy See could 'devote all its energies to promoting, without hindrance, the salvation of the human race'.[16] Nonetheless, Leo did not totally abandon the conservatism of his predecessors; he declared Anglican ordination invalid in 1896, and would not condone the movement that came to be known as Americanism.

Leo was distressed to hear that a liberal faction had supposedly emerged in the American Church, led by John Ireland, Archbishop of St Paul, and Cardinal John Gibbons, Archbishop of Baltimore, aided by Denis John O'Connell, rector of the American College in Rome. Among other things, it was charged that the movement favoured a separation of Church and state and sought to reorganize the Church along more democratic lines, imposing the ideals of the United States upon Catholicism, worldwide. Conservatives in the hierarchy complained that a 'party of advanced views' sought dominion over the American Church, perceiving O'Connell as their 'acknowledged agent and representative' in the Eternal City. It is believed that his identification with this liberal current, subsequently known as Americanism, contributed to his removal from the rectorship of the College.

Responding to the conservative outcry, Leo determined to end the Americanist controversy by his letter *Testem benevolentiae* of 22 January 1899 to Cardinal Gibbons, condemning the attempt to reconcile the Church with all aspects of the age. Without criticizing the American system of government, or the separation of Church and state that prevailed in the United States, the pope pointed to the difference between the Church, which is of divine right, and other associations, which subsist by the free will of man. Leo would not sanction the notion of a Church in America different from that which prevailed in the rest of the world, citing the unity of doctrine and governance. The pope dismissed the rejection of external spiritual direction and the disdain for the teaching of the infallible pontiff, and the preference for the natural virtues over the super-natural, the active over the passive virtues, along with the rejection of religious vows as incompatible with Christian liberty. When Cardinal Gibbons received the letter, he denied that any know-ledgeable Catholic espoused the cited accusations. Subsequently, the controversy more or less subsided.[17]

The resolution of the Americanist controversy allowed Leo to return to the other major objective of his pontificate – to end the diplomatic isolation of the papacy and have it resume an important role in international affairs. Like his social programme, his diplo-matic campaign commenced soon after he had donned the tiara and paralleled his social programme. He quickly wrote to President MacMahon of France, seeking rapprochement with the Third Republic in the hope of ending, or at least curtailing, its anti-clerical programme. This was followed by letters to the emperors of Germany and Russia, and the president of the Swiss Confederation, informing them of his election and hoping that this would serve as a first step in paving the way for reconciliation with Rome. He was assisted in this task by the fact that his newly appointed secretary of state Cardinal Alessandro Franchi was more of a moderate than an intransigent, and was welcomed in most capitals.

Determined to preserve the principles of the faith, Leo nonetheless sought to bring the papacy and the Church into some accommodation with the modern world. Unlike the contentious Pius IX, his successor showed himself willing to cooperate with a series of governments ranging from monarchies to republics. He softened his tone towards the German empire, and assumed the initiative in seeking a resolution of their differences by writing to both the German emperor and the German chancellor soon after ascending the papal throne; he was rewarded by a lax enforcement of the anti-clerical Falk laws after 1880. The legislation was formally modified and restricted in the Reichstag session of 1880–81, and all but eliminated by the six clauses of the Church bill of June 1883.[18] Leo's conciliatory diplomacy thus proved more effective than the confrontational course pursued by Pope Pius IX.

Eventually, most of the anti-Catholic legislation was repealed. In turn, Bismarck recognized the importance of the papacy by inviting Leo to mediate the dispute between Germany and Spain in the Caroline Archipelago in the South Seas in December 1885. Recognizing the ancient rights of Spain over the Carolines, the pope ensured protection and economic privileges to its German subjects. His judicious arrangement between the contesting powers was accepted by both to the satisfaction of each – and brought increased international prestige for the papacy.[19] Leo named Bismarck a Knight of the Order of Christ and relations between the papacy and this Protestant power became cordial. Thus in 1887, when the emperor Wilhelm celebrated his ninetieth birthday, Leo sent representatives to participate in the festivities. That same year he dispatched an envoy to Britain to transmit the pope's best wishes on the occasion of Queen Victoria's Golden Jubilee. Following her death, her successor, Edward VII, visited Leo in April 1903, further proof of the cordial relationship that the head of the Catholic Church had established with Protestant England.

Leo also continued his efforts for a reconciliation with the French Republic and a rapprochement between French Catholics and a string of anti-clerical ministries. Leo was seconded in his efforts for a *ralliement* by Cardinal Mariano Rampolla del Tindaro, who shared his vision of reconciliation, and the primate of Africa, Cardinal Lavigerie, who advised the pope to make some dramatic move in the matter. In October 1890 Lavigerie visited Rome, where it was decided that the cardinal would appeal to French Catholics to adhere to the Republic for the good of their faith. Meanwhile, Rampolla asserted that the Vatican had no preference among forms of government; the faithful in France could follow the course of the Holy See, which recognized all established governments in order to defend religious interests. In 1892 Leo explained that laws were the work of those in power rather than the form of government. The former, especially the anti-clerical measures introduced in France, might rightly be opposed, while the latter, the Republic, should be respected. Although difficulties remained between Catholics and the Republic, Leo's diplomatic initiatives had an impact and worked to improve relations between Paris and the Vatican.

While Leo devoted much of his pontificate to improving the papacy's position in international affairs and addressing social issues, he did not neglect the institutional Church. During his tenure, 248 new dioceses were created and regular ecclesiastical hierarchies were re-established in Scotland, Bosnia and Herzegovina, North Africa and Japan. He also revived and promoted the study of Thomistic theology, and promoted the study of Church history, facilitated by the opening of the Vatican archives and library to scholars.

Leo believed that the disclosure of archival documents would help rather than harm the Church. His decision in 1883 to make the Vatican archives accessible to scholars contributed to the positive reaction to his pontificate. His opening of the Secret Vatican Archives encouraged historical studies and Christian archaeology as well as biblical studies. At the same time, he reinvigorated and expanded the Church's missionary efforts by cooperating with the colonial powers and encouraging and supporting the efforts of a number of religious orders.[20] Disturbed and distressed by the persistence of slavery, he drafted two encyclicals on the subject. The first, *In plurimis* (5 May 1888), addressed to the bishops of Brazil, called for the liberation of slaves.[21] The second, *Catholicae Ecclesiae* (20 November 1890), was stronger; it reiterated Leo's previous condemnations of slavery and assigned certain missions to the abolition of this pernicious institution.[22] Leo's diplomatic achievements, social programme and missionary efforts were widely recognized and applauded by his contemporaries.

This positive image was somewhat diminished by Leo's handling of the Roman Question, his insistence on the need for the temporal power and refusal to recognize the loss of the papal state, along with his renewal of protests against the curtailment of religious instruction in Italy's schools and refusal to recognize the Kingdom of Italy. In 1881, Leo urged the Italian faithful to undertake vigorous action in provincial and municipal elections on behalf of the Church, the only domain open to them in light of the *Non expedit* or papal prohibition on Catholic participation in the national affairs of the Italian kingdom. Little indeed, and certainly no measurable progress was made in the Vatican's relations with the Kingdom of Italy. Despite the hostile attitude assumed by the Vatican, the prospect of a restoration of the Papal States remained as dim as ever. Indeed, even the black aristocracy, who remained loyal to the papacy and had long hoped and prayed for a restoration, reluctantly but increasingly considered a restoration improbable, if not impossible.

Relations deteriorated further in July 1881, following the violent demonstration orchestrated against the papacy when the body of Pius IX, the chief figure in the counter-Risorgimento, was transported from St Peter's to San Lorenzo fuori le Mura, in accordance with his wishes. Shocked and scandalized by an attempt to hurl his predecessor's casket into the Tiber, Leo harped on about the perilous position of the papacy in the Eternal City. His plea for foreign intervention, however, went unanswered, leading even some intransigent anti-nationalists to ponder the need for a change of course towards Italy. Leo was not included in this group.

Thus while Leo aimed for reconciliation with a number of states in Europe, Asia and the Americas, the Italian kingdom was virtually excluded from his diplomatic initiative.[23] Regarding the loss of the Papal States, Leo continued the policies of Pius IX towards Italy, proclaiming that the head of the Church was no longer free, having been deprived of the temporal power necessary for the full exercise of his ministry. In fact, the state proved a burden for the Vatican and Leo operated well without it. During the 25 years of his pontificate, the aged pope worked tirelessly on behalf of the Church and was prepared to do more. During the celebration of his ninetieth birthday, when a well-wisher commented, 'May your Holiness live to be a hundred', Leo responded: 'Why do you set limits to divine providence?'[24] Leo lived another three years and died at the age of 93 years, 4 months and 18 days. Almost immediately, he was judged an important pope and a great statesman, even though there had been limits to his reformism.

VI

Pius X: Confrontation with Modernity, Conciliation with Italy

POPE PIUS X (1903–14) WAS DISTURBED BY MODERNISM, A movement in the Church he deemed dangerous and heretical. He began his encyclical *Pascendi dominici gregis* of 1907 against it, contending:

> The partisans of error are to be sought not only among the Church's open enemies, they lie hid in her very bosom and heart, and are the most mischievous, the less conspicuously they appear . . . many who, feigning a love for the Church, lacking the firm protection of philosophy and theology, nay more thoroughly imbued with the poisonous doctrines taught by the enemies of the Church, and lost to all sense of modesty, vaunt themselves as reformers of the Church, and assail all that is most perfect in the work of Christ, not sparing even the person of the Divine Redeemer, whom with sacrilegious daring they reduce to a simple mere man.[1]

Following Leo XIII's death on 20 July 1903, it appeared that the aristocratic pope would be followed by his equally aristocratic secretary of state, Cardinal Mariano Rampolla del Tindaro, whom Leo supposedly favoured as his successor. When Rampolla, perceived by many as being pro-French, received 29 votes in the conclave that opened at the end of July, and the papacy appeared within his reach, this was said to arouse concern in Berlin and Vienna. His selection was reportedly vetoed by Cardinal Puzyna, Archbishop of Kraków, at the direction of Austria. It was also rumoured that the German empire's concerns about Rampolla's

alleged pro-Gallic proclivities and determination to reconcile the
Church and the French Republic, played a part in his exclusion.
Others pointed to the role and responsibility of the Dual Alliance
of Germany and Austria in preventing Rampolla's election. Franz
Josef's recourse to the 'veto' was deeply resented inside and outside the conclave, and many believed it torpedoed Rampolla's
election.

Whether the 'veto' was the determining factor in the rejection
of Rampolla remains uncertain. What is known is that the conclave
did not elect the internationally minded, aristocratic and liberal
prelate, but instead selected the parochial, conservative and pastoral
68-year-old patriarch of Venice, Cardinal Giuseppe Melchiorre
Sarto. He was chosen to don the tiara on the second day of the conclave, the 4 August, on the fourth ballot.[2] Word spread that Sarto
assumed the papal responsibility reluctantly. When asked what
name he would take, he replied: 'Since I must suffer, I take the name
of those who have suffered; I shall be known as Pius.'[3] Others claim
that he indicated he would take the name of Pius IX, the pope who
condemned error. Perhaps he said both – or neither. What is clear
is that very quickly he was seen as the 'Pope of the poor and
humble', who did not assume airs, retained his simple personality
and discouraged all signs and symbols of adulation.

Aware of his limitations in the realm of diplomacy, and his
limited ability to communicate in French, the language of
diplomacy, he selected the 38-year-old Monsignor Merry del Val as
his secretary of state, and explained his decision:

> I have chosen him not only because he speaks many languages,
> was born in England, educated in Belgium, is a Spanish
> national and has lived in Italy, not only because he is the son of
> a renowned diplomat and is well acquainted with the problems
> in various counties, but particularly because he is a very modest
> man and a holy priest.[4]

Some were surprised by Sarto's election, since he was not well
known outside the Italian delegation. Others believed that this
probably worked in his favour, for most of the cardinals did not

want another international personality like Leo XIII. The Italian
cardinals, who dominated the conclave, knew Sarto was unpreten-
tious, devoted and devout. It was also known that wherever he
served, he emerged as a beloved pastor and had been an effective
bishop. Perhaps most important of all, he was seen to cooperate
with the Italian authorities and offered the prospect of a resolution of the Roman Question, which many in the Church now
favoured.[5]

The personality and policies of this rural pastor of humble
background differed sharply from those of his predecessor. Unlike
Leo, who had focused on diplomacy and the importance of
restoring the papacy's international position and presence, his successor stressed Church practices, religious principles and clerical
structure and responsibility. One of his priorities was an extensive
reorganization of the Curia, or the Vatican bureaucracy, in his quest
to modernize the chaotic machinery governing the Church. He made
it clear that he was determined to modify means and not ends,
which he largely regarded as fixed. With this distinction in mind, it
soon became apparent that the new pope not only had different
aims but would also pursue different paths from his predecessor.
While Leo XIII tended towards the world of international diplomacy, Pius X deemed internal Church matters and theological
issues most important. He considered himself first and foremost a
priest and pastor rather than a politician or diplomat.

This was quickly made known in his inaugural encyclical of 4
October 1903, *E Supremi apostolatus*, which provided a brief
review of the evils in which the Church and society were
enmeshed, including the rejection of God, the attacks on the
dogmas of faith and the persecution of religion, among others.
Having described the evils afflicting the Church, the state and
society, he proceeded to outlined his programme for the 'restoration of all things in Christ'.[6] In structure, his critique followed the
critical encyclicals of previous popes, including the *Diu satis* of
Pius VII, the *Mirari vos* of Gregory XVI and the *Qui pluribus* of
Pius IX. To achieve his pastoral programme he called upon the
clergy to lead the laity to observe 'the laws of God and the
Church'.[7] He repeated his determination to reject all novelties and

restore all things in Christ in his first consistorial address, *Primum vos*, of 9 November 1903.[8]

In Rome and abroad it was generally recognized that Pius x's pontificate dealt primarily with matters of faith and aimed at fortifying the inner life of the Church. Among other things it initiated the codification of Canon Law (1904), and along with the revision of the breviary, or book of prayer for priests, invoked the reintroduction and reinvigoration of Thomistic theology for both the laity and clergy. Stressing the centrality of the sacraments, Pius x encouraged Catholics to receive Communion frequently, urging children to do so as well as adults. He chose the name Pius in honour of Pius ix, revealing at once his commitment to traditionalism, and his suspicion of the many lax developments of the present age and modern culture.[9] He deplored and denounced the departure of chants and sacred music from set norms and insisted on the return of established rules and formal regulations.[10]

The traditionalism and conservatism of Pius x led some to conclude that it contributed to his anti-Judaism. Recently, however, a number of Jewish as well as Catholic authors have challenged the accusations launched against him, rejecting the notion that his unwillingness to support a Jewish state in the Holy Land flowed from his anti-Judaism. These defenders of Pius x point to his long and close relations with Jewish individuals and even some Jewish causes before and after he became pope. In fact, the obituary of this pope in *Il Vessillo Israelitico*, Italy's leading Jewish periodical, praised Pius x for being the one and only European sovereign to protest against the pogroms in Russia.[11]

Privately, he questioned the benefits derived from the Holy See's estrangement from the Italian kingdom and Pio Nono's self-imposed imprisonment in the Vatican. His ideas had evolved over several decades of pastoral activity and life experiences in the Veneto. While patriarch of Venice, he had supported an alliance of Catholics and moderate liberals to contain and combat the more dangerous socialists. He sought conciliation rather than conflict with the Kingdom of Italy, so that when Umberto visited the Veneto, Sarto offered all the courtesies a monarch of Italy expected.

When the king was assassinated in Monza, Sarto did not hesitate to send warm condolences to Queen Margherita.

Giuseppe's boyhood shaped the man who became pope. Born on 2 June 1835, the second son in a large family of ten children – eight of whom survived – his peasant background differed dramatically from that of most popes, who came from aristocratic families.[12] His father, Giovanni Battista Sarto, was able to secure a steady, but very small income by supplementing his farm work with janitorial services for the commune. His wife's work as a seamstress contributed to their limited budget. Giuseppe's appreciation of the need for social justice did not flow from scholarly tracts or ideological considerations but from the poverty he, his family and most of his immediate neighbours had experienced first-hand over the years.

Life for the Sarto family in the Veneto – which remained under Austrian control until 1866 – though difficult, was rendered tolerable by their religious convictions, to which Giuseppe clung from an early age. His religious outlook was nursed by his profoundly religious mother, Margherita Sanson, who overcame her husband's opposition to Giuseppe's religious vocation for fiscal reasons and supported his entry as a day student in the junior seminary of Castelfranco in 1846. Following his graduation in 1850, he was awarded a scholarship – provided by the patriarch of Venice, Cardinal Jacopo Monica – for the seminary of Padua, where he studied philosophy and theology and prepared for the priesthood (1850–58). Although he was not perceived as an intellectual, during his years at the seminary he was always at the top of his class.[13] He was ordained on 18 September 1858.[14]

Following his ordination, he was assigned to assist the parish priest as chaplain at Tombolo, a small village of some 1,000 souls where he served for nine years; this was followed by another nine years of pastoral service at nearby Salzano in the Veneto. In the spring of 1875 Pius IX appointed him chancellor of the diocese of Treviso and spiritual director of the seminarians there. His hero since childhood was St Vincent de Paul, whose interest in serving the poor he shared.

In 1884 Leo XIII selected him to serve as bishop of Mantua, where he continued his pastoral activity, and in 1893 named him

Cardinal Patriarch of Venice. Over the decades his career was overwhelmingly pastoral and largely restricted to his native Veneto, a stronghold of Catholicism. It was well known that he was a traditionalist and a conservative who opposed any compromise between rationalism and religion. He described himself as 'intransigent to the core'.[15] During the course of this long pastoral career he came to regret not only the course of political developments but was also, like Pope Leo, troubled by many of the social and ideological consequences flowing from industrialization. He regretted the 'canonization of capitalism' with its emphasis on individual maximization, which emerged as a new gospel that challenged the old, sanctifying the amassing of wealth and the social survival of the fittest. He judged these excesses of capitalism unfortunate and unfair.

Sarto, however, found the dogmas of socialism and communism, or adherence to the 'goddess of reason' or 'god of progress' in the pantheon of modernity,[16] to be cures worse than the disease. He favoured Catholic action but not Catholic unions. Nonetheless, he deplored the attempt to have the Church ruled out of public life and in the process sought to undermine religion and the one true God. Thus in the new century Pius believed that the old Church faced a hostile climate, confronted by rationalism, liberalism and socialism, all of which he found dangerous and destructive.[17] Instead, he concurred with the stance elaborated by the Spanish priest Félix Sardà y Salvany in his book *El liberalismo es pecado!* (1884).[18] The only true solution to the problems of humanity would be found within the Catholic faith, not in the ideologies of those who sought to undermine it. Pius x, like Pius ix whose name he assumed, perceived himself the agent of truth and justice, which had been offended. He believed that not only was there no Church without the pope, but also no Catholic society without the Holy See.[19]

In light of his record and his conservative personality, it is hardly surprising that Pius x's pontificate would focus on matters of faith and doctrine rather than on politics and diplomacy, although the latter were not ignored, especially when they impinged upon the practice of the faith. 'The Pope must be willing to enter into relations with rulers of states', he said in 1903, to assure Catholic interests.[20] He was not willing, however, to tolerate the intervention of the powers in papal or Church affairs, as had occurred in the conclave of 1903. Indeed, he issued a decree demanding excommunication for anyone who attempted to use the veto or suggested or even encouraged its use.[21] At the end of 1904 his *Vacante sede apostolica* established new procedures during the vacancy of the Holy See, along with new regulations for the election of the next pope which barred any outside intervention.

In an encyclical letter of March 1904, Pius reviewed the nature and the course of the conflict between the world and the Church. Anticipating his subsequent condemnation of modernism, he denounced heresies, the denial of the supernatural, abandonment of true philosophy and the development of and recourse to a fallacious historical criticism. To cope with these 'evils', Pius x urged public and private prayer and called upon the bishops to carry out a programme of philosophical, theological and historical reconstruction to protect the faith from the abuses of the age.[22] While he did not share the political and diplomatic outlook of his predecessor Leo or his successor Benedict, he was very interested in protecting and expanding Church interests and the faith abroad. During the first year of his pontificate he praised the Society for the Propagation of the Faith for its missionary efforts and proclaimed St Francis Xavier patron of the missions. Subsequently, in 1908, he praised the Society's efforts on behalf of Native American children. He also displayed an interest in the work of the International Eucharistic Congresses, and elevated the Latin American College in Rome to a pontifical institution.[23] Like Leo XIII, he judged the imposition of slavery on the native peoples of Latin America as criminal and shameful, and urged the bishops of that continent to intervene on their behalf.[24]

Following the festivities and receptions that marked the beginning of his pontificate, Pius happily returned to his former simple way of life. He stressed the importance of the papacy, not to fulfil the vanity of its holder but for the good of the faith and the Church. Both as a man and pope, Pius disliked ceremony, which he constantly sought to avoid. For one thing, he could not bear to be carried about on a chair and refused to have visitors on their knees during the course of an interview or audience. He also disliked having visitors kiss his toe and other humiliating signs of respect. He refused to have visitors cheer and applaud him upon his entry into St Peter's, deeming such actions inappropriate in a church and ordered the practice stopped. He rejected outright the Curia's suggestion that he increase the Sarto family's prestige, and in doing so his own, by making his sisters countesses.[25]

He also refused to take his meals alone, as popes had done for the last 260 years, almost always eating in the company of his sisters, his secretaries or his friends. When the chamberlain informed him that this was an infraction of an age-old custom, Pius got him to acknowledge that St Peter did not follow that custom and nor did Popes Julius II or Leo X. After some additional banter, the chamberlain acknowledged that Pope Urban VIII had introduced the custom in 1623. 'Fine', Pius responded, 'our glorious predecessor Pope Urban VIII decided that the Pope should always eat alone, and he had every right to do so. I, Pope Pius X, decide by the same right that during my pontificate the Pope shall never eat alone.'[26]

There were some who applauded this papal position, appreciative of his simplicity, while others depicted Pius as a simpleton who could not follow papal customs. Assessments of his 'achievements' have also varied. Looking at his actions and record over his decade-long pontificate, some have hailed Pius as one of the great reformist popes, perceiving and proclaiming him the greatest reformer since the Council of Trent.[27] His reforms have been seen to range from the reorganization of the Curia to the teaching of the catechism, from the restoration of Gregorian chant to the revision of the missal and the breviary, and from the reorganization of seminaries to the re-codification of canon law. All this was accomplished in less than a decade.[28] Early on, he was perceived as saintly by some and demonic by others. Pius judged the criticism a small price to pay for restoring mankind in Christ.

He began his pontificate by concentrating on reforms within the Church and its hierarchy. Following his initial promise to restore all things in Christ, Pius X began his reign with a wide series of reforms that included his liturgical reform of Church music and the restoration of Gregorian chant in 1903–4. In March 1904 he established a commission of cardinals to codify canon law. That

same year, he ruled that all candidates for the priesthood had perforce to attend a seminary, and in 1905 initiated the reorganization
and curriculum revision for these seminaries. Again in 1905, a new
standard catechism was issued that encouraged frequent Communion and in 1910 he lowered the age for First Communion.
These papal measures sought at once to renew and revitalize the
ecclesiastical and curial structures, while reinvigorating Catholic
spirituality and faith. To strengthen the position of the Holy See and
assure its control over the Church, a decree issued in the summer of
1906 required its written permission before the founding of any
new religious congregation.

Pius X deemed these and other changes essential, in light of the
grave and growing threat against the Church and her teachings, and
repeatedly said so. He found the situation doubly dangerous
because criticism flowed not only from the outside but sprang from
within the Church as well. He expressed his concern about the
clergy in his encyclical letter of July 1906, *Pieni l'animo*, in which he
decried the spirit of insubordination and independence found
among some inside as well as outside the Church. He urged the
bishops to supervise their clergy carefully and to demand obedience in thought as well as practice, keeping a close watch on their
sermons, speeches and writings. Overall, Pius perceived the need
for close supervision of the clergy, especially those engaged in
writing and publishing.[29]

Pius was particularly distressed by the emergence of modernism, a movement of the early twentieth century that he believed
affected a preference for what was new or modern, with a disregard
for earlier developments, and assumed that everything new was
better than what preceded. Fearing its impact, Pius did not fully
understand either the message or the motivation for the movement
and was influenced by clerics who had their own agendas. He was
particularly concerned by its alleged radical transformation of
thought as regards God and his relation to man, the world here and
the hereafter. Pius feared the impact of the thought and writings of
Alfred Loisy (1857–1919), deemed the principal French champion
of modernism, who began a historical and critical analysis of the
Old Testament and the Gospels. Pius believed that Loisy and his

THE PAPACY IN THE MODERN WORLD

followers sought emancipation from clerical and ecclesiastical authority, rejecting all fixed truth and dogma, and adhering to the belief that scripture could, and should, be subjected to historical and critical scrutiny. At the end of 1903, with papal encouragement, the Holy Office condemned Loisy's writings.

Pius believed that modernist influence in France had contributed to the deterioration of Franco-Vatican relations following the fall of Napoleon III and the formation of the Third French Republic in 1870. It was the modernist philosophy, the pope charged, that led the assembly of the Republic to unilaterally suppress the Napoleonic concordat of 1801. When Pius X protested against the assembly's actions, it provided the pretext and justification for additional anti-papal measures, including the recall of the French ambassador from the Vatican. Still more anti-clerical measures were undertaken by the radical republic, which led its government to seize and place Church property and other clerical assets in the hands of lay associations in 1905. These *associations cultuelles* were charged with the administration of the confiscated Church property.

This was followed in 1906 by the separation of Church and state along the lines the modernists supposedly advocated. The Vatican felt constrained to protest against the state visit of Victor Emmanuel III to Paris in 1903, as well as the return visit of the French president Loubert to Rome in 1904. Pius was convinced that the Republicans exploited the Vatican's protest against Loubert's visit to Rome as a pretext for passage of the law of separation. The real reason, he believed, was ideological, and reflective of the modernist stance.

Pius struck back in a series of encyclicals to the bishops of France. The first was *Vehementer nos* of 11 February 1906, which denounced the French law of separation as disastrous to society as well as the Church. In many ways, the pope considered this legislation as the culmination of a series of anti-Catholic abuses which included their new marriage laws, the laicization of schools and hospitals, the conscription of clerics into the armed forces, and the dissolution of religious orders and congregations. In effect, he believed that the French were waging a war on the faith and the Church. Pius condemned these steps as a denial of God, a repudiation of religion and a violation of the natural law, as well as the law of nations. Pius branded these violations of Catholic rights and liberty nothing less than blatant injustice.[30]

Pius x's second letter in response to the persecution unleashed by the French in general, but with a particular condemnation of the *associations cultuelles*, decreed that these associations of worship were in violation of the sacred rights of the Church and therefore inadmissible. *Gravissimo officii munere* of 10 August 1906 urged clergy and laity to work together to resist this and other violations of the faith – but to do so peacefully. The third protest letter, *Une fois encore*, was dispatched in early January 1907. It praised the response of the French faithful to the persecution unleashed by the republican regime, along with their refusal to recognize the associations of worship. The pope had to conclude that the perpetrators of this abusive programme aimed at nothing less than an attempt to destroy the Church and to de-Christianize France.[31] Despite these and other hostile French measures, Pius hoped to regain the support of France by praising its missionary efforts on the occasion of the long-anticipated beatification of Joan of Arc in 1909.

The Holy See's relations with Portugal were little better than those with France. Both in the capital and the countryside the religious orders and regular clergy had been harassed and persecuted since the turn of the century. This led Pope Pius to complain of the government's persecutions, which included the banishment of the religious orders and the confiscation of their property, the elimination of all aspects of religion in public life, the passage of an extreme divorce law that undermined marriage and the prohibition of all religious instruction in schools. The proclamation of the Republic in 1910 only made things worse and contributed to the separation of Church and state in May 1911. During this year Pius continuously complained about these hostile measures, which he charged violated the rights of the Church. He deemed their impact disastrous by reducing the Church in Portugal to poverty, depriving priests of the right to regulate worship, interfering with the training of seminarians and attempting to corrupt the clergy. Pius also deplored and condemned the Portuguese proposal that the country's 800 priests accept pensions from the Lisbon government, viewing this offer as a belated attempt to justify their seizure of clerical property while imposing unjust measures on ministers of the Lord.

The Holy Office issued a denunciation of modernism – the ideology that Pius believed provoked the Third Republic's and the Portuguese anti-Catholic campaigns – in its *Lamentabili sane exitu* decree of 3 July 1907. It condemned 65 errors attributed to the modernist movement. Described as the synthesis of all heresies, the first 38 errors focused on the mistaken view of scripture espoused by this ideology. The remaining 37 included errors in interpreting dogma, while listing modern misconceptions concerning the authority of the Church, Holy Scripture, revelations, the faith, dogma, the person of Christ and the sacraments, along with the principles of evolution.[32] All the condemned propositions in one way or another focused on scriptural studies, the content and history of dogma, and the role of the Church and the clergy.

On 8 September 1907 Pius issued his long encyclical *Pascendi dominici gregis*, on the doctrines espoused by modernism, which he explained was not a unified heresy but a collection of heresies. Furthermore, he warned that these errors were launched not only by the Church's enemies, but also by some members of her own clergy. Pius proceeded to catalogue the errors infecting the modernist philosopher, believer, theologian, historian, critic, apologist and reformer, describing what they believed and where, and how, they went astray. Their religious practice, Pius continued, was individualistic and autonomous, not reducible to dogma or subject to any external authority. The encyclical denounced in detail the philosophical, theological and historical errors that led to agnosticism, evolutionism, the denial of divine inspiration and the historicity of the scriptures. He warned that, should it prevail, it would contribute to the destruction not only of Catholicism but of all religion.[33]

To ensure this did not occur, article 55 of *Pascendi* created a secret society to combat the errors of the movement:

We decree therefore . . . a 'Council of Vigilance' be instituted without delay. The priests called to form part in it shall . . . meet every two months on an appointed day under the presidency of

the Bishop. They shall be bound to secrecy as to their deliberations and decisions, and their functions shall be as follows:
They shall watch most carefully for every trace and sign of
Modernism both in publications and in teaching, and to
preserve from it the clergy and the young, they shall take all
prudent, prompt and efficacious measures.[34]

The anti-modernist 'obsession' was aided and abetted by
Monsignor Umberto Benigni's Sodalitium Pianum (also known as
the Sapiniere), a secret network of informers that resorted to
dubious means to implement the papal condemnations against
modernism. Its efforts contributed to the decline of modernism,
but aroused criticism both inside and outside the Church. It placed
not only modernists under suspicion but also all scholarship, con-
stituting a sort of 'ecclesiastical secret police'.[35] Liked and supported
by Pius x, Benigni continued to scrutinize scholarship and harass
scholars throughout the pontificate, and was eliminated as a power
only following the election of Benedict xv. Benigni ended his career
as a fascist!

The papal campaign against modernism marched on and
gained momentum following a ruling of the Biblical Commission
in November 1907 that outlawed a series of works branded modernistic. At the same time it confirmed the decree *Lamentabili* and
the encyclical *Pascendi*, enforcing excommunication for those who
failed to adhere to their decisions. In 1908, on the fiftieth anniversary of his priesthood, Pius explained what a priest should be and
do, providing an indirect description of his own career and actions.
Among other things, he emphasized the need for sanctity, humility
and obedience, along with self-abnegation, fidelity to the apostolate,
preaching the word of God, hearing confessions, visiting the sick
and dying, comforting the sorrowful, and very likely the most
important of all for this opponent of modernism: instructing the
ignorant and reclaiming the erring.[36] In light of these last goals,
Pius felt the need to continue his campaign against modernism.

In April 1909, the encyclical *Communium rerum* outlawed the
reading of all works branded as modernistic and likewise reaffirmed
the condemnation against it, while the *Motu proprio Sacrorum*

antistitum, the oath against modernism, of September 1910 recalled and reiterated the proscriptions against it catalogued in *Pascendi*. This last decree outlined and established means for combating the dangers of modernism, including the requirement for clergy to pursue scholastic and Thomistic philosophy along with traditional Catholic theology. September 1910 also witnessed one of the most controversial steps in Pius x's 'crusade' against modernism: the imposition of an anti-modernist oath on all priests and seminarians. On a somewhat more positive note, it promoted the theology and scholastic philosophy advocated by Leo xiii and called for triennial reports by the bishops on these prescriptions.[37]

These and other anti-modernist measures led some to assume that this pope's preoccupation with this 'heresy' not only dominated his pontificate, but also prevented action on the other problems confronting the faith and society. This was not true. In fact, his increasing preoccupation with the socialist threat in general, and the problems this posed in Italy in particular, led Pius to reassess the papal reaction to the Kingdom of Italy. Even before he became pope, Sarto had questioned the continuation of the *Non expedit* that kept many Catholics from voting in national elections or sitting in the Italian parliament. While some voted and served in local political events, many continued to boycott the political life of the Italian kingdom. Sarto concluded that this self-imposed exclusion benefited neither the faith nor the Church – and in fact favoured its opponents. As a remedy, he quietly sought a revision of the *Non expedit*.

The crucial change Sarto invoked was facilitated by the political ascendancy of Giovanni Giolitti in Italy from 1901 to 1914. Liberal to the core, he favoured the separation of Church and state and was unwilling to grant the pope a territory the size of a postage stamp. He welcomed Catholics into the political life of the national state, however, and recognized that they shared many of the values of the moderate liberals, who favoured order but did not condone repression. He compared Church and state to two lines that moved side by side, but never crossed.[38] He deemed those liberals who remained preoccupied with the Church–state conflict tied to the past and claimed that they failed to recognize the pre-eminence of social issues. Furthermore, from the first he viewed hostility towards the Church and Catholics as counter-productive and contrary to his policy of conciliation. Thus, in 1901–2, while serving as Minister of the Interior in the cabinet of Giuseppe Zanardelli, he did not support the divorce bill proposed by the prime minister and strongly opposed by the Catholics. It was well known in Catholic circles that he did not lift a finger on its behalf, and Catholics very much appreciated his refusal to sanction this 'odious' measure.

The moderation shown by Giolitti towards Catholic goals, his refusal to pursue a policy of persecution, and his open invitation to have them participate in the nation's political life, encouraged the Vatican to mitigate its opposition to Catholic participation in national affairs. Pius x led the movement to reconsider the Vatican's policy of 'absentee antagonism' towards the Italian kingdom for a number of reasons, including his realization that their absence hurt rather than helped the Catholic cause, along with Giolitti's refusal to pursue an anti-clerical policy. Finally, the pope realized that socialism and communism represented a far greater danger to the Church than Giolittian liberalism.

Hence in 1903 when Giolitti replaced Zanardelli as prime minister, the prospect of Catholic–liberal cooperation increased. This was reflected in the parliamentary elections of 1904, when there was a real understanding between Catholics and liberals, transcending the usual support bishops had provided candidates of order. Catholics benefited indirectly by securing the election of a number of moderate liberals who opposed anti-clericalism, and directly by having a number of their own enter the Chamber of Deputies, with some four firm Catholics securing seats. This disturbed some anti-clerics, who accused Giolitti of concluding some sort of pact or deal with the Vatican and thus betraying the liberal state. The charge was without foundation and was fuelled by resentment rather than reality. It was also provoked by the fear that Catholic participation in Italy's political life would increase – and it did.

Following the elections of 1904, in June 1905 Pius x issued the encyclical *Il fermo proposito*, which provided that the various bishops in the kingdom would decide individually whether the population of their diverse dioceses should vote in national elections. Thus the *Non expedit* was effectively bypassed. Equally important, the Vatican and the Italian kingdom were now talking to one another and even negotiating. In 1906 the Vatican of Pius x, and the government of Giovanni Giolitti, concluded an important, though still little-known, agreement. By its terms the Italian government paid the Holy See 9 million lire for its appropriation of the principal houses of the religious orders in Rome, and its acceptance by Pius x provided a de facto recognition of the fait accompli and acceptance of the Kingdom of Italy. It was a crucial step that paved the way for a resolution of the Church–state conflict, facilitated the Lateran Accords of 1929, and provided a de jure resolution of the Roman Question.

Relations between the Holy See and the Rome government moved even closer in 1907 when the religious congregations in the Ottoman empire were placed under the protection of the Italian government. The following year Giolitti and his majority in the Chamber won the gratitude of the Vatican by refusing to support the legislation of the reformist socialists calling for the secularization of primary education and thereby assuring its defeat.[39] Indeed, Giolitti moved in the opposite direction and had his Ministry of Education issue instructions permitting individual communes to introduce religious instruction in schools.[40] Understandably, Catholics preferred the Giolittian regime to an anti-clerical liberal or socialist one.

The close cooperation between the Vatican and Italy and the Giolitti ministry and Catholic political organizations was clearly manifest in the parliamentary elections of 1909. During that campaign Catholic organizations such as the 'Azione Cattolica' and its offspring the 'Unione Elettorale' brought a large number of votes not only for Catholic candidates but Giolittian ones as well, provoking an outcry among some socialists, anti-clerical liberals and Catholics who sought their own Catholic political party. Giolitti was accused of plotting that undermined and compromised the liberal agenda, while the Catholic organizations were seen to compromise the Catholic political future for the crumbs that Giolitti offered.

The outcry and opposition of 1909 led to a storm of protest during, and after, the parliamentary elections of 1913, which witnessed an increased Catholic participation. Both dissident liberals and members of the Catholic camp who wanted their own party, resented the role played by Count Ottorino Gentiloni and the Catholic Electoral Union over which he presided. The outrage increased when the count revealed to the press that the fate of some 220 candidates had been determined by his organization and that some seven conditions had been required for its support. Quickly branded the 'seven commandments', Golitti and Gentiloni were accused by critics on the Left and the Right of plotting to subvert the liberal state with the complicity of Pope Pius x.

Despite the criticism of the close cooperation between the Vatican and Italian Catholics on the one hand, and the Giolittian liberals on the other, the cooperation continued during the pontificate of Pius x. It was furthered by the Libyan War of 1911, which some chose to depict as a crusade against a religious rival. Giolitti, for his part, very much appreciated the papal policy allowing Catholics to participate in the nation's political life but opposed the formation of a separate Catholic political party. This was the position that Giolitti and his close collaborators supported.

The barrage of bitter criticism launched against the pope, Giolitti and Gentiloni proved largely ineffective, for none of the three intended to chart a radical change, of course. Gentiloni, for his part, did prove more careful in granting interviews to the press, while Giolitti and the pope had other, more immediate concerns. Having ensured his majority in the Chamber in the difficult, tiring and often bitter political campaign of 1913, Giolitti looked forward to a holiday following his temporary resignation, confident that his control of the Chamber would allow him to return to power the moment he desired. The pope, meanwhile, was haunted by the premonition of an impending, bitter and destructive war which he feared would prove ruinous for the people and institutions of Europe. His nightmare materialized following the assassination of the Archduke Franz Ferdinand in Sarajevo on 28 June 1914, which by the end of summer 1914 led to a Europe-wide war that would eventually become the First World War. Unable to prevent its outbreak or mediate peace, the depressed pontiff died on 4 August 1914 – some said of a broken heart.

Recognized for his goodness, humility and dedication by almost all, as well as his concern for all humanity regardless of race or religion, some considered Pope Pius x a living saint. In fact, during the course of an audience a lady supposedly remarked: 'Holy Father, I hear that you work miracles and that you are a saint, *un santo*.' With a broad smile Pius said: 'I beg your pardon, Signora, you are wrong in one letter: my name is Sarto, not Santo.'[41] The process for his canonization began during the pontificate of Pius xi in 1923; he was beatified in 1951 and canonized in 1954 during the pontificate of Pius xii. He was the first pope to be proclaimed a saint by the Church since the sixteenth century.

Benedict xv: The First World War, the League and the Missions

WHILE PIUS X (1903–14) WAS PREOCCUPIED BY CHURCH matters and events in Italy, the pontificate of his successor Benedict xv (1914–22) would be dominated by international affairs, papal diplomacy's search for peace, and coping with the economic disruption and political confusion unleashed by war and its aftermath. Pope Benedict's peace proposal to the belligerent Powers dated 1 August 1917 and dispatched on 7 August was described by the pope as a more concrete and practical one for their consideration. Among other things it read:

> First of all, as a fundamental principle, moral right must be substituted for the material force of arms. Out of this shall arise a just agreement for a simultaneous and reciprocal diminution of armaments, according to rules and guarantees to be laid down hereafter, without impairing, however, the force needed for the maintenance of public order in each State. In place of armed force should be substituted the noble and peaceful institution of arbitration according to regulations to be made and penalties to be imposed on any State which might refuse either to submit a national question to such a tribunal or to accept its decisions.[1]

Following the death of Pius x on 20 August 1914, the conclave to select his successor opened as a destructive war raged in Europe. The cardinals sought a pope who could resolve the problems that the conflict posed for the Church, states and society. They turned to Giacomo Paolo Giambattista della Chiesa, who had a strong background in law and diplomacy and possessed superb negotiating skills. The relatively young prelate of 59, elected on 3 September 1914, took the name Benedict xv, in light of his appreciation of Benedict xiv's missionary efforts (1740–58) and his special devotion to St Benedict. When della Chiesa donned the tiara, war had burdened the Continent for a month. The cardinals in the conclave hoped that while the pastoral Pius x had proved unable to prevent the outbreak of war, his diplomatic successor might prove capable of bringing it to a rapid conclusion. It was believed that the aristocratic della Chiesa had the education, diplomatic background and skills to do so. His election followed that of Woodrow Wilson as president of the United States.

Both pope and president sought an alternative to the prevailing international system, sharing the conviction that it did not resolve conflicts peacefully.[2] Cooperation between the two was difficult, not only because of the anti-Catholicism that still prevailed in the United States, but primarily because the papacy did not have diplomatic relations with the u.s. when the war erupted. Such relations had existed from 1848 until the mid-1860s during the pontificate of Pius ix, but came to an end in 1867, when the American Congress prohibited the financing of any diplomatic post to the Papal States. Contacts of a sort were maintained through the apostolic delegates and the hierarchy. Papal action was also hindered by the fact that the papacy's relation with a number of other powers was also curtailed as a result of Pius ix's self-imposed imprisonment and his condemnation of liberalism, communism and nationalism. This, along with Benedict's poor health, posed problems for papal diplomacy.

Born prematurely at Pegli, in the diocese of Genoa, on 21 November 1854, the sickly sixth child of the Marchese Giuseppe Antonio and Marchessa Giovanna Migliorati della Chiesa was baptized immediately, because it was feared he would not survive. Since his health remained precarious, he remained largely housebound in childhood and learning was his main diversion. His early education was provided at home by a private tutor. Subsequently he pursued his secondary education at the Catholic Istituto Danovaro e Giusso, studied philosophy at the diocesan seminary, and law at the University of Genoa, all while he continued to live at home. On 5 August

1875, when he was not yet 21, he received a doctorate in law and then enrolled in the Roman seminary of the Capranica, where he lived and studied at the Gregorian University. From there he passed on to the Academy for Noble Ecclesiastics in Rome – the training ground for Vatican diplomats – where he studied and then taught from 1878 until 1883. On 21 December 1878 he was ordained a priest by Cardinal Patrizi in the Lateran Basilica. Following his ordination, he earned a doctorate in theology in 1879, and another in canon law in 1880.

On reaching manhood Giacomo remained short and frail, and was referred to as 'Il piccoletto', 'the little one'. The fact that the right side of his body was visibly shorter than the left contributed to his limp and awkward gait and movement. These physical shortcomings were more than compensated by his native intelligence, remarkable memory, great learning and profound determination. His intellectual ability, knowledge of civil and canon law, and diplomatic skill were recognized in the Curia and led to his admission into the Congregation of Extraordinary Ecclesiastical Affairs in 1882. At the end of that year, when Archbishop Mariano del Tindaro Rampolla was appointed nuncio to Spain, he chose della Chiesa as his private secretary, and both arrived in Madrid in February 1883. There Giacomo, who had been trained in diplomacy and was fluent in French – then the chief language of diplomacy – as well as Spanish, did well. His knowledge of German along with his native Italian made his input into the Vatican's diplomatic relations indispensable. He remained in Spain for four years.

Impressed by his service and ability, in 1887, when Rampolla was recalled home and made secretary of state, della Chiesa was brought into the Secretariat of State, serving as under-secretary from 1901–2. He was happy there, remaining for another four years, but less than happy at being named Archbishop of Bologna in 1907. Perhaps this is why Giacomo was not made a cardinal quickly, as was customary for one who held that position. The fact that he was critical of the excesses of the anti-modernist campaign, which very likely disturbed some in the Curia, most notably Merry del Val, who was named secretary of state, might have been another factor in denying him the red hat for some seven years.

He was made a cardinal only in 1914, the year Pius x died and just three months before the conclave assembled to select his successor. The newly named cardinal became one of the 65 eligible to vote in the conclave, but only 57 were able to take part in the election: two were absent because of illness, while the others could not make it because of time or age.[3] The war remained the major preoccupation of the Curia and the hierarchy, including the newly minted cardinal. He wrote and presented a remarkable address on an issue troubling both the clergy and laity in the Church – what position should the Church take towards the various combatants in the war? The short answer was that the pope could attempt to mediate a peace, assist the victims of the conflagration and undertake a series of humanitarian measures, but in all his efforts he would have to preserve a strict impartiality. The speech, along with Giacomo's diplomatic reputation, probably played a crucial role in his election. He led in each of the tallies and was finally elected on the tenth, taking the name Benedict xv.

Once pope, he determined to pursue a number of aims, and above all to end the catastrophic war. In the interim, he pledged to provide all the assistance his means allowed to aid the victims of the conflict; to help to ensure a just and lasting peace; to reorganize the missionary effort to assist both bodies and souls of the native populations; and finally to assist in the creation of a new framework for international relations. This was meant to replace the balance of power system that had long prevailed and which had led to the catastrophic conflict, with its adverse moral and material consequences.

The pope's first and most pressing priority was to end the destructive war, which soon became one of the most costly in terms of lives taken and property destroyed. Benedict made it clear that he would use all the legitimate means at his disposal to bring it to an end. He thus assumed an awesome responsibility in confronting the plague he perceived as the 'scourge of the wrath of God'. Although Benedict understood the need to preserve the Vatican's impartiality scrupulously in pursuing a policy of pacifism, his intentions aroused suspicion in both camps. Nonetheless, seasoned diplomats such as the British ambassador to Italy were convinced that Benedict would pursue a vigorous course to restore peace.[4] It proved an accurate assessment, for following his election he called on the faithful to pray for peace,[5] and prepared to use both spiritual and diplomatic means to end the war.

In his determination, some said mania, to restore peace, Benedict had recourse to the nuncios and internuncios, who represented the Holy Father and his secretary of state before civilian representatives. From time to time he used the apostolic delegates, who represented the Vatican before ecclesiastical authorities, as well as employing encyclicals and other papal messages and exhortations to the powers and the broad public to achieve his objectives. Following the death of Cardinal Domenico Ferrata, whom the pope had initially appointed secretary of state, Benedict selected another experienced diplomat, Pietro Gasparri, to take the post. Gasparri, the son of a shepherd, proved to be a brilliant and shrewd diplomat and quickly emerged as Benedict's indispensable confidant and close collaborator in the quest to restore peace. It was with him alone that the generally aloof Benedict maintained an intimacy of friendship.[6]

The diplomatic bent of Benedict differed from Pius x's pastoral approach, both in terms of the issues confronted and the solutions proposed. The two also differed in their response to modernism. Nonetheless, there was some continuity between them on a number of other matters. Both, for example, sought to revitalize the missionary efforts of the Church – which Pius had addressed in a number of pronouncements. In his *In Apostolicum sublecti munus* of 25 March 1904, Pius x commended the Society for the Propagation of the Faith for spreading the Gospel, proclaimed St Francis Xavier patron of the missions, and urged a united effort to spread the faith.[7] Subsequently, he praised the Society of St Jerome for its diffusion of the Gospel, and the work of the Society for the Preservation of the Faith among Indian Children.[8] Deploring the enslavement of Native Americans, allegedly for their own good, and other crimes committed against them, Pius called upon the combined effort of Church and state to remedy the situation and to support institutions for their physical as well as spiritual well-being.[9]

Pope Benedict xv shared his predecessor's concern for the missionary activity of the Church, as well as that of Benedict xiv, whose name he assumed. In 1741 Benedict XIV had issued the bull *Immensa pastorum principis*, which insisted that the native populations of Brazil be treated more humanely. In subsequent bulls he criticized the Jesuit recourse to Chinese and Japanese methods in their missionary work in East Asia and the Americas. In turn, Benedict XV regretted that the missionary effort of the Church, which he deemed crucial, had fallen into disarray through neglect during the course of the world war and the chaos of its aftermath. He pleaded for broad public support for the revitalization and reorganization of the missions. The latter was necessary because European participation in the destructive war had undermined their claims of moral superiority over the population under missionary jurisdiction. In his long apostolic epistle *Maximum illud* of 30 November 1919, issued in the sixth year of his pontificate, Benedict examined the propagation of the faith throughout the world, recounting and reviewing missionary efforts worldwide over the centuries and foreseeing the need for future efforts on their part. Like Pius X, he challenged the Eurocentric pre-war approach towards the population of the mission territories, which from time to time degenerated into racism.

In *Maximum illud* Benedict XV reminded missionaries that their goal was essentially a spiritual one, which must be carried out in a selfless way, calling for them to respect native culture and foster native clergies and hierarchies rather than having them permanently under European control and domination.[10] At the same time, he underlined the necessity of proper preparation for the work in foreign cultures and the need to acquire language skills before going there. By these and other terms Benedict disassociated the Catholic Church from European imperialism, since he prohibited nationalism among the missionaries, insisting that they respect the native culture. Upset by the paucity of native vocations, he ordered the Congregation for the Propagation of the Faith to determine the causes for the failure – and fix them. He requested a continued striving for personal sanctity and praised the selfless work of females in the missions. At the same time, Benedict declared that the missionary effort was not only the responsibility of the missionaries, but urged all Catholics to participate, through the Apostolate of Prayer, by supporting vocations and by helping financially. He concluded by calling on a number of organizations to arrange and supervise mission activities within the Catholic Church. For his continuous concern for the missions, Benedict was dubbed 'Pope of the Missions'.

Benedict XV, like Pius X, was also very much concerned with the future of the Holy Land – an issue that assumed greater importance once the British liberated it from the Muslim Turks in the autumn of 1918. Pope Benedict confirmed the position of the Franciscans there, providing the funding for their maintenance of the shrines and other holy places. To further bolster the Catholic position, he supported a Jesuit plan to establish a branch of the Roman Biblical Institute there. While both popes understood and supported the desire of Jews to return and settle there, both had reservations about the creation of a Jewish state. The prospect provoked religious rivalry as well as conflicting political claims. Decisions regarding the future of the Holy Land were temporarily tabled for the consideration of a future conference of the Allies. The conference met at San Remo in April 1920. Britain, responsible for the Holy Land's liberation, was awarded the mandate. All but the British regarded this as a temporary solution at best – and this assessment proved accurate.

Benedict also followed Pius X's policy of reconciliation with Italy, sharing his conviction that the conflict of the Roman Question was counter-productive. Like Pius, he believed that the Vatican's nineteenth-century policies towards the Italian state were no longer appropriate. He therefore moved quietly to establish de facto relations with the Kingdom of Italy, recognizing Victor Emmanuel III as 'His Majesty' rather than the 'duke of Savoy', and raised no objections to Catholic rulers visiting the Italian king in Rome. This was readily transmitted to the prime minister who succeeded Giolitti, Antonio Salandra. Benedict also shared Pius's efforts to stop the war from expanding and his particular concern to keep Italy out of it. Knowing of the Italian determination to take control of *Italia Irredenta*, or unredeemed Italy, in January 1915 Benedict proposed by means of his nuncio to Vienna that Austria cede the Trentino to Italy in order to keep her neutral during the conflict. The Kaiser, the military and patriotic Germans considered the proposal both stupid and treasonous and believed it would render their task of winning the war more difficult.

Franz Josef and the Austrian military considered the papal suggestions suicidal, which led both Vienna and Berlin to suspect the motives of the Vatican. Benedict's mediation efforts were also deemed suspicious by the Italian government, which dreamed of broader territorial acquisitions. Nor was the papal intervention welcomed by the Entente powers, who believed that Italy's entry would alter the prevailing balance of power and enable them to impose whatever terms they liked upon the Central Powers. Unknown to the Vatican, Italy and the Entente were in the process of negotiating the secret Treaty of London, which in exchange for the promise of considerable territorial compensation brought Italy into the war on the Allies' side in 1915.

Disappointed but not discouraged by the negative responses of the powers to his initial mediation attempts, which they denounced as meddling, Benedict decided to intensify his appeal to a broader audience. In fact, two days after his coronation he delivered his first consistorial allocution – an address to the cardinals assembled in the consistorial hall. In *Ubi primum* of 8 September 1914, the pope pledged to do all within his means to hasten the end of the calamity, and proved true to his promise. Benedict also called on the faithful to pray for peace, and urged rulers to respond positively to their pleas.[11] This message and the call for peace were repeated in his inaugural encyclical *Ad beatissimi* of 1 November 1914, the first of twelve, which borrowed from the works of Pius x. In it, Benedict attributed the present unrest to lack of love in human relationships, contempt for authority, injustice in social and class relationships, and greed for material objects and possessions.

The pope called for change as a preliminary condition for a more peaceful world.[12] Awaiting the broader transformation, Benedict had his secretary of state Gasparri urge the belligerents to suspend hostilities on Christmas Day 1914 – an appeal, like so many others emanating from the Vatican, that was ignored. In fact, from 1914 to 1917 Benedict posed a number of requests to the belligerents invoking the negotiation of a just peace, including those of 8 September and 6 December 1914; 25 May, 28 July and 6 December 1915; 4 March and 30 July 1916; and 10 January and 5 May 1917. All were ignored. Benedict was not discouraged, and at the beginning of 1915 drafted a prayer to Jesus for the faithful to recite, asking him to 'Pity the countless mothers in anguish for the fate of their sons; pity the numberless families bereaved of their fathers; pity Europe over which broods such havoc and disaster.' It concluded: 'Hear our trustful prayer, and give back to the world peace and tranquillity.'[13]

Benedict issued an exhortation in July 1915, on the first anniversary of the outbreak of war, once again invoking a just peace.[14] His plea unanswered, he encouraged President Wilson to launch a peace appeal. The papal message was carried to the White House by Cardinal Gibbons, who spent half an hour there. He reported to Rome that the president was gratified to hear from the pope, but cautiously indicated that the United States would make no overtures unless its mediation was acceptable to both camps. Gibbons went from the White House to the State Department, where he met Secretary of State Lansing for another half an hour.[15] Benedict hoped that President Wilson, who had shown fairness and good will, might nudge the belligerents to negotiate, calling upon both sides to make concessions.[16] The two hoped for a peace without victory.

While the pope, like Wilson, invoked a fair and negotiated peace, the belligerents sought military victory. Having failed in his diplomatic initiatives to end the war, the pope focused on humanitarian efforts to lessen its impact, such as attending to the needs of the populations caught in the storm. At the start of 1916 Benedict's secretary of state responded to the pleas and petitions of the American Jewish Committee of New York. He reported that the Holy Father, like the 3 million Jewish citizens of the United States the committee represented, deplored the suffering of Jews as well as others during the conflagration. Gasparri concluded by asserting that the pope rejoiced in the religious harmony that prevailed in the United States, convinced that it contributed to the peaceful prosperity that prevailed there.[17]

Although both camps sought the moral support of the papacy, Benedict steadfastly refused to assume a partisan stance. Prepared, indeed anxious, to condemn and catalogue the violations of justice and international law, he was unwilling to name those responsible for these crimes. Thus, while he empathized with the suffering endured by the Belgians and prayed for their relief, and was willing to provide religious, material and moral assistance, he refused to condemn the German invasion. Likewise, he did not condemn the Russian invasion and occupation of Galicia. Both the pope and his secretary of state refused to assign responsibility, insisting that the Church and papacy should not take sides.[18] Benedict explained that the Holy See did not wish to be neutral in the European war, but perforce had to remain impartial – a distinction neither understood nor appreciated by the Allies or the Central Powers.[19]

For Benedict, neutrality entailed the inability or unwillingness to judge principles or actions, something the Holy See had not only a right but a responsibility to do. Impartiality represented the Vatican's determination not to favour one side over another.[20] The 'silence' on responsibility was deemed by some to be not only an obvious political failure, but a moral and religious one as well. This was reflected in the press and other publications of a number of states, which found the Vatican's impartial stance inexplicable and unsupportable. The charges were summarized in a pamphlet of 1916, 'The Silence of Benedict xv', which claimed that papal 'silence' represented not only a sad commentary on the papacy but compromised the Church as well. Vienna and Berlin on the one hand, and Paris and London on the other, hoping to win the war and impose punitive terms on the defeated states, considered the papal call for peace without victory subversive.

Georges Clemenceau and the French branded Benedict 'le pape boche', while von Ludendorff denounced him as 'der französische Papst'.[21] Unable to end the war, Benedict renewed his efforts to alleviate the suffering it provoked by expanding his already extensive charitable efforts, aiding prisoners of war and refugees, and providing money, material and food across the Continent from France to Lithuania. Under his direction, and with the assistance of his secretary of state, Pietro Gasparri, and Monsignor Eugenio Pacelli, secretary of the Congregation for Extraordinary Ecclesastical Affairs, numerous Catholic agencies were established to minister to the sick, wounded, homeless and destitute.

Benedict was primarily concerned about the fate of the children, expressing his concern in an encyclical. In 1916 he appealed to the people and clergy of the United States to help him feed the starving children of German-occupied Belgium. His aid to children was not limited to Belgium but extended to children in Lithuania, Poland, Lebanon, Montenegro, Syria and Russia. Benedict's 'mission of mercy' created a virtual 'Second Red Cross', attempting to alleviate the suffering of combatants and civilians. He did not, however, abandon the hope of securing peace. Consequently, Pope Benedict was among the first to praise Wilson's peace note of December 1916 to the belligerents, seeing it as a positive step towards achieving a negotiated settlement.[22] Indeed, he characterized Wilson's speech as 'the most courageous document which had appeared since the beginning of the war'.[23] Benedict believed that it contained 'many truths and revived the principles of Christian civilization'.[24] He would borrow from it, and subsequently Wilson would borrow from Benedict's peace proposal.

With the thought of peace in mind, Benedict drafted a more specific proposal and appointed Monsignor Pacelli to present its outline to the Germans, who were called upon to make the most concessions. In order to make him a more acceptable papal representative to the status-conscious Germans, Pacelli was named Nuncio to Bavaria and made titular archbishop of Sardes. Shortly thereafter, Pacelli left for Munich, arriving there on 25 May 1917. In June he met the German chancellor Theobald von Bethmann-Hollweg (1856–1921) and presented Benedict's proposal for a peaceful resolution of the conflict. It entailed four basic points: the general limitation of armaments; the establishment of international courts; the restoration of Belgian independence; and leaving issues such as Alsace-Lorraine to be resolved by the contending parties.

The chancellor appeared receptive, but Kaiser Wilhelm II (1859–1941), whom Pacelli met at the end of June 1917, was less so, and the German military proved even more sceptical. Although Pacelli received no commitment on, or acceptance of, the papal proposal in Germany, he nonetheless encouraged Benedict to dispatch his peace note to the belligerents. Dated 1 August, it was dispatched on 7 August and called for mutual disarmament;

arbitration rather than military measures to settle disputes; freedom of the seas; the renunciation of war indemnities; territorial disputes such as those between Italy and Austria and France and Germany to be decided peacefully with recourse to equity and justice; and a similar approach to disputes concerning Armenia, the Balkan states and Poland.[25] Benedict proposed that these terms could be implemented sequentially: first the suspension of the fighting, second the reduction of armaments, and finally the institution of arbitration to resolve differences. The papal proposal anticipated much that was later included in Wilson's Fourteen Points, including his call for a League to replace the prevailing international anarchy. Perhaps this explains why it was praised by the American press, the *Evening Press* of New York dubbing it an international event of the highest rank and importance.[26]

The pope acknowledged that his peace proposal followed the lines of President Wilson's December address. Thus when the Belgian and British ministers accredited to the Vatican were received by Benedict and enquired about his references to the freedom of the seas in his peace proposal, the pope responded that he intended to give the same meaning that President Wilson had provided in his earlier message.[27] The British government let it be known that it had reservations about both the president's and the pope's endorsement of freedom of the seas.

In turn, President Wilson, in his Fourteen Points of January 1918, borrowed from and elaborated upon the papal points. The American programme called for the warring states to agree to: 1) renounce secret diplomacy and accept open agreements; 2) respect and accept the freedom of the seas; 3) strive for the elimination of economic barriers between nations; 4) support the reduction of armaments; 5) abide by the impartial adjustment of colonial claims; 6) evacuate and restore Russian territory; 7) restore Belgian sovereignty; 8) evacuate French territory and return Alsace-Lorraine to France; 9) redraw the Italian frontier along national lines; 10) grant autonomy to the various nationalities of Austria-Hungary; 11) evacuate Montenegro, Romania and Serbia; 12) grant self-determination to the peoples of the Ottoman empire and freedom of passage through the Dardenelles; 13) establish an independent Poland with

access to the sea; and, to ensure the maintenance of this and subsequent agreements; 14) create an association of nations to govern
international relations.[28] Benedict approved of these Fourteen
Points, even as his own peace proposal was rejected by both camps,
who found it nebulous and inconclusive and proved unwilling to
return to the status quo antebellum.

Benedict was convinced that critics of his proposal sought to
silence him and was determined not to let them succeed.
Paradoxically, President Wilson's fourteen-point peace proposal,
though strikingly similar to that of the pope's, received a much
more serious hearing and would serve as the basis for Germany's
surrender. Varied explanations were provided as to why one plan
was accepted while the other rejected, as though the two were
mirror images. In New York the Reverend Joseph McMahon, pastor
of Our Lady of Lourdes Catholic church, in an address on the
papacy as peacemaker, provided an answer. Repeating that the
terms of Pope Benedict and President Wilson were identical, he
added that this was not generally recognized due to the work of a
worldwide 'League of Hatred of the Catholic Church'.[29]

The Vatican recognized that the United States, which had played
a major role in the war, could not be ignored like the 'impartial'
papacy. In early December 1918 Benedict, Cardinal Gasparri and
Monsignor Pacelli responded positively to the General Armistice
of 11 November, which brought an end to the destructive 'suicide
of nations'. In January 1919 Benedict xv met Woodrow Wilson, the
first president of the United States to be received by a pontiff, and
called for a just treaty that would ensure the peace. Benedict was
unable to be present at the peacemaking, barred by the Italians who
feared that he would raise the Roman Question.

The pope and his two major assistants in diplomatic affairs,
Gasparri and Pacelli, were all disappointed with the Treaty of
Versailles, which violated many of the Fourteen Points on which
Germany had surrendered. Benedict criticized the conditions
imposed upon the Central Powers, particularly decrying the consequences for Catholic Austria, and was concerned that the treaties
did not provide the protection he desired for the Catholic missions, to
which he was so dedicated.[30] Finally, he believed that the economic

conditions imposed on Germany were too harsh, threatening European economic stability as a whole and leading to unrest and disorder throughout the Continent, to the detriment of both victors and vanquished. Cardinal Gasparri proved equally pessimistic, believing that the peace conditions and the humiliation of the Germans would probably result in another war, as soon as Germany would be in a military position to start one, while Pacelli branded the treaty 'an international absurdity'.[31] *La Civiltà Cattolica*, representing Vatican sentiment, described the treaty's 440 'articles of peace' as 'articles of war'.[32]

Although Pope Benedict xv did not believe that humanity could or should rely solely on secular means and institutions to preserve the peace, it is not true that he was hostile to the projected League of Nations proposed by President Wilson and accepted by the powers at Versailles. Pinpointing the inability of the current international configuration to resolve conflicts peacefully, and painfully aware of the horrific consequences resulting from that failure, as early as 1914 Benedict had proposed an alternative. In his encyclical *Ad beatissimi* (1 November 1914) he appealed to the nations of the world to find some other means of resolving differences. Until some new structure emerged, the pope implored the powers to adhere to existing international law. Deploring both the violation of laws and the disrespect for harmony, Benedict believed that this contributed to the carnage of the world war and prayed that a new code and international organization would ensure a more tranquil future.[33]

In his peace note of August 1917, Benedict called for the institution of universal arbitration as a substitute for armies.[34] Subsequently, Cardinal Gasparri clarified and elaborated on the pope's peace proposal, focusing on Benedict's call for a new order that included 'the suppression, by common accord of compulsory military service; the constitution of a Court of Arbitration for the solution of international questions; and lastly, for the prevention of infractions, the establishment of a universal boycott'.[35] In an encyclical of May 1920, 'On Peace and Christian Reconciliation', the pope again, and even more forcefully, expressed his support for the League that President Wilson had proposed, the forerunner of the United Nations:

Things being thus restored, the order required by justice and charity re-established and the nations reconciled, it is much to be desired, Venerable Brethren, that all States, putting aside mutual suspicion, should unite in one league, or rather a sort of family of peoples, calculated both to maintain their own independence and safeguard the order of human society. What specially, amongst other reasons, calls for such an association of nations, is the need generally recognized of making every effort to abolish or reduce the enormous burden of the military expenditures which States can no longer bear, in order to prevent these disastrous wars or at least to remove the danger of them as far as possible. The Church will certainly not refuse her zealous aid to States united under the Christian law in any of their undertakings inspired by justice and charity, inasmuch as she is herself the most perfect type of universal society.[36]

Rather than engineering or even gloating over the American failure to enter the League, as some in the anti-Catholic camp charged, the pope regretted this turn of events.[37]

Although many of the solemn principles advocated by the League of Nations were similar to those advocated by the papacy, there were obstacles to the Church's participation in an international community organized on the basis of independent sovereign states. Nonetheless, the pope believed that the two could cooperate in overcoming the famine and misery in Europe, which led to confusion, chaos and the prospect of revolution. In particular, Benedict sought to work closely with the new organization in providing humanitarian assistance, calling upon the League of Nations to help the starving masses of Russia and other stricken areas of Europe.[38] He was disappointed by the lack of response and leadership shown by the League, while the papacy established relations with the many new states that were created because of the demise of Imperial Russia, Austria-Hungary and Germany.

It has been suggested that Benedict's failure to mediate a peace meant that his pontificate was a failure – a sentiment that Benedict shared during his bouts of depression. It was not. Unquestionably, Benedict's seven-point peace proposal, rejected by both camps, influenced Wilson's Fourteen Points, which formed the basis of Germany's surrender and the peacemaking of 1919. Furthermore, Benedict reinvigorated the papacy's international role by establishing relations with a number of 'new' states, including Britain, which dispatched a *chargé d'affaires* in 1915. He also re-established relations with states that had broken contact with the Holy See, such as with France in 1921. Under his leadership the Vatican became increasingly engaged in international affairs, and the countries sending representatives to the Vatican more than doubled. This increased representation and added participation and peace efforts combined to enhance the post-war prestige of the papacy.

Pope Benedict even attempted to establish diplomatic relations with the Soviet Union and sent a telegram to the League exhorting its members to help the Russian people as they confronted mass starvation.[39] In 1922 he opened secret talks with the new Mussolini government in the hope of resolving the Roman Question. He also helped to revitalize and reorganize the missions by calling on the faithful worldwide to pray for and financially support them. Benedict made improvements in internal Church affairs by issuing in 1917 the first Code of Canon Law of the Catholic Church, whose creation he had prepared with Pietro Gasparri and Eugenio Pacelli during the pontificate of Pope Pius x. It is believed that this new Code stimulated religious life and activities throughout the Church. Benedict's charitable work, massive humanitarian assistance and peace efforts secured his recognition as the 'Pope of Peace'; as early as 1920 the Muslim Turks erected a statue in Istanbul to 'The Great Pope of the World Tragedy'.

VIII

The Crusade of Pius XI against Anti-Semitism

IN 1938 POPE PIUS XI SECRETLY COMMISSIONED THE American Jesuit father John LaFarge to draft an encyclical denouncing racism and anti-Semitism, reflecting the pope's opposition to both. Together with two fellow Jesuits,[1] he prepared *Humani generis unitas*, paragraph 105 of which reads:

> Those who have placed race illegitimately on a pedestal have rendered mankind a disservice. For they have done nothing to advance the unity to which humanity tends and aspires. One naturally wonders if this end is faithfully pursued by many of the principal advocates of a so-called racial purity or if their aim is not rather to move the masses to very different ends . . . It is further increased when it becomes clear that the struggle for racial purity ends by being uniquely the struggle against the Jews.[2]

The death of the 67-year-old Pope Benedict xv towards the end of January 1922 came as a surprise, partly because his health had always been poor and yet he had survived. Equally surprising was the election as pope of the 65-year-old Achille Ratti – only recently made Cardinal Archbishop of Milan – on the fourteenth ballot of a very divided conclave. The new pope differed from his predecessor, even though both hailed from northern Italy, and both were born in the 1850s and were in their sixties when elected to the Chair of Peter. There were, however, major differences between Benedict and his successor. Physically and personality-wise the differences between the frail Giacomo della Chiesa and the athletic, mountain-climbing Achille Ratti were striking. While Benedict, a diplomat by training and inclination, took Leo XIII (1878–1903) as his model, Pius XI looked to the outspoken Pius IX (1846–78) – whose name he assumed – for inspiration. Pius XI also had serious reservations about the papal policy of 'impartiality' that Benedict and Gasparri had elaborated during the course of the First World War. While Benedict XV was often solitary, Pius XI was far more gregarious. Finally, while Benedict had a short pontificate of just over seven years, that of Pius XI spanned some seventeen.

Despite these real differences, the two popes shared certain sentiments and characteristics, including a strong intellectual strain and the desire for a resolution of the Roman Question, which required reconciliation with the Kingdom of Italy. In fact, the secret talks with Italy that Benedict XV had his secretary of state, Pietro Gasparri, initiate were brought to a successful conclusion by Gasparri, who remained secretary of state to Pius XI. This was an unusual step taken by Pius – one of the few instances when a new pope retained the services of a secretary of state appointed by his predecessor. Benedict and Pius also agreed to tolerate the principle of the separation of Church and state, as elaborated in the still largely Protestant United States – rather than alienate that upcoming power. Furthermore, they sought improved relations not only with Italy and the United States but also with the newly formed Soviet Union and Polish state. In 1919 Benedict dispatched Ratti on an important diplomatic mission to Poland and two years later made him archbishop of Milan and cardinal. Both were also devoted to the worldwide missions, as well as supportive of the League of Nations. They hoped that the newly formed League would curb the international anarchy that had culminated in the disastrous and destructive world war. Like Benedict, Pius XI sought a reasonable resolution of the reparations issue that would promote peace and prosperity.[3]

Both popes were not only intellectually gifted but also broadly educated. Ordained a priest at the end of 1879, following study at the Gregorian University and the Sapienza in Rome, Ratti received degrees in philosophy, theology and law. Appointed to the Ambrosian Library in 1883, he later became its director in 1907. He was summoned to Rome in 1910, to serve as vice-prefect of the Vatican Library, becoming its prefect in 1914. He was constrained to abandon his bibliographic refuge when he was named apostolic visitor to Poland in 1918 and, following the creation of the Polish state, made nuncio in 1919. Two years earlier Benedict had named Eugenio Pacelli nuncio to Bavaria and subsequently to Germany, and Ratti kept him there when he was elected pope in 1922. In 1930 Pius recalled Pacelli to Rome and made him secretary of state in place of Gasparri. This long, sometimes close collaboration between Pius XI (1922–39) and Pacelli, who succeeded as Pius XII (1939–58), has led some to conclude that the two saw eye to eye on how to respond to the 'totalitarian' regimes and their racist and anti-Semitic policies that culminated in the Holocaust. Indeed, much of the Italian historiography, and the English one dependent on it, has stressed this close relationship and collaboration between Pius XI and Pacelli, who took the name Pius XII when he assumed the tiara. Indeed, Pius XI's decision to make Eugenio Pacelli a cardinal, and his secretary of state in place of Pietro Gasparri in 1930, surprised few. Since Pacelli was known to be Gasparri's protégé, it seemed logical that the pope would replace the mentor with his main pupil.

There were some similarities between Papa Ratti and his secretary of state, for both were accustomed to getting their way. Additionally, the two had become staunchly anti-communist while serving as nuncios: Ratti in Poland and Pacelli in Bavaria. Furthermore, both sought to assure the position of the Church by means of concordats. While Ratti was spontaneous, outgoing, outspoken and openly assertive, however, Pacelli was studied, aloof and indirect in speech and diplomatic in action. Those who perceived a continuity between the two also noted that Pius XI and Pacelli were serious scholars who shared a distrust of communism but were seen to be less critical of the fascist dictators. Both were criticized for favouring a policy of accommodation and appeasement towards the repressive fascist regimes, which later led one author to brand Pius XII Hitler's pope. They were also linked in their profound distrust of the inclination and ability of political parties to ensure Church and clerical interests, and preferred agreements made by the Church with the various governments, whether they were democratic, liberal, socialist or fascist. During his pontificate the agreements concluded by Pius xi, with the assistance of Pacelli, were numerous and important – including the Reich Concordat negotiated by Pacelli with Hitler's Third Reich,[4] and the Lateran Accords negotiated by Gasparri and Eugenio's brother with Mussolini's Italy.[5]

Ratti and Pacelli both supported an agreement with the Soviet Union and opened negotiation with the Stalinist state, but neither proved able to attain an accord that they considered reasonable. The failure contributed to the overriding opposition to commun- ism during both pontificates. In the words of one author they were 'of one mind in their hatred and fear of Bolshevism'.[6] Furthermore, Ratti and Pacelli could, and did, cooperate on a series of issues. They collaborated in drafting the three major encyclicals launched against the totalitarian regimes that threatened Catholicism and the Church: *Non abbiamo bisogno* of 1931, against the abuses of fascist Italy; *Mit brennender Sorge* of 1937, against the vices and violence of Nazi Germany; and *Divini redemptoris*, likewise of 1937, against the evils of atheistic communism.

Many of the assumptions concerning the solidarity of Ratti, Pacelli and Gasparri have been questioned as new documents have become available, which confirm what some had suspected – that the three disagreed on how to respond to fascist and Nazi abuses, with the pope determined to denounce those features of the dictatorships that conflicted with the faith. It is true that Pacelli contributed to a number of the condemnations of the fascist and totalitarian regimes, but this was done at the behest of the pope, while his secretary of state quietly nursed serious reservations about this critical policy. Nonetheless, some believe that Pius xi was grooming Pacelli to be his successor by sending him abroad so that he would be better known.[7] Reportedly, Pius xi predicted that Pacelli would make 'a splendid pope'.[8] Perhaps these assignments abroad served as a safe and pragmatic means of eliminating Pacelli's diplomatic but persistent opposition to papal policy.

This has led some to ponder whether the cooperation and supposed similar outlooks of Pius xi and Pacelli extended to their attitude towards Nazi Germany. Did Pius xi set the stage for the policy of accommodation with the fascist regimes that his successor pursued? This, and other charges, have been launched against Pius XI. Among other things he has been criticized for Vatican policies towards the fascist dictatorships, including Mussolini's Italy and Hitler's Reich, and denounced for concluding concordats with the fascist state in 1929 and the Third Reich in 1933 – thus legitimizing these regimes. The collaboration was allegedly furthered by Pius XI's failure to prevent the Catholic Popular Party from joining the Mussolini cabinet in 1922, and by providing the dictator with moral support during the Matteotti crisis of 1924–5, when it appeared that Mussolini's regime might collapse.

During his tenure the achievements of fascism were often praised, and some suspected that the infallible pope concurred with the policies of Il Duce, who claimed always to be right.[9] Finally, the anti-Bolshevik crusade of fascism was seen to have found resonance in Rome, which embraced the regime as a natural ally against communism.[10] This supposedly resulted in an axis between the pope and Mussolini, both of whom were seen to adhere to the leadership principle. It appeared to some that Pius XI looked with favour upon the authority exercised by Il Duce.

Others charged that the clerical anti-Judaism in the pre-Vatican II Church, facilitated, if it did not provoke, the anti-Semitism of fascist Italy and Nazi Germany.[11] Radical fascists such as Roberto Farinacci believed that Mussolini's racist legislation was the logical culmination of the anti-Judaism that had persisted in the Church for centuries.[12] These and similar statements has led one scholar to write that Pius XI 'offered few objections to the Italian racial laws',[13] implying that Pius XI did not find fascist anti-Semitism reprehensible. This accusation was also launched by a number of Italian observers who claimed that Pius XI 'failed to assume a determined opposition against the racism of fascist Italy'.[14]

While some complained that Ratti had imbibed the anti-Judaism that lingered in certain Vatican circles, what is known is that he remained suspicious of religious rivals; Protestantism as well as Judaism. Not surprisingly, during the Lateran Accord negotiations he opposed granting religious equality to either.[15] Anti-Semitism based on race was another matter, and Ratti believed it represented a violation of Christian precepts and principles, and was absolutely inadmissible for the faithful. He continued to denounce racism, refusing to acknowledge any relationship between discrimination against the Jews on the basis of what they believed – or did not believe – and who they were. Later, when informed that in some states racism had been approved by law, the pope would not be silenced. He responded that when politics or political figures infringed upon the realm of religion, the pope had the right and duty to issue directives to the faithful.[16] Therefore in 1926 he did not hesitate to condemn Charles Maurras' anti-Semitic Action Française.[17]

Racism, in Ratti's opinion, represented not only a danger for the Jews, but also a challenge to Christianity.[18] Throughout his papacy he conducted a crusade of sorts against what he perceived as Nazi excesses before Hitler's Final Solution led to the horror of the Holocaust. As early as September 1922, he proclaimed that Christian charity extends to all, without distinction of race.[19] At the end of that year the Holy See pleaded on behalf of the persecuted Armenians.[20] In 1926 Pius condemned Charles Maurras's reactionary and racist movement.[21] Two years later, the Holy Office struck out against anti-Semitism, when it suppressed the Friends of Israel (formed in 1926), issuing a clear condemnation. This pope did not hesitate to denounce those who fostered race hatred,[22] and he influenced the German hierarchy.

The bishop of Mainz charged that the Nazis wished to establish a new trinity of blood, people and state, warning Catholics that they could not belong to such a party. In March 1931 six bishops of the Cologne province deemed the errors of National Socialism similar to those of the Action Française condemned by Pius XI, while the three bishops of the Paderborn province ruled that membership of the Nazi Party was impermissible for Catholics.[23] Edith Stein, a convert from Judaism to Catholicism, wrote to the pope in 1933, seeking help for the persecuted Jews of Germany,[24] prompting him to instruct the nuncio in Berlin to intervene on their behalf.[25] Confronted with Hitler's intransigence, the nuncio failed to challenge the Führer.[26] Pacelli's recently opened pre-war correspondence reveals that he did not press the nuncio to do more.[27]

An objective examination and analysis of the records of Pius XI and his two secretaries of state in this correspondence reveals that Gasparri openly, Pacelli quietly but consistently, disagreed with the pope on the course to pursue towards Nazi Germany and fascist Italy, with a broadening divergence on how to respond to German and Italian anti-Semitism, and what the Vatican could or should endure to retain the concordat of 1929 with fascist Italy, and that of 1933 with Nazi Germany. Pius XI's opposition to racism was one of the reasons he was suspicious of National Socialism. Hitler, appreciating the influence of the Catholic Church, sent Hermann Göring to Rome in May 1931, but Pius XI did not receive him and forbade his pro-German secretary of state Pacelli from doing so. Later, in 1933, when Hitler had become chancellor, the Catholic vice-chancellor Franz von Papen visited Rome and dangled the prospect of a concordat before Pacelli, who had become secretary of state in 1930.[28] Berlin rather than Rome assumed the initiative and sought to bind the Church to the Reich.[29] The pope did not seek an agreement with this 'evil regime'.

Pacelli diplomatically disagreed, backed by Cardinal Gasparri, who wielded considerable influence in the Secretariat of State and Curia he had shaped. Following the Nazi assumption of power, the old cardinal drafted a memorandum in favour of an agreement with the Reich – calling on the Church to cease its criticism of Hitler's regime. He advised that if the Nazis sought the dissolution of the Catholic Centre Party, the Vatican should comply. Finally, he proposed that the Holy See and the hierarchy remove the restrictions imposed upon Catholics that prohibited them from joining the Nazi party, which Gasparri believed reflected national sentiments. This appeasement was seconded by the German bishops, who withdrew their declaration of August 1932, which forbade the faithful from joining the Nazi party. Pacelli concurred with his mentor's programme, supporting both the negotiation of a concordat and the adoption of a more conciliatory policy towards the Third Reich. Neither the persecution of Jews or Catholics prevented the secretary of state from concluding the controversial concordat with the Nazi regime in 1933. The pope hesitated, but not Pacelli, who was backed by Cardinal Gasparri, who still wielded considerable influence in the Secretariat of State and the Curia.

Aware of the pope's ambivalence in negotiating with the Nazis, Pacelli confessed that the Holy See deplored the anti-Semitism of the German government, its violations of human rights and the 'reign of terror' it imposed on the Reich. The Vatican signed the accord, he explained, because it appeared the sole means of preventing the destruction of the Church and its lay organizations in Germany.[30] On paper the agreement made broad concessions and provided numerous assurances to the Holy See, for more than two-thirds of its 33 articles seemingly made concessions to the Church.[31] An additional protocol guaranteed the right of the Church to collect funds in the Reich.[32] Pacelli was congratulated for his achievement by his predecessor, Cardinal Gasparri,[33] who belatedly forgave his protégé for taking his post. Convinced that the Reich Concordat best assured the future of the Church in Nazi Germany, Pacelli made its preservation a prime concern which in large measure accounts for his 'impartiality' and 'silence' vis-à-vis Nazi action.

The Vatican's reliance on impartiality can be traced back to the pontificate of Benedict XV (1914–22) and the diplomacy of Pietro Gasparri, Pacelli's mentor and patron and Benedict's secretary of state. Gasparri insisted that, as Vicar of Christ, the Holy Father could condemn principles in conflict with the faith, but as universal father he must remain impartial and not favour one side or state against another in conflict – a maxim that Pacelli accepted, extended and internalized. Like Gasparri, Pacelli also believed that in the realm of diplomacy, principle had to be tempered by prudence lest it produce more harm than good. Convinced that neither fascism nor Nazism would survive for more than two or three decades, the pragmatic cardinal believed that unless vital Church interests were threatened, the Vatican should remain politically impartial, avoiding a confrontation with regimes that could wreak havoc upon the Church. Pius XI disagreed with this appeasement, which led to Gasparri's ouster at the end of 1929. Unrepentant, Gasparri continued to call for conciliation and the avoidance of conflict.

Many wonder and question why Pius XI, who did not agree with Gasparri, long retained him as secretary of state, and why he selected his student, Pacelli, as successor. These are valid, important

and interesting questions. Pius XI never explained his rationale, but
he apparently retained Gasparri because of his crucial role in the
negotiation of the Lateran Accords that this pope very much
wanted. Pius forced Gasparri to resign following their successful
conclusion in February 1929. He selected the younger, less assertive
Pacelli to succeed as secretary of state because he had been out of
the country as nuncio in Germany for more than a decade, and
presumably did not have the support structure to pursue an
independent course. Furthermore, the younger prelate was far more
deferential to his superiors than his blunt mentor, and kept most of
his opinions to himself – especially in regard to his superiors. This
also explains why Pius XI did not know how committed Pacelli was
to appeasement. Finally, the pope hoped that his selection of
Gasparri's protégé would soothe the legion of supporters of the old
cardinal in the Secretariat of State.

Pius XI, however, continued to resist Gasparri's contention
that impartiality could be invoked to sanction silence, even when
matters of faith were involved. He was scandalized, though not
surprised, by the numerous Nazi violations of the concordat, provoking him to launch a series of complaints.[34] The Nazi sterilization
law was published days after conclusion of the concordat, while
Catholic clergy, charitable organizations, schools and publications
were all attacked.[35] In response, *La Civiltà Cattolica* condemned
the Nazi mythology of race, while the Pontifical Society for the
Preservation of the Faith noted that even those having a mediocre
knowledge of Catholic doctrine recognized that anti-Semitism was
forbidden.[36] Pius, for his part, distrusted Hitler and the Nazis more
than ever.

Some claimed that the Nazi's destruction of Jewish works in
May 1933 was reminiscent of the earlier Christian burning of Jewish
texts, but Pius denounced the comparison. At the end of October
1934 he approved a condemnation of the errors of National
Socialism by the Holy Office. Not all in the Curia concurred with
this course, invoking diplomacy rather than confrontation to preserve Catholic organizations. Rome faced a real dilemma: should it
remain silent to avoid the wrath of the regime or speak out against
obvious Nazi abuses, exposing the Church to grave peril. Papa

Ratti, and his secretary of state Pacelli, the future Pius XII, disagreed on this and other matters.[37] Pius XI, for his part, believed that Christianity had public as well as private responsibilities, and the Christian life required action.[38]

Troubled by Nazi neo-pagan policies, Pius XI rejected their contention that the Jewish question was an internal racial issue rather than a religious one.[39] He likewise dismissed Hitler's conviction that the Nazi restrictions on the Jews worked for the benefit of the Church as well as the State.[40] Pius considered such talk a frontal challenge to ecclesiastical teaching and felt a moral obligation to say so, assuring a delegation of visiting German students that he would do all within his means to defend the faith.[41] Firmly convinced that the Vicar of Christ had to be involved in world affairs, he rejected impartiality for an interventionist course. This promise and prospect prompted a series of voices to invoke his assistance against the Nazi persecution, including Edith Stein.[42] Pius XI responded by calling upon the nuncio in Germany to intervene on behalf of the Jewish victims, and it was at his prodding that the bishops of Germany proclaimed: 'God gave his only son for the salvation of all of mankind.'[43]

Differences between Pius XI and his new secretary of state soon emerged – although were largely ignored until the opening of the papers of Pius XI in the Archivio Segreto Vaticano. While the pope did not hesitate to resort to confrontation, his secretary of state continued to favour conciliation. Both opposed the anti-Semitism of Hitler's Germany, later copied by Mussolini's Italy, conscious that this violated Catholicism's universal ministry. They disagreed on how to respond to those who violated these principles, and the pope eventually realized that Pacelli, like most in the Curia, did not share his intransigent opposition and confrontational course.

The differences between the two are subtly but unmistakably manifest in the reports that Pacelli made of his meetings with the pope from 1930 to 1938 and made partially available in published form in 2010. Pacelli obediently followed the pope's orders, knowing that Pius XI had fired Gasparri, who had not. Pius XI became increasingly annoyed by Pacelli's passive resistance to his policy, making it clear that he reserved the right to follow his own opinion. Pius xi's vocal opposition to Nazi policy and anti-Semitic measures led some in the Vatican to fear for the future of the Reich Concordat. Once the anti-Jewish measures were backed by law, the nuncio in Germany, Cesare Orsenigo, wrote to Pacelli that the pope had to terminate his crusade against the persecution of the Jews or face unfortunate consequences.[44] Pacelli agreed, but dared not openly challenge the pope lest he be fired like his mentor. Meanwhile, others praised Pius xi for his efforts on behalf of the persecuted. In September 1933 the *Jewish Chronicle* of London applauded the pope's stance, while so many others remained silent:

> The Pope, having received reports of the persistence of anti-Semitic persecution in Germany, has publicly expressed his disapproval of the movement . . . He recorded . . . that Jesus Christ, the Madonna, the apostles, the prophets and many saints were all of the Hebrew race, and that the Bible is a Hebrew creation. The Aryan races, he declared, had no claim to superiority over the Semites.[45]

Papal opposition continued in the condemnations of Nazi principles and practices by the Holy Office in 1936, which rejected race as a principle of organization.[46] Publication of the condemnation was blocked by its secretary (Cardinal Francesco Marchetti-Selvaggiani), who, like Pacelli, opposed an open conflict with Nazism.[47] The pope, on the other hand, believed that the dignity of the Holy See required him to denounce Nazi outrages.[48] In February 1936, when Hitler sent Pius xi a congratulatory telegram to commemorate the anniversary of his coronation, the pope responded by deploring German developments.[49] Following the remilitarization of the Rhineland, he confided to the French ambassador: 'if you [French] had called forward 200,000 men you would have done an immense service to the entire world'.[50] Attempts to implicate the Church in the Nazi persecution of the Jews were rejected by Pius xi, who differentiated religious anti-Judaism from racial anti-Semitism and found Nazi racism in conflict with Church teaching.[51]

The continued Nazi attacks on the Church and its doctrines led Pius xi to speak out despite the subtle restraining influence of his secretary of state. On 14 March 1937 the pope issued the encyclical *Mit brennender Sorge*, which was secretly printed and distributed to the various parishes and read from Catholic pulpits throughout Germany on Palm Sunday.[52] 'With deep anxiety and increasing dismay', Pius wrote, he had witnessed the 'progressive oppression of the faithful'.[53] He protested against the treatment of the Church in the Reich while negating the principle of the division of humanity on a racial basis.[54] Denouncing the racism of the regime, and all social theories derived from the myth of blood and race, he catalogued the articles of faith trampled upon by the Nazis. He was shocked by their attempt to revive the pagan belief in a national god or a national religion, restricting the universal faith to one people or race.[55] His action earned him respect in Western capitals, but condemnation in Berlin.[56] Although Pacelli, under papal orders, played a part in drafting this encyclical, the secretary of state still sought to prevent a break between Berlin and the Vatican.[57] He was told that Hitler was infuriated by the encyclical and deplored the Vatican's secrecy in its transmission, along with its anti-Nazi message, vowing to take revenge at an appropriate time.[58] In the interim, the Führer had his police bring a number of Catholic priests to trial for 'immoral conduct' and sexual abuses.[59]

When in May 1937 Cardinal George William Mundelein of Chicago made insulting references to the Führer as a poor paperhanger, Pius refused to censure him, as some demanded, but praised him instead.[60] The following month *La Civiltà Cattolica*, which occasionally issued anti-Jewish pronouncements, proclaimed that the Church condemned all forms of anti-Semitism.[61] Like the Pope, its editors refused to recognize any relationship between clerical anti-Judaism and Nazi anti-Semitism. By the end of the year, Pius deplored anti-Christian developments in Germany no less than those in the Soviet Union.[62] In fact, Nazism soon displaced communism as his major concern.[63] Distressed by the prospect of a break in relations with the Reich, in 1938 Pacelli proposed going to Berlin to negotiate a settlement, but his offer was ignored both by Berlin and the pontiff.

In April 1938 the Sacred Congregation of Seminaries, presided over by the pope, condemned the racism championed by Nazi

Germany and charged Catholic academic institutions to combat these erroneous theories.[64] These protests did not stop the Nazi persecution of the Jews and its attempts to uproot Christianity from its Jewish origins.[65] This offended Pius XI, who complained to the German ambassador to the Holy See, Diego von Bergen, who warned Berlin that the pope might take drastic action. In fact, Pius seriously considered breaking with the Nazi state and terminating the concordat, but was persuaded by his secretary of state from taking this step. Even before he became pope, Pacelli invoked conciliation rather than confrontation with the Reich, deeming the latter course detrimental to the Catholic population of Germany. Pius XI, on the other hand, found it difficult to pursue a policy of conciliation towards regimes that frequently and flagrantly violated the precepts of the faith.

The pope continued his denunciations throughout 1938,[66] and deplored the extension of racism to Austria following the Anschluss.[67] He was outraged by Cardinal Innitzer's support for the Nazi absorption of Austria, summoning him to Rome and demanding a retraction. When Hitler visited Rome, in May 1938, the pope left for Castel Gandolfo, unwilling to see a cross, other than that of Christ, parade in the Holy City.[68] The *Osservatore Romano* ignored the Führer's presence, printing instead the April condemnation of racism. In June 1938, when Mussolini's Italy embraced anti-Semitism, Pius XI could not contain his outrage, despite the warnings of his secretary of state about the adverse consequences that would flow from a disruption of relations with fascist Italy and the Third Reich. Pius refused to keep quiet, letting Il Duce know through intermediaries that this action made him 'ashamed' of being Italian and regretted to see Italy imitate Germany's anti-Semitism.[69] Soon thereafter, in mid-July 1938 when the 'Fascist Manifesto on Race' was issued, Pius branded it 'a true form of apostasy'.[70]

Exasperated by the 'exaggerated nationalism' and racism of Nazi Germany, the old pope resolved to take further steps to denounce this misguided policy.[71] Convinced that he could not rely on his secretary of state for an unequivocal condemnation of anti-Semitism, in June 1938 Pius XI sought the assistance of the

American Jesuit John LaFarge to condemn these moral evils. Pius concurred with LaFarge's *Interracial Justice* (1937), which denounced the notion of 'pure race' as a myth, noting that the teachings of Christ proclaimed the moral unity of the human race and warning that the fostering of racial prejudice was a sin that could not be ignored.[72] Pius XI supported LaFarge's critique. Skirting his conciliatory Secretariat of State, and its head, the pope secretly commissioned the American Jesuit to draft an encyclical demonstrating the incompatibility of Catholicism and racism.[73]

Like LaFarge, the pope invoked a spiritual defence of human rights, outlining the topic and its method of treatment with the Jesuit. Pius XI thus planned to condemn the anti-Semitism of Hitler's Germany without involving his secretary of state. He was also working on a speech cataloguing fascist abuses and errors. Aware of the opposition to his confrontational course, Pius swore LaFarge to secrecy,[74] not even informing Pacelli of his plans. During an audience to a group of nuns, however, Pius XI let slip that he was preparing an encyclical condemning racism.[75]

When LaFarge informed Father Wlodimir Ledóchowski, the Polish General of the Order, of the pope's desire to have the encyclical quickly, the latter suggested that he collaborate with two other Jesuits: the Frenchman Gustave Desbuquois and the German Gustav Gundlach. They worked throughout the summer of 1938 to meet the papal deadline, and in late September placed a draft of the encyclical in the hands of Ledóchowski for transmission to the pope. Ledóchowski, a close ally and associate of Pacelli, did not transmit their draft to the pope. Instead, he brought it to the attention of some within the Curia and the Secretariat of State, who judged it dangerously confrontational, leading Ledóchowski, without papal authorization, to submit it to another Jesuit to moderate its message.

The projected letter condemning anti-Semitism did not renounce the Church's anti-Judaism. Apparently, the pope and the Jesuit authors of the document considered them distinct. At the end of July, during an audience to the students of the Propaganda Fide, the pope praised their universal mission at a time of so much racism.[76] He harped on the universality of the Catholic Church, reminding the students that humanity consisted of one great, universal family, the theme of his unreleased encyclical. Between mid-July and mid-September 1938 Pius XI made four speeches against racism.[77] Human dignity, he repeated, rested in a unified humanity, branding the Fascist Aryan Manifesto of 14 July 1938 a 'true form of apostasy', urging Catholic groups to combat it and initiating a chorus of opposition to the racism of the totalitarian regimes.[78] Pius regretted that Italy had imitated the German example in espousing a racism contrary to the beliefs and teachings of the Church.[79] Count Ciano, Mussolini's son-in-law and foreign minister, described the pope's speech as violently anti-racist.

Pius XI continued to espouse the sentiments of the 'encyclical' he had authorized, upset by the racist and anti-Semitic policies that fascist Italy adopted as it moved closer to Nazi Germany. Despite his failing health, he made his opposition to racism clear in early September 1938, announcing that the Vicar of Christ could not remain silent in the face of grave errors and the violation of human rights. On 10 November 1938 Mussolini published a decree forbidding marriage between Italian Aryans with persons of 'another race'. Pius responded by writing to the king and Mussolini that this was a violation of the concordat of the Lateran Accords. He made public his displeasure in his Christmas address.

The pope's public denunciation of racism worried Pacelli, who sought to prevent a break with the Nazi regime.[80] It was a difficult task in light of the pope's visceral opposition to the racism of the Berlin government, and the prospect of its adoption by fascist Italy only increased his anger. Despite Pacelli's conciliatory stance, relations between the Vatican and the Reich deteriorated during the course of 1938 as the documents of the newly available files of the Vatican Secret Archives confirm. In July Pius XI stressed the absolute incompatibility between racist nationalism and universal Catholicism.[81] 'No, it's not possible for we Christians to participate in anti-Semitism', the Pope told a group of visiting Belgians on 6 September 1938. 'Spiritually, we are Semites.'[82] 'I shall speak out, I will not be afraid', he proclaimed in October: 'I am impelled to do so . . . by my conscience.'[83] There was still no hint of the release of LaFarge's encyclical. Father Gundlach convinced LaFarge to write directly to Pius XI, enquiring about his reaction to their efforts and indirectly letting him know it had been submitted.

In fact, Pius XI was not officially informed that the anti-racist encyclical he had commissioned had been delivered until he heard from LaFarge. Once informed that it had been delivered at the end of September 1938, the seriously ill and angry pope demanded to have it sent to him immediately, which prompted the reluctant Ledóchowski to comply. Only when the pope demanded that it be delivered at once did the encyclical materialize. Reportedly, Pius XI received the projected encyclical on 21 January 1939, but it is uncertain if he read it before his death on 9 February.[84] Some believe he was silenced by being murdered. This is pure conjecture, based on the fact that his primary physician was Dr Francesco Petacci, father of Claretta Petacci, Mussolini's mistress.

Pius XI's campaign against racism was frustrated not only by the hostility of the dictatorial regimes, and his poor health and advanced age, but also by those in the Vatican seeking a more conciliatory successor. The group in the Vatican that favoured appeasement of the totalitarian regimes rather than antagonizing them, signed an agreement behind the pope's back with Mussolini's regime on the racial issue. According to Father Angelo Martini of the Society of Jesus, who was granted access to these Vatican documents, the 'pact' of 16 August 1938 provided that in return for fascist consideration of papal sensibilities on Catholic Action and its organizations and activities in Italy, the papacy was to leave the 'Jewish Question' entirely to the regime.[85] Those who negotiated the pact knew that the pope would never have agreed to such a bargain, so their action was apparently based on the belief that Pius XI did not have much longer to live! What part, if any, Pacelli played in this is unknown.

On the basis of what Pius XI thought and said, and his willingness to confront the totalitarian regimes, one can only conclude this pope would have issued the 'encyclical' that reflected his stance on anti-Semitism had he lived longer. We also know that following the death of Pius XI, Pacelli decided to shelve the two critiques of the fascist regimes that the pope had planned. Indeed, Domenico Tardini reports in documents recently opened in the Vatican Secret

Archives that by a series of telephone calls on 15 February 1939, the secretary of state Pacelli ordered the Vatican printing house to destroy all evidence of the papal speech, which he feared would widen the rift with Mussolini's Italy and its Nazi allies.[86] Pacelli had the draft of the 'secret' encyclical against Nazi racism returned to its authors. His reasons for doing this are still debated.

Both documents reflected Pius XI's confrontational course towards the fascist regimes, which Pacelli opposed. Following his mentor Gasparri, Pacelli favoured a more diplomatic policy and chose not to release either. This was symptomatic of the new course he would pursue towards fascist Italy and Nazi Germany from the first days of his pontificate. Pius XII's 'impartiality' and 'silence' replaced Pius XI's crusade against anti-Semitism!

Pius XII: The Second World War, the Holocaust and the Cold War

IN 1942, WHEN THE MILITARY CHAPLAIN FATHER PIRRO Scavizzi personally related the horror of the Holocaust to Pope Pius XII, his response was intense:

> The Pope, standing besides me, listened with great emotion; then he raised his hands and said: 'Tell everyone you can that the Pope is in anguish for them and with them! Say that many times he has thought of hurling excommunications at Nazism, of denouncing the bestiality of the extermination of the Jews to the civilized world. Serious threats of reprisal have come to our ears, not against our person, but against our unhappy sons who are now under Nazi domination. The liveliest recommendations have reached us through various channels that the Holy See should not take a drastic stand. After many tears and many prayers, I came to the conclusion that a protest from me would not only not help anyone, but would arouse the most ferocious anger against the Jews and multiply acts of cruelty because they are undefended. Perhaps my solemn protest would win me some praise from the civilized world but would bring down on the poor Jews an even more implacable persecution than the one they are already enduring . . .'[1]

Eugenio Maria Giuseppe Giovanni Pacelli, elected pope on his sixty-third birthday, in one of the shortest ever conclaves, assumed the name Pius XII. He had something in common with his immediate predecessors; like Leo XIII and Benedict XV he was a diplomat and had the linguistic diversity and great intellectual capacity of the latter. He concurred with Pius XI on the importance of concordats and found himself in agreement with Pius X on the need for reconciliation with Italy – a sentiment also shared by Pius XI. While Benedict and Pius XI had limited pre-papal pastoral experience, Pacelli had virtually none. Finally, while all the popes from Pius IX to Pius XII had to confront difficulties, those that Papa Pacelli had to confront were particularly troubling and included the Second World War, Nazi, fascist and communist totalitarianism, the Holocaust and the Cold War.

When Papa Pacelli donned the tiara the clouds of war were thickening, and the new pope devoted the first few months of his pontificate to attempting to prevent the outbreak of another disastrous war. In his quest for peace he had recourse to the need to preserve impartiality – which has a long history but is all too often neglected by historians. In the modern age some trace it back to the pontificate of Pius VII (1800–23), when the pope refused to align the papacy with Napoleonic France. Rejecting the French alliance, Pius explained that God willed that the papacy should pursue a peaceful policy towards all, 'even towards those from whom evil may be expected'.[2] In the opening decades of the twentieth century the trio of Pope Benedict XV, his secretary of state Pietro Gasparri and Pacelli, further developed the policy of impartiality, which they differentiated from neutrality. Gasparri insisted that, as Vicar of Christ, the Holy Father should condemn principles in conflict with the faith, but as universal father he must remain impartial and not favour one side or state against another in a conflict – a maxim that Pacelli helped develop and accepted. A central feature of this policy was the unwillingness of the Holy See to take sides in disputes, but it called upon all to make concessions.

Initially, the new pope was little appreciated by Adolf Hitler, who assumed that Pacelli's long collaboration with Pius XI, and assumption of the name of his outspoken predecessor, meant that he would continue his confrontational policies. Most likely, this is why Berlin had reservations about his election at first.[3] These concerns proved premature, for Papa Pacelli was convinced that his predecessor's confrontational course towards the totalitarian regimes was dangerous and counter-productive, and he determined

to change direction. Consequently, German reservations about the
new pope were soon dispelled as Pius XII made a sustained effort to
improve relations with the Nazi state. He confided his intention of
pursuing a more conciliatory policy towards the Reich to the Italian
foreign minister, Count Galeazzo Ciano.[4] He proved true to his
promise, even though the Hitler regime proved increasingly anti-
Semitic, aggressive and expansionist, as well as anti-Christian. This
did not deter Pius XII. One of his first actions was to meet the
German cardinals, revealing to them his new conciliatory course
and intention of sending a personal letter to Hitler announcing his
accession – and he did so. He showed himself extremely sympathetic to Germany when he met a group of pilgrims from the
Reich in April 1939.

As a result, Nazi reservations about the new pope were soon
dispelled as the change of papal policy found favour both in Rome
and Berlin. Count Ciano, Mussolini's son-in-law and foreign minister,
expressed his satisfaction with Pius XII and wrote in his diary: 'I
believe that we can get along with this Pope.'[5] Berlin was equally
enthusiastic, since Nazi officials were convinced that they could
achieve a modus vivendi with him.[6] Not surprisingly, Pacelli's paci-
fist policy found favour in the Curia and the Vatican's Secretariat of
State, whose sentiment and policy it reflected.

On the other hand, this pro-German policy flowing from papal
impartiality was resented by Britain and France, who were the
potential victims of fascist expansionism and aggression. Not surprisingly, while Pius XII perceived his actions and proposals to be
that of an 'Apostle of Peace', the Allies viewed his suggestions and
behaviour as that of an 'Advocate of Appeasement', which would
have unfortunate consequences. Indeed, some later charged that
this impartiality contributed to the papal decision to remain relatively silent during the course of the Holocaust. Here, too, Pius XII
followed the path paved by Benedict XV and his secretary of state
Gasparri, who did not condemn the genocide of the Armenians in
order to preserve Vatican impartiality during the First World War.

Some later charged that Pius XII's public silence was motivated
by the Vatican's indifference to the plight of the Jews because of
anti-Semitism or at least anti-Judaism – a charge challenged by its

other silences where Jews were not involved. Such was the case with Benedict's 'silence' during the Armenian genocide in the First World War and Pius XII's public silence during the invasion of Catholic Poland and the genocide of Catholic Poles and Orthodox Serbs during the course of the Second World War. Determined not to alienate Nazi Germany, Pius XII did not protest against its invasion of Catholic Poland at the beginning of September 1939. In an address to the Polish colony in Rome at the end of that month, the pope offered condolences and consolation, but once again issued no condemnation of Nazi aggression. Instead, he revealed his determination to remain neutral to a group of visiting German pilgrims and remained true to this commitment. This pope held his tongue even after the Nazis murdered some 20 per cent of his Polish priests!

The papal silence towards the Nazi atrocities committed in Poland served as a prelude to the subsequent broader genocide of the Jews – neither of which was clearly and publicly condemned by Pius XII. Indeed, in an interview Rolf Hochhuth gave in February 1964 the playwright admitted that he originally conceived of focusing on the plight of the Poles before turning to the Holocaust endured by the Jews.[7] Pius was distressed to learn that some Poles felt abandoned by the Holy See, claiming they were misinformed, and was shocked to think that anyone might suspect him of not caring for Poland and the Poles.[8] Critics responded that actions speak louder than words.

Despite the critique of some, Pius XII continued to adhere to his policy of impartiality, which he believed allowed him to play the part of an honest broker in the search for peace. On a more practical plane, he sought to ensure that the Church would not become Hitler's main target and hoped to preserve the structure of the Church in Germany. Pacelli claimed that the Holy Father as Vicar of Christ could make moral judgements between competing principles, but as the father of all should remain neutral in specific conflicts. Supposedly, this policy was pursued both by Pius XII and his predecessor Pius XI, a conclusion accepted by the greater part of the Italian historiography.

A small group of historians contested the contention that Ratti and Pacelli agreed on the policy to pursue towards the anti-Semitism of the Axis powers. Early on, Carlo Falconi contrasted 'The silence of Pius XII' with the outspoken criticism of his predecessor. Peter Kent, of the University of New Brunswick, likewise saw important differences in the reactions of Pius XI and his successor towards anti-Semitism in his article of 1988, 'A Tale of Two Popes'. Emma Fattorini, in a series of works, has come to a similar conclusion.[9] Their findings, based on solid documentation, were confirmed by the availability of new sources during the first years of the third millennium. From 2000 to 2010 the Vatican released thousands of pre-Second World War documents from when Pacelli was nuncio in Germany, and then secretary of state. Also opened were Pacelli's *Fogli di udienza* or records of audiences, one volume of which has been published. These sources at times clearly, sometimes more subtly, contrast the confrontational course of Pius XI with the more conciliatory one of Pacelli. Those close to Pacelli, such as Domenico Tardini, noted that he lacked the fighting spirit of Pope Pius XI and seemed to prefer contemplation to action.[10]

Apparently, the cardinals in the conclave were aware of the differences between Pius XI and Pacelli and elected the latter Pope not to continue the confrontational course of the old pope towards the fascist regimes, but to change course and pursue a more conciliatory one. Pacelli did not disappoint them. Immediately following the death of Pius XI, he decided to abandon the two condemnations that the deceased pope had planned to launch: the first against Mussolini's violations of the concordat with Italy of 1929; the second against Nazi Germany's racism and anti-Semitism. Domenico Tardini reports in documents recently opened in the Vatican Secret Archives that in a series of telephone calls on 15 February 1939, secretary of state Pacelli ordered the Vatican printing house to destroy all evidence of the papal speech that he feared would widen the rift with Mussolini's Italy as well as its Nazi allies.[11] Once pope, Pacelli determined not to release the encyclical *Humani generis unitas* against Nazi racism that he knew would antagonize the fascist regimes. Both documents reflected Pius XI's confrontational course, which Pacelli had long opposed. Following his mentor Gasparri, Pacelli favoured a more diplomatic policy and chose not to release either in order to pacify rather than provoke the fascist dictators. This reflected the new course Pius XII determined to pursue vis-à-vis the totalitarian states.

Apparently Pius XII concurred with Gasparri that the fascist regimes would not survive for many decades, but while they did they could create havoc for the Church and its clergy. Hence the need not to antagonize them. This objective was responsible for the pope's limited public criticism of their activities – sometimes dubbed silence – justified by his recourse to impartiality. On the eve of the Second World War the French ambassador to the Holy See, François Charles-Roux, regretted Pius XII's impartiality towards aggressor and aggrieved alike, asserting that the Holy See should pursue an ethical rather than an expedient course based on the principles of religion rather than narrow self-interest or pragmatic considerations.[12] Pius concurred, asserting that though adhering to impartiality, the Holy See could and should condemn principles contrary to the faith but for various reasons – above all its mediation efforts – it should not become embroiled in the conflict. Some denounced this division as unrealistic and a pretext rather than a programme.

Critics judged as unrealistic the explanation that impartiality and silence were required for papal mediation. They noted that Pius XII's attempts at mediation proved no more successful than those of Benedict XV during the course of the First World War, and, like Benedict, Pius XII proved unable to prevent Italy from entering the conflict. Critical of his silence, some refused to recognize any positive papal role, including his aid to the civilian and military victims of the conflagration. In fact, Pius XII initiated another 'crusade of charity', outlined in *Crusade of Charity: Pius XII and POWs, 1939– 1945* by Sister Margherita Marchione. Although admittedly partisan, this sister of the Religious Teachers Filippini has found and reported on the work of the Vatican Information Office formed by Pius XII in 1939 to monitor and mitigate the suffering and separations provoked by the Second World War. Part of this vast correspondence has been drawn from the earlier printed eleven-volume *Actes et documents du Saint Siège relatifs à la Seconde Guerre Mondiale* (1965–81), but many more documents have now been made accessible by the Secret Vatican Archives.

Some 10 million wartime documents of the prisoner of war/ missing persons service presently available have been catalogued in two large volumes entitled *Inter arma caritas: L'uffizio informazioni Vaticano per i prigionieri di guerra istituito da Pio XII* (2004). The first volume includes an inventory of files and description of how the service operated; the second includes a selection of the millions of requests received, and in some cases the responses made by this service. The Marchione volume, in turn, catalogues and explores the wide range of requests for papal assistance from Christians and Jews and lists the aid granted. It entails how and when the Vatican intervened on behalf of the families of prisoners and the dispossessed, and the concrete assistance provided. Marchione asserts that the millions of requests made to Pope Pius XII indicates he had the trust of his contemporaries and was not deemed indifferent to the victims of the conflict – especially the Jews.

Nonetheless, Pope Pius XII, who was broadly admired in the West during the Second World, its immediate aftermath and during the early Cold War, was increasingly criticized by the early 1960s. A number of factors led to a more critical evaluation of him and his polices, some suggesting that Pius XII was not only anti-Judaic but also anti-Semitic. Papal impartiality between the anti-Semitic and 'brutal totalitarian regimes' and the 'democratic Allies' who were the victims of Nazi aggression, became increasingly incomprehensible to the post-war generation, who learned the extent of Nazi Germany's Final Solution during the trial of Adolf Eichmann in 1961. The trial revealed the terrible consequences of the Shoah or Holocaust, which led many to question the limited public condemnation or 'silence' of Pius XII.

This critique was given a widespread audience following the performance of Rolf Hochhuth's drama *Der Stellvertreter* (*The Deputy: A Christian Tragedy*) in 1963, which depicted Pius XII as a cold and calculating figure preoccupied by narrow clerical concerns, institutional constraints and the Vatican's financial interests who virtually ignored the plight of the Nazi victims. The negative image was reinforced by the appearance of such books as Daniel Jonah Goldhagen's *A Moral Reckoning: The Role of the Catholic Church and its Unfulfilled Duty of Repair*, Carlo Falconi's *Il silenzio di Pio XII* (1965) and John Cornwell's *Hitler's Pope: The Secret History of Pius XII* (1999). The denigrators and detractors of this pope encouraged the emergence of his defenders. Together they have contributed to the 'Pius War', which has generated more heat than light.[13] The contentious debate on Pius XII's silence reveals that a good part of this vast literature is motivated by the mania to denounce or defend this Pope and has proved unable or unwilling to address objectively the issue of his silence.

Many of these works are polemical rather than objective, with the combatants talking at one another rather than to one another. Consequently, many aspects of Pius XII's policy during the Holocaust have not been clearly defined, including the nature of his silence, the origin of this papal policy and its relationship to papal impartiality, and Papa Pacelli's motivation for recourse to silence during the genocide.

Despite the excuses of his defenders and accusations of his denigrators, Pius XII recognized early on the moral dimension of his wartime discretion and the ethical dilemma inherent in adhering to the papacy's cautious policy of impartiality. There was a rationale for the course he pursued that transcended his alleged indifference and hostility towards the Jews. This included the strict censorship in the Reich, which he recognized would prevent his criticism from reaching the masses and serve only to invite reprisal from the Nazi regime; it might lead to a disruption of the concordat and eliminate the remnant of rights retained by the Church in Germany; it might provoke the Nazis to make the plight of the Jews worse, while increasing the persecution of Catholics. Still, Pius worried that his intentions might be misunderstood and perceived as anti-Semitism or indifference to the suffering of the Jews of Europe, of which he was well informed.[14]

Furthermore, an objective assessment of papal policy reveals that while Pius did not unleash clear and direct public protests aimed at influencing the masses, he was not totally silent. From 1939 to 1945 he issued a series of pronouncements, allocutions and encyclicals that indirectly struck at the practices and policies of the Hitler regime. Written in Latin, often in a convoluted style, critics complained that they were designed to fulfil the papacy's moral responsibility and failed to arouse Catholics against the odious practices of the regime. In fact, Pius acknowledged the need for the Holy Father to denounce evil, admitting as much to both the French and Italian ambassadors. 'The Pope at times cannot remain silent. Governments only consider political and military issues, intentionally disregarding moral and legal issues in which, on the other hand, the Pope is primarily interested and cannot ignore', Pius XII told the Italian ambassador Dino Alfieri on 13 May 1940. Quoting St Catherine of Siena's warning to an earlier pope, he too feared 'that God would subject him to the most stringent judgment if he did not react to evil or did not do what he thought was his duty'.[15]

Pius himself acknowledged that he would have liked to have uttered 'words of fire' in condemnation of Nazi abuses but did not, lest he make the situation worse.[16] Consequently, although he denounced the violation of treaties and the preparation for war in his Easter Message of April 1939 and his radio appeal of 24 August 1939, he did so without abandoning his impartiality by naming those responsible for the sad state of affairs. Likewise, Pius XII's first encyclical, *Summi pontificatus*, which condemned the forgetfulness of the law of human solidarity, ignored Pius XI's explicit condemnation of Nazi racism.[17]

Those who claim that the Holy See was unaware of Nazi atrocities and especially the brutalization and genocide of the Jews, and others deemed undesirable, are mistaken. Almost immediately, distressful news reached the Vatican of Hitler's genocidal 'Final Solution', and the systematic persecutions and executions in Nazi-occupied Europe. The Vatican had been alerted to the grave Nazi crimes against humanity by a series of sources within and outside the Church. In fact, the metropolitan Sheptyckyi warned the pope that the German regime, perhaps to a higher degree than the Bolschevik one, was evil and diabolical, committing the most horrible crimes against the Jews and others, falling upon the helpless like a band of rabid wolves. In May 1942 Pius was told of the mass extermination (*uccisioni di massa*) of Jews from Germany, Poland and the Ukraine. Meanwhile, the military chaplain Father Pirro Scavizzi personally reported to Pius that the elimination of Jews through mass murder was almost total, without regard for children or even infants.

The under-secretary of state Giovanni Montini, who later became Paul VI, concluded that the massacre of Jews had assumed atrocious and frightening proportions. The members of the World Jewish Congress, among others, urged the pope to issue a proclamation against the destruction of the Jews and other crimes against humanity. Some within the Church hoped that the pope would speak out frankly, but Pius XII hesitated. His long-awaited Christmas message of December 1942 offered only an indirect criticism of the brutal Nazi policy, expressing concern for those who without fault, and sometimes only because of race or nationality, had been consigned to death or to a slow demise.[18] He remained reluctant to say more.

In response to Father Scavizzi's plea for a more public defence of the Jews, Pius responded that he thought of denouncing the bestiality of the extermination of the Jews to the civilized world, but did not do so because he feared it would make their plight worse.[19] In a letter of 30 April 1943 to the bishop of Berlin, Konrad Graf von Preysing, who had earlier asked the pope to issue an appeal on behalf of the persecuted Jews, Pius claimed that in his Christmas message of December 1942 he had referred to what was being done to the non-Aryans under German occupation. 'We have spoken briefly but we have been well understood', he wrote. He appreciated the plight of the persecuted, but added: 'as the situation is at present we are unfortunately not able to help them effectively in other ways than our prayers'. He promised, however, to raise his voice on their behalf again, if it were necessary and circumstances permitted.[20] Some claimed that he did not speak more openly due to his desire to avoid greater evil – which Pius confirmed on a number of occasions.

Although the Vatican of Pius XII received repeated reports of Nazi atrocities in 1940 and 1941, and was alerted to the genocide of the Jews during the conflagration, it preserved its public neutrality. In fact, in November 1941 the pope told the new Spanish ambassador, José Yanguas Messía, that he had a 'special love' for the Germans, adding that he had 'nothing against' Germany, which he

'loved and admired', nor against the Hitler regime, although he
acknowledged he was saddened by some of its measures.[21] This was
a startling and unfortunate statement in light of the atrocities perpetrated by the Nazi regime, of which Pius XII was well informed.
Adhering to his diplomatic and impartial course, the pope did not
cite, much less condemn, the atrocities committed by the Nazi
regime. Instead, he resorted to general condemnations of the evils
of war and desire for the end of suffering, lamenting the evils
affecting not only soldiers but also entire populations: the old,
innocent, peace-loving, and those bereft of all defence. 'To the
powers occupying territories during the war, we say with all due
consideration: let your conscience guide in dealing justly, humanely
. . . with the peoples of occupied territories', Pius advised.[22]

The pope once again attributed his restraint to 'the fear of
making the plight of the victims even worse',[23] alongside a series of
legal, political and security considerations that were also important
in the formation and implementation of Pius XII's cautious, conciliatory and impartial policy throughout the Second World War.
For diverse reasons, both his advocates and antagonists have over-
looked or discounted the legal constraints motivating his actions.
'With regard to the sovereignty pertaining to it in the field of
international relations', article 24 of the treaty with fascist Italy
proclaimed, 'the Holy See declares that it wishes to remain and will
remain extraneous to all temporal disputes among nations'.[24]
Apparently, this was viewed as a mandate by the legally minded
pope, who did not want to provide any pretext for a fascist Italy
incursion or intervention into Vatican City.

Pius resented the pressure of the chargé d'affaires of the United
States during the war, Harold H. Tittmann, Jr, to denounce Hitler
and Nazi atrocities openly and explicitly. He explained why he
could not and would not do so:

> First, there are over forty million German-speaking Catholics.
> If I should denounce the Nazis by name as you desire and
> Germany should lose the war, Germans everywhere would feel
> that I had contributed to the defeat, not only of the Nazis but
> Germany herself; for the German population not to be able to

make the distinction between the Nazis and the fatherland would only be human in the confusion and distress of defeat. I cannot risk alienating so many of the faithful. One of my predecessors, Pope Benedict xv, in the First World War, through an unfortunate public statement of the type you now wish me to make, did just this and the interests of the Church in Germany suffered as a result. Second, if I denounce the Nazis by name I must in all justice do the same as regards the Bolsheviks whose principles are strikingly similar; you would not wish me to say such things about an ally of yours . . .[25]

The reluctance of Pope Pius xii to say or do more for the persecuted Catholic Poles distressed them as well as the Americans. From his exile, the president of the Polish government urged Pius to launch an unequivocal denunciation of the diabolical Nazi forces, informing the Vatican of the evils perpetrated during their brutal occupation. The pope did not heed the advice of the Catholic Poles, and continued to move cautiously, rigidly adhering to his impartiality. Various voices, including a number of cardinals close to the Holy See, pressed Pius xii to follow the example of Pius xi and publicly denounce the Nazi persecution of the Church in Germany. Pius xii, however, continued to rely on his diplomatic course, carefully weighing his words following the German invasion of the Soviet Union in June 1941. Preserving its neutrality, the Vatican also refused to support the Nazi's anti-Bolshevik 'crusade'.

Privately, Pius xii continued to question whether he had chosen the proper path – more so than many of those who later defended his policies. He knew that his veiled accusations and generalizations did not reach or influence the German masses. One had to search for these critiques, as opponents of the regime abroad and newspaper reporters were prone to do, but he realized that such scrutiny was impossible within the Nazi state with its repressive censorship. He also recognized the need for the Vicar of Christ to say more as regards the Nazi brutalization of the Jews. When he met his apostolic delegate to Greece and Turkey, Angelo Giuseppe Roncalli (the future Pope John xxiii), in October 1941, he clearly worried about how his 'inaction' was perceived abroad and enquired whether his silence on Nazi behaviour and mistreatment of the Jews was judged badly.[26] John does not indicate in his diary entry if he responded to the papal question, how he responded to the query, and, if he did address the issue, how his response was received by the pope. Despite his concerns, Pius XII did not abandon his cautious diplomatic approach.

Critics continued to question Pius XII's reticence to denounce Nazi atrocities and strict public neutrality during the war. The Allied invasion of Sicily in July 1943 paved the way for Italy's surrender that September. This prompted a German drive into the peninsula from the north and occupation of Rome on 10 September. Hitler threatened to enter the Vatican, indicating to those around him that at the war's end concordats would disappear, and he would settle his accounts with the Church. Rumour circulated of a Nazi plot to seize the Vatican, kidnap the pope and cardinals in the Curia, and hold them hostage, as Napoleon had done in the previous century. In fact, in September 1943 Hitler reportedly ordered the seizure of the pope, but was apparently dissuaded from implementing this serious step by subordinates, so Pius remained in the Vatican throughout the German occupation. The Germans, however, ordered the arrest of the Jews in occupied Rome and began to transport them to Mauthausen, an Austrian concentration camp. Pius instructed Monsignor Alois Hudal, the rector of Santa Maria dell'Anima, who championed a compromise between Catholicism and Nazism, to complain to the German commander, General Stahel, while the secretary of state, Cardinal Maglione, summoned the German ambassador and privately protested against the arrest and deportation of the Jews. No public protest was issued.

Although the pope did not personally denounce the outrage conducted 'under his very windows', behind the scenes papal efforts and protests saved many Italian Jews, with a good number housed in the extra-territorial religious houses.[27] Pius quietly encouraged the religious orders in the Eternal City to shelter some 5,000 of the 8,000 Jewish community. The fact that he did not do more and publicly protest against the Nazi action led some to suggest that he substituted 'immoral silence' for the 'moral leadership' of Pius XI. The reality was far more complex, and the times different. Furthermore, all the pope's moderation and prudence could not prevent increased tensions between the Vatican and the German occupiers, and renewed threats of a possible papal deportation. Pius let it be known that he would not leave Rome under any circumstances, protesting against any violence contemplated against the Vicar of Christ. Meanwhile, the advance of the Allied forces in the peninsula, the breaching of the Gustav line in May 1944, followed by the fall of Cassino on 18 May, and the piercing of the German line in the Alban hills, paved the way for the Allied advance on Rome. The German commander, General Albert Kesselring, proposed that Rome be considered an open city and withdrew his forces, as Pius issued an address to the cardinals reviewing the afflictions of Rome. In June 1944, when the Allies entered Rome, Pius clung to his neutrality, claiming that the mutual collaboration of the contending parties had saved the Eternal City. Pius, however, assumed a very different policy once the war ended.

Both the pope and the Curia opposed the unconditional surrender of Germany, fearing that this would prolong the conflict and bring the Soviet Union and communism into central and western Europe, and questioned the American optimism vis-à-vis the role envisioned for Stalin. As early as his radio address of 1 September 1944, the pope insisted that Christians could not admit a social order that denied the right to, or rendered impossible, the possession of private property.[28] Critics complained that no concern about the need to preserve papal impartiality prevented Pius XII's vocal criticism and virtual crusade against Stalin's Soviet Union in the post-war period, during which he disdained silence and seemed to pay little heed to the consequences of his condemnations. The Vatican deplored the central role that it appeared the Soviet Union would play in post-war Europe, and opposed the projected veto to be granted to the Soviet Union in the Security Council of the United Nations.

A decree of 1 July 1949 (*Responsa ad dubia de communismo*) excommunicated those who supported communism, a condemnation that had never been launched by the Vatican against the adherents of Nazism or fascism.[29] During the thirteen years of his pontificate following the close of the war (1945–58), Pius generally pursued a conservative and anti-communist course. At this time, he finally found his voice as he called for the banishment of atheism and the indestructibility of spiritual values in the struggle against communism. He continued to support the efforts of the Europeans and Americans against 'godless' communism, and in 1956 he denounced the Soviet invasion of Hungary.

In Italy, Pius embroiled himself in the peninsula's affairs, by means of Catholic Action groups, under the leadership of Professor Luigi Gedda and the supervision of the bishops. The pope appreciated and applauded the efforts of Gedda's 'civic committees' to swing support to conservative parties and policies in Italy, supporting those that had a Western orientation, while opposing the communists, Socialists and a multiplicity of other parties of the Left. Although Pius XII disdained partisan politics, he nonetheless encouraged Catholic organizations and groups to support the Christian Democrats, in order to keep the communists out of power. Indeed, there were those in the Vatican who characterized the post-war struggle in Italy and Europe as one between Moscow and Rome.

In the process, Pius was seen to jettison his impartiality, hesitation and discretion in his denunciation of the Soviet Union and its communist ideology, refusing to remain silent in the post-war period as he became involved in the Cold War and pursued a policy of condemnation and containment of the Soviet Union. He favoured the European Recovery Program (Marshall Plan) of 1947, as well as the initial steps towards European economic integration, as a means to block communist subversion.

Throughout most of the years of his pontificate after the end of the war, Pius generally pursued a conservative, anti-communist course. Some have charged that his entire post-war pontificate remained defensive, desperately attempting to preserve Catholic civilization in a world shaken by militant Bolshevism. Whatever the motivation, Pius did range the moral weight of Catholic preaching against the USSR and its allies, while moving closer to the West. He was especially reassured by the promise of American aid to Italy, and American determination to maintain a military presence in Europe. Indeed, the common interests of the United States and the

Vatican multiplied following Roosevelt's death, during the increasingly hostile reaction of the Truman administration towards the
Soviet Union. Charging that the totalitarian, anti-religious state
demanded the silence and acquiescence of the Church, he rejected
these conditions. 'What was in the opinion of many a duty of the
Church, and what they demanded of her in an unseemly[!] way',
Pius protested, 'is today . . . a crime in their eyes and a forbidden
interference in domestic affairs of the state: namely resistance
against unjust restraint of conscience by totalitarian systems and
their condemnation all over the world'. Repeatedly setting forth
the tenets of the faith contradicted by communist doctrines and
policies, he fought Soviet political designs in Europe and abroad.

During these years, Pius called for the banishment of atheism
and the indestructibility of spiritual values in the struggle against
communism and the Soviet Union. 'Can, may the Pope be silent?',
Pius asked the assembled crowd in St Peter's Square, on 20 February
1949, adding: 'Can you imagine a successor to Peter who would
bow to such demands?' The crowd shouted an unequivocal 'No!'
The response pleased the pope, who used the support of the faithful
for his diplomacy of condemnation and containment of the Soviet
Union – a position endorsed by the United States. This policy was
accelerated by Russian actions, and by the outbreak of the Korean
conflict in 1950.

The papal willingness to abandon its impartiality and openly
and publicly oppose communism and launch a crusade against it in
the Cold War contributed to the reassessment of Pius XII's much
more muted opposition towards Nazi Germany and its atrocities
during the Second World War. There now emerged criticism of this
pope's 'sin of omission', which focused on his refusal to denounce
Nazi atrocities publicly, and above all the Holocaust. It was suggested that Pius's failure to condemn Nazism, which attacked the
Jews, but his hesitation to condemn communism, which attacked
the Church, revealed his true sentiments and priorities. This conclusion failed to take a number of important factors into consideration. For one thing, the communists had already dismantled the
churches in the territories they controlled, so little would be gained
by coddling them. Secondly, they did not circle and surround the

Vatican as the fascists did during the age of the Second World War, nor did they have the support of the United States as the Vatican had in the post-war period. Finally, there was the question of timing. The Vatican did not attack the Soviet Union during the war and had no need to attack Nazi Germany or fascist Italy – both of which no longer existed.

Furthermore, this pope's earlier and more cautious approach and lack of public protest, did not entail papal inactivity; he provided assistance to the Jews of Slovakia, Romania, Hungary and Turkey, among others. When the government of Slovakia promulgated its anti-Semitic Jewish Code in 1941, Pius had his secretary of state issue an official protest to its government. When Monsignor Tiso, its president, indicated that he perceived no conflict between Nazi principles and Catholic doctrine, the Vatican threatened to strike him from the list of monsignori if he did not retract.[30] Only the repeated Vatican protests against the deportation of Jews and their annihilation led Slovakia in 1943 to discontinue their contribution to the Final Solution.[31]

At war's end, Pius was effusively praised for his efforts on behalf of the persecuted, and this tribute reached a culmination at the time of his death in 1958. By the turbulent 1960s blame increasingly replaced praise, provoking a controversy concerning his role during the Holocaust. Paradoxically, at present many of this pope's most severe critics are Catholics, while some of his staunchest supporters are Jews, including one prominent rabbi historian. Although the debate continues, most objective observers have concluded that Pius was neither an anti-Semite nor 'Hitler's Pope', and not indifferent to the suffering of the Jews and other victims of the Nazi terror. There is far less consensus on the choices Pius XII made and the stance he assumed, however.

The records clearly reveal that Pius XII followed a diplomatic policy vis-à-vis the Nazis, issuing no clear condemnation of their aggression, expressing no explicit public outrage against their racism, which violated Christian principles and culminated in genocide, nor assigning responsibility for the war. Pius XII defended this decision to those inside and outside the Church time and time again. He deemed it unwise to denounce the Axis regimes' racist policies publicly, providing them with the pretext to dismantle the concordats and thereby endanger the institutional Church. Furthermore, he apparently feared that if it weakened fascist Italy and Nazi Germany, it might aid Soviet Russia or make worse the plight of the people it sought to rescue and prove detrimental and disturbing for German Catholics. For these and other reasons, he did not issue his predecessor's encyclical denouncing anti-Semitism and alerting the faithful to the sin of racism, fearing the diplomatic problems its issuance would undoubtedly unleash. These same concerns prevented the pope from explicitly denouncing the Nazi aggression and genocide he vehemently opposed.

Undeniably, Pius XII did not – some have said could not – take such a strong stance against the Hitler regime. Instead, he sought to conciliate or appease Nazi Germany. Only at the end of the war, in an allocution to the College of Cardinals, did he denounce Nazism as Satanic. He justified his conclusion of, and adherence to, the concordat of 1933 as avoiding greater evil and harm to the Church.

Criticized by some for having expediency triumph over ethics, others have cited the tangible benefits of this 'prudent policy'. Above all, the conciliatory papal course allowed the Church in Germany to survive the totalitarian coordination of the Nazi state. It was the only organization in the Reich to do so, and Pius XII was largely responsible for this achievement. But did the end justify the means? A price was paid for the papal adherence to impartiality because it necessitated the Vatican's cautious and quiet reaction to the abuses of Hitler's Germany. Cardinal Tisserant, prefect of the Congregation of the Eastern Church, worried that history would reproach the Holy See 'for following a policy of convenience for itself, and not much more'.[32] The cardinal found this course distressing for those who remembered and had lived under Pius XI. Others, both Catholics and Jews, appreciated the prudent diplomatic course of the pontiff, which allowed the Church to survive and provide refuge for many victims of Nazi abuse and quietly saved tens of thousands of lives. We do not know, and cannot know, what impact more spirited and public papal protests of the Holocaust would have had on the Nazi genocide of the Jews and the lives of the Catholic minority in Germany. Very likely it would have better preserved the reputation of Pius XII.

It was Hochhuth's pinpointing of this dichotomy between the moral imperative of the Holy Father to denounce evil and the cautious and diplomatic response of Pius XII to the Nazi regime that accounts for the impact of his drama rather than its literary quality or historical accuracy. The critique of Hochhuth and his play – which have become embroiled in the 'Pius War' – cannot and has not undermined this message, which continues to resonate for many.[33] A historical analysis of the dichotomy between Pius XII's moral code and pragmatic policies vis-à-vis Nazi Germany, dramatically expressed by Hochhuth, has been explored with greater objectivity, if less literary flair, by José Sánchez, author of *Pius XII and the Holocaust: Understanding the Controversy* (2002). This historian concludes that Pius XII was torn between two roles: diplomat and pastor.[34] Some posit that his role as pastor during this difficult time virtually mandated the diplomatic course that he pursued. Others perceive the tragedy of his pontificate flowing from the fact that success in one area was often attained at the expense of the other, with expediency triumphing over ethics. It is unlikely that this division will be resolved by the opening of Pius XII's papers or the finding of additional sources. This debate continues.

X

Aggiornamento and *Aperturismo*: The Second Vatican Council and Beyond

POPE JOHN XXIII (1958–1963), WHO FOLLOWED PIUS XII, WAS committed to updating the Church for the faithful and providing social justice for humanity. He sought to achieve the first goal by means of an Ecumenical Council (1962–5) and the second through his encyclical on social justice *Mater et magistra* (1961). The encyclical concluded:

> We therefore consider it our duty to reaffirm that the remuneration of work is not something that can be left to the laws of the marketplace; nor should it be a decision left to the will of the more powerful. It must be determined in accordance with justice and equity; which means that workers must be paid a wage, which allows them to live a truly human life and to fulfill their family obligations in a worthy manner.[1]

The papacies of John XXIII, Papa Roncalli, who envisioned and opened the Second Vatican Council, and of Paul VI (1963–78), Papa Montini, who brought it to a successful conclusion, are among the most important ones in the modern age. Angelo Giuseppe Roncalli, who followed Pius XII in October 1958 as Pope John XXIII, opened the Second Vatican Council in October 1962, and was beatified in 2000, was one of the most beloved popes of the twentieth century and named one of the greatest popes of all time. Although his pontificate lasted fewer than five years, from 1958 to 1963, he is remembered in Italy as 'The Good Pope' or 'The Smiling Pope' for his human warmth and kindness. His encyclicals,[2] such as *Princeps pastorum* ('On the Missions') of November 1959, *Mater et magistra*

('On Christian and Social Progress') of May 1961 and *Pacem in terris* ('On Universal Peace in Truth') of April 1963, are among the best known and have had an impact worldwide.[3]

In the missionary component in *Mater et magistra* John stressed the role of the Church as the mother and teacher of all nations. In it the pope applauded the collapse of imperialism and the attainment of independence of the peoples of Asia and Africa, while denouncing the persistent international disproportions of people and wealth, and seeking a peaceful remedy. In his words, 'the solidarity of the human race and Christian brotherhood demand the elimination, as far as possible of these discrepancies'.[4] From the first days of John's pontificate, Monsignor Montini, who later became Pope Paul VI, shared the pope's social consciousness and concerns. Not surprisingly, he immediately supported John's reformism and defended his programme, which was condemned by some traditionalists and conservatives. Despite this criticism, Roncalli and Montini forged ahead, with John providing the vision and Montini the agenda for social change and religious justice. Montini admired many attributes of John XXIII – described as the first modern pope – and shared his views on how the Church and clergy should face the modern world; from the opening of John's pontificate he supported his vision and programme. For this, among other reasons, following John's death Montini, who succeeded him, continued the Council John had convoked for change.

Although the official papers of the pontificates of both John XXIII and Paul VI in the Archivio Segreto Vaticano remain closed, John XXIII is one of the best-known popes of the twentieth century. This flows from the fact that, unlike a number of other popes of the age, and especially Pius XII (1939–58) – who just before his death had ordered many of his private papers burned[5] – the outgoing and talkative Roncalli expressed himself openly and often, on religious and secular issues, verbally and in writing. Indeed, from time to time Roncalli concluded that he had to be more reserved, that he talked too much and needed to curb his tongue – even with those with whom he was close.[6] Much is known about Paul VI from his early writings for Catholic newspapers and periodicals, his correspondence while chaplain to university students, and the fund of documents accessible in the Istituto Paolo vi in Brescia.

Unlike the aloof and taciturn Papa Pacelli, who kept no personal journal and was little prone to reveal his inner thoughts, his outgoing and talkative successor traced his spiritual development in a host of writings including *Il giornale dell'anima e altri scritti di pietà* ('Journal of a Soul'), published posthumously, and his *Lettere ai familiari* ('Letters to Intimates'). Through these and numerous other published writings and correspondence we know a good deal about Pope John's life and ecclesiastical career. Light has also been shed on his pontificate, including his threefold programme of convoking a diocesan synod for Rome, calling an Ecumenical Council for the Universal Church, and determination to revise the Code of Canon Law, which was in part outdated.

While many of John's predecessors called for the preservation of all aspects of the Church, retaining without change its practices and policies, John sought an updating of the means to transmit its message without altering the message or doctrine.[7] As a consequence, much attention has been paid to his call for *aggiornamento* or updating of the Church and his call for its *aperturismo*, or opening up to the world. He was the first pope to do so.

Born in Sotto il Monte, some half a dozen miles from Bergamo in northern Italy, on 25 November 1881, he was the third child and first son of a family of thirteen children from a poor but pious peasant family of sharecroppers. 'We were poor, but happy with our lot', Roncalli later wrote, 'confident in the help of Providence.'[8] In fact, Angelo was the recipient of providential assistance in the form of scholarships which allowed him to receive an extraordinary education for one of his class. At the age of twelve he entered the diocesan seminary, where he was influenced by clergy active in the Italian Catholic Social Movement. A good student, he was awarded additional scholarship aid, enabling him to continue his education at the Apollinare seminary in Rome, where he studied theology and history.

Ordained in August 1904, he served as a parish priest, seminary professor and member of Catholic Action in the diocese of Bergamo, as well as secretary of the progressive prelate and reform-minded bishop of Bergamo, Count Giacomo Radini-Tedeschi, whom Roncalli served for nearly a decade from 1905 to 1914. Roncalli was impressed with the piety and policies of Radini-Tedeschi, whom he called 'my bishop'. Radini-Tedeschi for his part alerted Roncalli to prevailing social and economic injustices and the pressing need to address these problems plaguing the peninsula.[9] Roncalli, in turn, readily acknowledged his debt to the bishop and was very clearly influenced by his programme and policies.

Angelo's correspondence during his years in Bergamo and Rome reveal his commitment to doctrine and dogma while also calling for a degree of reformism in practices and procedures, and show that he shared Radini-Tedeschi's aim of bringing about a re-Christianization of state and society. He was also impressed with, and influenced by, the bishop's call for social justice. Indeed, in much of his daily commentary he depicts Radini as the ideal priest and bishop. Roncalli therefore resented the unwarranted aspersions of modernism against his bishop, whom he judged eminently faithful to the Church and the papacy. In September–October 1906 Roncalli travelled with Radini to the Holy Land, which represented for him the first experience of the Middle East, initial contact with the Muslim world and interaction with non-Catholic Christians. It also contributed to his love of travel, which would remain with him for the rest of his life. At this stage he tended to reflect traditionalist sentiments and lamented Christians who remained outside the Church.

He was drafted into the Italian army in the First World War, serving as chaplain and stretcher-bearer. Despite the persistence of the Roman Question and the ongoing conflict between Church and state both during and after the war, Roncalli, like the greater part of the Italian hierarchy and clergy, remained faithful to the Italian cause. Indeed, he was convinced that God favoured and blessed the Allied camp, which championed liberty and justice. The complete Allied victory for him seemed a dream come true. Love of country and concern for social issues influenced Roncalli's initial positive assessment of Mussolini's fascism, which he hoped would resolve the Roman Question and ensure the triumph of the Church of Christ. The price imposed for these promises was too high for

Roncalli, who soon concluded that Il Duce's means were iniquitous. For these reasons Roncalli wrote in 1924 that he could not in good conscience vote for the fascists.

After the First World War Roncalli was made spiritual director of the diocesan seminary, and in 1920 helped organize the first national Eucharistic Congress held in Italy. In 1921, Pope Benedict xv appointed him head of the Society for the Propagation of the Faith before beginning his diplomatic career. In 1925 he was named apostolic visitor to Bulgaria, a difficult assignment given the strained relations between Bulgaria and the Vatican.[10] Roncalli was both surprised and somewhat disappointed when the secretary of state, Pietro Gasparri, informed him of his impending consecration as titular bishop and nomination as apostolic visitor to Bulgaria – which appeared to be a secondary appointment that would take him away from *patria* and family. He submitted, however, to Pius xi's 'request' and preserved his loyalty to the papacy.

Subsequently, during the 1930s, Roncalli served as apostolic delegate to Turkey and Greece, countries that were even more estranged from Rome and presented even greater difficulties than Bulgaria. Mustafa Kemal Atatürk had turned Turkey into a blatantly anti-clerical country, while Greece was under the dictatorial thumb of General Ioannis Metaxas.[11] Roncalli catalogued a series of events during his stay there in his diary, *La mia vita in Oriente*.[12] Following his appointment at the end of 1934, Roncalli would spend twenty years in the Middle East, with a few brief interruptions, returning permanently to western Europe only in 1944 – while Europe was in the throes of the last stages of destructive war and Italy was suffering from a dual occupation.

During the course of his long tenure in the Middle East, Roncalli confronted a number of difficulties there and from the first had to adjust to a series of changes. Among the latter were the death of Pius xi on 10 February 1939 and the election of Eugenio Pacelli as Pius xii. He supported the new pope's abortive peace efforts in the face of the impending threat of war and the Nazi invasion of Poland. He also adhered to Pius xii's recourse to impartiality, but Roncalli wrote at the end of September 1939 that his duty to remain outside the realm of politics – championed by Gasparri and Pacelli

– did not stop him from crying over Poland, which he believed was slain and martyred. He regretted that this great Catholic nation was once again subjected to slavery. In fact, Roncalli would subsequently take steps against Nazi iniquities, which can be seen from a reading of the second volume of his diaries from the East, covering the years 1940–44.[13]

Although the latter half of Roncalli's stay in the Middle East was dominated by the Second World War, he was able to move freely from neutral Turkey to occupied Greece, and occasionally return to Rome, Milan and his family home in Sotto il Monte. He was, however, acutely aware of the hardships faced by the civilian populations of Europe and the flood of refugees seeking to escape persecution. To his dismay, during the second half of his stay in the Middle East he witnessed the brutality of the Final Solution.[14] In Turkey he met Jews almost on a daily basis and sympathized with their plight. While he adhered to Pius XII's policy of impartiality, and would not publicly take sides in the conflict, internally he classified the villains and the victims, but watched carefully what he wrote in his diary.

John followed Pius XI's defence of the Semitic and eastern origins of Christianity, and like him condemned anti-Semitism, but did so quietly. He took steps, however, to aid the Jews escape from persecution by providing them with baptismal certificates. By this and other means he intervened to prevent the removal of some 20,000 Jews from Slovakia. Before and during the war, Roncalli was credited with helping to save thousands of Jewish refugees in Europe, and for this and other reasons some Jews consider him to have been a 'Righteous Gentile'.

Reports probably reached the Vatican of Roncalli's actions on behalf of the Jews, for during his 45-minute audience with Pius XII on 10 October 1941 the Pope raised the Jewish issue. He asked whether his silence on Nazi behaviour was judged adversely (an admission that many admirers of Pius have consistently denied). Roncalli neither relates the context in which Pius XII brought up the topic of 'silence' nor how he responded. Whatever was said and done by Roncalli apparently did not disappoint Pius XII, who in December 1944 named him nuncio to Paris. He did so despite the opposition of some in the Secretariat of State, who questioned his credentials for this most important post.[15] In fact, his performance there was spectacular and more than satisfied the demanding pope. In 1953 he was given the red hat and made patriarch of Venice, where he remained until the death of Pius XII on 9 October 1958. On 12 October 1958 he left Venice to attend the conclave to elect a new pope, and on 28 October was elected to succeed Pius XII. His appointment of Monsignor Domenico Tardini as secretary of state led some to believe that he would pursue a conservative course,[16] but this notion was soon dispelled.

Roncalli was then almost 77 years old and in the eyes of many would have a short and uneventful pontificate. This was not his intention. On 20 January 1959, some three months after his election, he startled Tardini by revealing his determination to convoke an Ecumenical Council. Some days later he revealed his plan to a small group of cardinals, who were equally surprised – indeed stunned. Although John loved tradition, from the first he sought to make the papacy more accessible, emphasizing its pastoral rather than its dogmatic role. To fulfil this goal, not long after his election on 25 January 1959, John proposed three major undertakings: an Ecumenical Council for the universal Church, a synod for the Roman diocese, and the reform of the Code of Canon Law for all the faithful. The Council, which he decided to call the Second Vatican Council, was the most important of his initiatives and would become the major achievement of his pontificate. The division between those who favoured change and those who opposed it emerged almost immediately, on the first day of the Council. Although the conservative opposition suffered a setback, it did not surrender.

Initially, it was not clear whether the Council John envisioned sought to renew and update the religious life of Catholics or was convoked to condemn the errors of the modern age. With the assistance of Giovanni Montini – whom John had recently made a cardinal – the two outlined a reformist course. Its major goals were renewal of the Church, dialogue with the modern world and the promotion of Christian unity.[17] The opening of the twenty-first Ecumenical Council took place on 11 October 1962 in St Peter's

Basilica in Rome. In his opening address to the first session of the Council, John called upon the members to speak to a world that was rapidly changing, as was its perception of the faith. He also invoked the modernization of the Church and its reconciliation with other faiths.[18]

While John's decision to convoke the Council was appreciated and applauded by some, it was vehemently denounced by others, especially by the conservatives in the Curia, who attempted to torpedo his *aggiornamento*. Their vocal opposition aroused and angered the usually jovial Pope, who responded:

> In the daily exercise of our ministry our ear is sometimes offended by suggestions from persons who, though ardent in their devotion, are not over abundantly endowed with discretion or a sense of proportions. Modern times to them mean only falsehood and ruin; they are always saying that our age, in comparison with those of the past, is steadily deteriorating; and they behave as if they had learned nothing from history, which is nonetheless the teacher of life . . . it is our duty to disagree with these prophets of doom who constantly foretell disastrous events as if the end of the world were at hand.[19]

There was a positive aspect to the conservative opposition to John's Council, for it inspired his friend Monsignor Giovanni Montini, who shared the pope's programme of *aggiornamento*, to take a more active role in its deliberations. Montini, who followed John as Paul VI, shared John's concern with social justice and ecumenism and increased his support for both. His assistance proved invaluable, for he was much more familiar with Roman developments and the Curia's tactics than John, who had spent decades abroad. From 1933 to 1937 Montini had served as the assistant to the under-secretary of state Monsigor Domenico Tardini, then replaced him as under-secretary of state to Cardinal Eugenio Pacelli. Within a year, Pius XI was dead, and Pacelli, Montini's boss, became pope, taking the name Pius XII.

Montini, who served in the Vatican's Secretariat of State from 1922 to 1954, played a crucial role in establishing the agenda for the

Council. The first session, which opened in autumn 1962, was short but important, since discussion of the liturgy and Divine Revelation led to dissension and division between 'traditionalists' and 'progressives' and the rejection of the Curia's attempt to control the course of events. Although few documents were approved when the first session closed on 8 December 1962, new ground rules were established for the subsequent sessions, which John would never see.

John's cancer was advanced and inoperable, and he had barely six more months to live. Thus he would not be able to see the Council to its successful conclusion. He died of cancer in early June 1963, and his last recorded words expressed the hope that the Council would continue to reform and strengthen the Church and the faith and complete its reconciliation with state and society. John had done much, including abandoning the Cold War mentality of Pope Pius XII towards the communist states of Eastern Europe. Indeed, his Ostpolitik or eastern policy has been seen as paving the way for the collapse of Soviet control of Eastern Europe and the total communist domination of Russia. Nonetheless, John regretted not having been able to do more.

He lived for 81 years, had been a priest for 58 years, a bishop for 38 and a pope for fewer than 5 years. During his short pontificate, more than 30 monarchs and heads of state visited him. His death was mourned by much of the world. Khruschev's Soviet Union joined the other powers in sending condolences. Only a few knew much about John's efforts to reach accommodation with the states of Eastern Europe and the Soviet Union.

After his beatification, his body was moved from the crypt of St Peter's to the basilica above to be venerated. In June 2000 his remains were found to be unusually well preserved, though the Vatican said this was not a miracle but was due to the sealed triple coffin. When John closed the first session of the Second Vatican Council with a Mass on 8 December 1962, the great expectations that the Council had aroused had yet to be fulfilled. During the course of the two crowded months of the first session, which caught the imagination of the world, there had been no overall plan or structure and no decrees had been approved.

John's successor, Papa Montini, took the name Paul to call attention to the worldwide mission of the Church. The new pope sought dialogue not only with members of the faith, but also with other Christians, Muslims and Jews, as well as agnostics and atheists. Indeed, he hoped for dialogue with the entire world and the whole of humanity, which explains why he became the most travelled pope to date, as well as accounting for his deep commitment to the Council. Later, he would be the first pope to visit Africa. He also made it clear as early as his coronation Mass in 1963, a week after his election, that the Council would resume and would hopefully fulfil all the objectives that John and he had outlined. Following his coronation, he set the tiara aside and was the last pope so crowned.

He set the date of 29 September 1963 for the opening of the second session. Soon thereafter he issued an allocution in which he emphasized John's goals, invoking both renewal and *aggiornamento*. In his eulogy for his predecessor, Paul noted that death would not, and indeed could not, stifle the spirit that he had infused into the mission of the Council. Like John, Paul called for a reform of the Curia and the Vatican bureaucracy – as have all popes since. Paul also favoured an examination, reassessment and reform of canon law, and above all greater attention to the need for social justice that John had invoked in his encyclicals. He recognized and clearly stated that the peace desired by all men of goodwill ultimately depended on justice for all. In his call for justice and peace he proved supportive of the United Nations, as well as recourse to John's encyclical *Mater et magistra*. Paul VI noted that his papal predecessors had all welcomed the League of Nations and its successor the United Nations, commenting that their temporal universality complemented the spiritual universality of the Church.

By continuing the Council convoked by John, Pope Paul not only revealed his commitment to his departed friend, but stressed the convictions and programme they both shared. At the opening of the second session of the Council, Pope Paul addressed the delegates at length and expressed his full support for their efforts. He frankly acknowledged that, like John XXIII, he sought dialogue not only with other Christians but with other religions as well. In pursuit of these and other goals the Council considered changes in the liturgy and the role of the laity in the structure of the Church, along with the re-establishment of a permanent and married diaconate. Despite some dissension on the nature of the Church as well as its governance, Paul remained optimistic regarding the outcome.

The second session of the Council, which ran for 67 days from 29 September to 4 December 1963, was productive and included some 40 working sessions with more than 600 speeches. Among other things it approved 'The Constitution on the Sacred Liturgy', along with 'The Decree on Social Communications'.[20] This provided for the use of the vernacular which in many areas replaced the Latin. Although this suited the vast majority, a minority had a longing for the Latin Mass and an even smaller minority joined the opposition to the Council.[21] In his closing address to the second session of the Council, Paul announced his plans for a pilgrimage to the Holy Land that would include a visit to Israel. Before his departure in December, he outlined and proposed an agenda for the third session of the Council.

In his campaign to increase participation and productivity, Paul prepared for the opening of the third session of the Council, making provision to have some women attend as auditors but without the right to speak or vote during the debates which lay men had. At the opening of the third session Paul indicated that the Council still had many important matters to decide, but the most delicate concerned the nature of the episcopacy. Soon thereafter he told the non-Catholic Christians who attended as observers that the Church was ready to participate in ecumenical dialogue.

The debate on the Church continued during the third session, with a special focus on the nature of the episcopacy and the issue of religious liberty. By the time the third session ended, three important measures had been approved: *Lumen gentium*, the Dogmatic Constitution on the Church, explaining the relationship of the pope, the bishops, priests and laity within the Church; *Orientalium ecclesiarum*, the Decree on the Catholic Eastern Churches; and *Unitatis redintegratio*, the Decree on Ecumenism.[22] Paul, like John, was convinced that a crucial aspect of the Council was to promote unity and this was reflected in the selection of the Jesuit cardinal

Augustin Bea, for years the rector of the Pontifical Biblical Institute, as well as confessor to Pius XII, as head of the new Secretariat for Promoting Christianity Unity.

On 28 September, under his leadership, the Council reached the controversial declaration on the Jews, in fifteen sentences that sought to denounce and reverse 2,000 years of hatred and oppression. Interestingly, this reform was undertaken under the leadership of Pius XII's confessor. In response to those who sought to avoid consideration of *Nostra aetate*, which changed the nature of Catholic– Jewish relations, Cardinal Bea responded that it had to be done. The document asserted that the Church reproves as foreign to the mind of Christ any discrimination on the basis of race, colour or religion. Indeed, the Council recognized the contribution of various faiths to the spiritual, social, moral and cultural welfare of humanity.

At the end of the year Pope Paul ventured to Bombay in India to be present at the 38th Internal Eucharistic Congress and on 3 December 1964, during the course of that visit, expressed the love and respect that the Church had for all the peoples of Asia. In a country of 500 million people with less than 1.5 million Catholics, Paul revealed his hope for Christian reunion to non-Catholic leaders of India's Christian minority. He also indicated his desire to narrow the gap between the world's Christians and non-Christians, continuing the dialogue that he claimed the Church intended to pursue with all the peoples of the globe.[23] A champion of dialogue, Paul proved willing to talk with Communist authorities on several levels, and in 1966 and 1967 received the Soviet foreign minister, Andrei Gromyko, and president, Nikolai Podgorny, in the Vatican.

Between the closure of the third session and the opening of the fourth, Pope Paul VI issued a note on the primacy of the papacy. In mid-September 1965 he established the Synod of Bishops as a permanent institution of the Church and an advisory body to the papacy. At the same time he revised, some said revolutionized, the process for the election of a pope. He unilaterally decided that only cardinals below the age of 80 would be allowed to vote in the conclave. Subsequently, he insisted that bishops and cardinals retire after reaching the age of 75.

The pope's plan had four major elements. First, relations between states should be governed by reason, justice, law and negotiation rather than fear, violence, deceit or war. This, in turn, required disarmament. The money saved from the stockpiling of weapons could, and indeed should, be used to assist the developing nations and solving the problems of hunger and poverty. Finally, the pope saw the need to protect fundamental human rights and freedom, and above all religious liberty. It contained the radical assertion that the Roman Catholic Church rejected nothing that was true and holy in other religions. Some Conservatives were scandalized by this declaration, which they claimed was tinged by indifferentism, which had been condemned by all the popes from Gregory XVI to Pius X.

As he prepared for the fourth and final session of the Council, scheduled to open on 14 September 1965, Paul recognized that even though considerable accomplishments had been made in the first three sessions, much still had to be done. At the opening of the fourth session he did not discuss any themes that would be examined by the Council, preferring to have the Church fathers enjoy freedom of opinion on such matters. The following day, however, Paul announced that the Vatican Council had motivated him to establish a special conference of bishops or Synod of Bishops to collaborate with him in an advisory capacity in the governance of the Church.[24] He hoped to persuade by reason and example rather than by exercising authority.

Pope Paul, who backed the United Nations' quest for disarmament and its fight against hunger, agreed to address that body on the occasion of the twentieth anniversary of the organization. On 4 October 1965, as he left for New York, he explained that his aim was to encourage, strengthen and bless the efforts that people of goodwill were making to safeguard, guarantee and promote peace. He repeated his programme when he arrived at John F. Kennedy Airport in New York, and when he addressed the General Assembly of the United Nations. His message there was a simple one, delivered with disinterest, humility and love for all peoples. It was 'no more war, war never again'.

Paul's support of the peace efforts of the United Nations was appreciated by most of its member states. The warm reception he received from President Johnson, the American people and the United Nations made the visit a public relations triumph and confirmed the Vatican's position as an important transnational force. Though his message that there should be no more war was widely acclaimed both inside and outside the Church, it was not easily or readily attained. On a more positive note on 7 December 1965 there was promulgated *Dignitatis humanae*, or Declaration on Religious Liberty; *Ad gentes divinitus*, or Decree on the Church's Missionary Activity; *Presbyterorum ordinis*, or Decree on the Ministry and Life of Priests; and finally *Gaudium et spes*, or Pastoral Constitution on the Church in the Modern World.

Following Paul's address to the United Nations in October 1965, which supported the organization's efforts to preserve the peace, the pope returned to Rome. At the end of October 1965 he promulgated five important Council documents, including *Christus dominus*, on war and the pastoral office of bishops in the Church; *Perfectae caritatis*, on the adapation and renewal of religious life; *Optatam totius*, on the training of priests, *Gravissimum educationis* on Christian education; and *Nostra aetate*, on the Church's attitude towards non-Christian religions.[25]

Nostra aetate proved particularly important for the Jews, who had endured persecution at the hands of the Church and more recently had to endure the Nazi pogrom of the Holocaust. The papal initiative to effect a reconciliation between Christians and Jews read:

> True, the Jewish authorities, and those who followed their lead pressed for the death of Christ; still, what happened in His passion cannot be charged against all the Jews, without distinction, then alive, nor against the Jews of today. Although the Church is the new people of God, the Jews should not be presented as rejected or accursed by God, as if that followed from the Holy Scriptures.[26]

When Paul closed the fourth session and the Council on 8 December 1965, assessments of its efforts varied. In certain conservative circles he was criticized for having 'pushed' for too much, too soon. On the other hand he was criticized by liberals both for his insistence on priestly celibacy and his opposition to birth control.

Nonetheless, both friends and foes acknowledge that while the inspiration and opening of the Council was due to the efforts of John, the passage and implementation of the sixteen documents of the Second Vatican Council was the work of his successor, Paul. Together, their focus on social justice and the use of national languages in the Mass in addition to Latin, along with other changes, made the Church more accessible for the laity. At the same time the call for social justice found resonance in the developing world, and some believed that this encouraged Pope Paul to further his programme of internationalizing the Church and its clergy while curbing its European and Italian domination. Like the apostle Paul, whose name he assumed, Paul vi delivered his message to the entire world.

This new direction was reflected in his selection of a non-Italian secretary of state and his naming new cardinals in 1969, many more of whom were non-Italians, making the College of Cardinals more international and less European. Internationalization was also reflected in his travels to such places as the Middle East, Africa, the Philippines and India. Finally, Paul followed John in abandoning the Cold War policy and mentality of Pius xii towards the Soviet states of Eastern Europe in favour of reconciliation with these regimes, and he not only continued but also accelerated and expanded John's policy of Ostpolitik. Subsequently, when adopted by the Polish pope John Paul ii (1978–2005), this policy contributed to the collapse of communism in Eastern Europe and the Soviet Union. At the same time, Paul understood and appreciated the nostalgia among part of the clergy and the laity for the old practices, and moderated the pace of innovation to prevent division and schism. In the eyes of critics this reasonable approach was perceived as indecision and led some to underestimate the important contribution of this pope and his pontificate to the Church and the faith.

XI

The Papacy of John Paul II and the Aftermath of the Council

When John Paul took office in 1978, the new pope inherited
an institution eager to embrace ecumenism, relevance, and
renewal. Although the Holy Father also sought the same goals, his
interpretation and means to achieve them were very different from
those of progressive members of the hierarchy and clergy . . .

John Paul was quick to recognize and seize his broad authority –
to centralize it, to make critical appointments and to control the
actions of the pivotal office of the church.

Jo Renee Formicola, *Pope John Paul II: Prophetic Politician* (2002)

FOLLOWING THE PONTIFICATES OF JOHN XXIII (1958–63) AND
Paul VI (1963–78), the two popes most identified with the work of
the Second Vatican Council (1962–5), the Catholic Church
remained divided in its assessment of the Council's accomplishments and the position of the faith in the modern world. Conservatives including Marcel Lefebvre rejected many of the 'reforms' the
Council introduced, denounced and derided the use of the
vernacular in place of Latin in the Mass, and longed to return to the
order that he and his comrades associated with the pre-war papacy.
Liberals, on the other hand, complained that Paul VI had not
fulfilled John XXIII's call for *aggiornamento* and renewal, while
deploring his conservative stance on a wide range of issues
including the ordination of women, birth control and abortion, the
celibacy of the clergy and papal infallibility. These divisions were
reflected in the Curia and the College of Cardinals, as well as in
society as a whole. Conservatives hoped for the election of a 'real

pope', by which they meant one who shared their goals and agenda. The more liberal Catholic theologians, led by Hans Küng, on the other hand, sought a pope attuned to contemporary civilization rather than one buried in the past.

In the eyes of some, the post-war popes from Pius XII to Benedict XVI increased the influence of the papacy, which assumed a political, diplomatic and social as well as religious role, and functioned as one of the leading transnational institutions of the modern age. Others complained that the price paid for this expanded political and diplomatic role came at the expense of its religious mission. These critics blamed the Council for this and other difficulties confronting the Church, including changes in the liturgy that they judged unnecessary and unwanted, imposed rather than invoked. On the other hand, champions of change and the Council questioned the commitment of the four popes elected following the death of Pope Paul (John Paul I, John Paul II, Benedict XVI and Francis) to the changes in the liturgy and governance of the Church that Vatican II had introduced.

Two of the four revealed their support of the Council's policies by the names they chose: Pope John Paul I (d. 1958) and Pope John Paul II (d. 2005). The pontificate of the first pope to assume a double first name in honour of his predecessors John and Paul proved unfortunately short-lived, lasting only a month, while the second had a far longer pontificate and greater impact. The third post-conciliar pope, elected in 2005, Benedict XVI, claimed to have no programme of his own, seeking only to implement the policies and texts of John XXIII, Paul VI and John Paul II.[1] He moved from a liberal stance during the Council to a more traditional one in its aftermath. The rules governing the two conclaves held in 1978 barred cardinals over the age of 80 from exercising a vote, which curtailed but did not eliminate the conservative strain in the conclave.

In 1978 a number of cardinals suggested that it was time for a pastoral pope, rather than a diplomatic or curial one such as Paul had been. Ideological and functional divisions were compounded by national rivalries. The Italians, who constituted about half of the 57 European cardinals, expected the 455-year-old tradition to continue, and that the next pope would be Italian – he was after all bishop of Rome. Others believed that the time had come to smash this convention, denouncing it as an Italian lock on the papacy, which they perceived as a transnational institution. Nonetheless, on 26 August 1978, the first day of balloting, Cardinal Albino Luciani, the patriarch of Venice, was elected 'almost by acclamation' as the 262nd successor of Peter. The new pope, who had an unshakable and uncluttered faith, explained in his first address why he had assumed the name of John Paul – the first pope to choose a double name. Acknowledging that he had neither the 'wisdom of heart' of John, nor the 'preparation and learning' of Paul, he shared the vision of both to serve the Church and bring it into harmony with the modern world.[2]

In fact, once pope, John Paul dedicated himself to pursuing a policy of continuity with the policies outlined by John and Paul, determined to implement the guidelines proposed and the decisions reached by the Second Vatican Council. In the process, the new pope dispensed with the imperial 'We' and tried to avoid being carried about in the *sedia gestatoria*, the portable throne on which pontiffs were borne. Following Pope Paul's example, he also refused to follow the 1,000-year tradition of being crowned with the tiara, opting instead for a simple ceremony. From the first, his pontificate promised to be more pastoral than authoritarian, favouring prayer over politics, calling for 'more prayers and fewer battles'.

Although the new pope promptly confirmed Cardinal Jean-Marie Villot as his secretary of state, and nominated him prefect of the Council for the Public Affairs of the Church, John Paul almost immediately realized the enormous responsibilities of his office. The challenges confronting the papacy proved a heavy burden and his long days, which began at 4.30 a.m., taxed the stamina and undermined the health of the smiling, humble and serene pope, who suffered from a series of physical infirmities. The Church, he explained, could never do too much to help solve the problems of freedom, justice, peace and development and had to promote friendship between individuals and peoples. Not violence, but love could do everything.[3] John Paul's health had never been robust and he had suffered from a tubercular condition early in life, complicated by several heart ailments and phlebitis, a painful circulatory disease that was aggravated by the series of small heart attacks he had endured during the past years.

He had kept his poor health a private matter when he was in Venice, fearing that Paul might have constrained him to retire, but once pope he acknowledged his difficulties. His smiling and cheerful disposition hid the gravity of his condition, aggravated by the numerous, enormous and burdensome tasks imposed by the papal office. When he died after a pontificate of only 33 days, one of the shortest in modern times, the public, unaware of his persistent health problems, was surprised and shocked, suspecting the worst. Small wonder many refused to believe that coronary occlusion, heart fibrillation or myocardial arrest was responsible for the death of the 65-year-old pontiff, convinced that some form of foul play was responsible for his untimely death. Such suspicions were fed by the fact that the Curia and College of Cardinals refused to authorize an autopsy, as preparations were begun to select his successor.

Despite his very short pontificate, interest in this pope continues in Europe and the United States. In October 2012, on the centenary of his birth, an international conference entitled 'John Paul: A Man of Faith for our Time' was held in New York.[4] His pontificate and simplicity were seen as an important transition for the modernization of the papacy and the accommodation of the Church with the contemporary world. The cause for his beatification began in 2003, with some believing that Pope Benedict XVI would beatify both Paul VI and John Paul I in 2013. He did not.

Karol Wojtyla, who succeeded Luciani as John Paul II, shared his determination to implement the proposals of the Vatican Council. Born in Wadowice, Poland, he was the first non-Italian to be elected pope since Adrian VI (1522–3) and the youngest since Pius IX (1848–78). In his address to the Council of 7 November 1962, he invoked a call for a more biblical, less clerical tone to the Church. This was repeated in a speech of 21 October 1963, in which he pleaded that the Church should never again appear as an authoritarian institution. Although his interventions in the Council were few, he affected the compromise that produced the pastoral constitution *Gaudium et spes*, or 'The Church in the Modern World', of 7 December 1965. In Poland he was one of the leading supporters of the strikes of 1976, which culminated in the creation of the student solidarity committee in Kraków. As archbishop of Kraków he maintained close contact with the city's Jewish community and cordial relations with its head.[5] Like Paul, as pope he travelled widely, visiting North America on various occasions, the Middle East, Africa, Asia and Australia, which had a broadening effect on his mind and personality.[6]

The first Polish pope, and the tallest in the twentieth century, Karol Wojtyla, like Luciani, indicated his support of the Council by assuming the name John Paul II. He was seen to combine the charisma of John XXIII with the administrative agility of Paul VI. Like his predecessor, he refused to be crowned and preferred the more personal and informal 'I' to the traditional and intimidating use of 'We'. He also followed John Paul I in declaring his total support for the Second Vatican Council, indicating that his task would be to implement its teachings and further the new mentality and atmosphere it envisioned in the Church.[7] Again, like Paul, he refused to remain closed in the Vatican or preoccupied with narrow Church affairs, revealing an interest in the outside world, viewing the papacy as a participant in international developments. In rapid succession he visited Assisi and Siena, and the shrines of the patron saints of Italy; inspected the papal residence at Castel Gandolfo; flew by helicopter to the mountain shrine of La Mentorella; and quickly planned a series of visits outside Italy.

On 21 October 1978, only five days after his election, John Paul II held a press conference for some 2,000 journalists in the Vatican, and later that day addressed the 125 members of the diplomatic corps in the Sala del Consistorio. After this address the pope surprised and pleased the diplomats by talking privately with most of them. In his speeches he revealed his commitment to the reforms of Vatican II, his international goals and desire for dialogue with all nations. Recognizing that the pope could not do everything, he assumed as his first task to gather the people of God in unity. His claim of modern-day universality for the papacy was repeated in a talk at the Piazza di Spagna on 8 December 1978. From the beginning of his pontificate, he assumed a political role far greater than any of his modern predecessors. He also revealed that the Christian concept of human relations did not succumb to the individualistic logic of profit and gain, but sought to put into practice the teaching of the Second Vatican Council, which intended that the earth be used for the well-being of humanity as a whole. In his homily following his investiture, the pope revealed his intention of serving all humanity, calling for the opening of the frontiers of states as well as open economic systems.[8] He reflected at once the accommodation and confrontation of the papacy with the modern world.

On his way to Mexico during his first transatlantic trip as pope, he made a one day stopover on 25–26 January in Santo Domingo, where he called for a more just and humane international order,[9] declaring himself a pilgrim of peace and hope. In Mexico he met President López Portillo and formally inaugurated the Latin American Bishops Conference at Puebla, in which he warned of the excesses of Liberation Theology. The pope made it clear that while he sympathized with the plight of the workers of town and city and supported their call for fair wages, he would not accept a theology based on a non-Christian ideology.[10] In his words, 'the real liberation of man demands profound changes in the modes of thinking, evaluating and acting that the civilizations based on materialism imposed on humanity'.[11] His traditional approach was also seen in the order to the Jesuit father Tom Drinan to give up his seat in the American Congress, and the decision that Hans Küng could no longer be deemed a Catholic theologian or teach as such. The pope also insisted that the Jesuits end their criticism of papal policy and their conflict with the Church, and exacted a promise to that effect from their dying general, Pedro Arrupe.

In April, following the death of Villot, John Paul named Agostino Casaroli, who had helped to orchestrate John's and Paul's Ostpolitik, establishing bonds with the regimes in eastern Europe as his new secretary of state. In September 1979 the pope visited Ireland, where he preached that violence destroyed the work of justice, and in October arrived in the United States for a seven-day visit, his first there as pope. From the moment of his arrival in Boston, John Paul II spoke of the need for obedience, assuming a traditional stance on such issues as divorce and birth control. Some charged that he took Pius XII, whose contributions he praised, as his model.[12] At the same time, the pope decried the emphasis on materialism, permissiveness, drugs and violence, using his popularity and magnetic personality to reinforce his orthodox positions. John Paul repeated similar messages in New York, where he addressed the United Nations, and in Washington, DC, where he was received by President Carter at the White House and met Church officials at the Catholic Univeristy of America. In his visits to Philadelphia, Des Moines and Chicago, he revealed his determined traditionalism.[13]

John Paul II inherited the host of difficulties confronted by Pope Paul VI, who had sought to implement the reforms of the Second Vatican Council, while restraining those who pressed for 'excessive' and 'unwarranted' innovations. He relied on traditional means to achieve the reformist programme outlined in his encyclical of March 1979, *Redemptor hominis* ('The Redeemer of Man'). This encyclical stressed the worth of human life from the womb to natural death, and argued that true freedom was best preserved in the Church. In John Paul's words it represented a confirmation of the traditions of the schools from which he came, as well as his personal pastoral style.[14] In his letter the pope insisted that the pressing problems of the age could be resolved only by the implementation of Christ's revelation, as announced by the Church and papacy. These themes were repeated in his encyclical *Dives in misericordia* of December 1980. Conscious that the Church and its leadership confronted grave tasks, John Paul did not hesitate in assuming the burden, revealing a remarkable capacity for work.[15]

Confronted by financial problems and a deficit of more than $20 million – which jumped to $28 million in 1980 – out of a total budget of some $60 million, John Paul called the College of Cardinals, usually convoked only to elect a pope, to Rome, revealing to them that the Vatican had been in serious economic difficulties since 1975. The deficit, which escalated to some $460 million by 1987, continued to bedevil Rome.[16] It did not, however, curtail the pope's voice, activities or travel. In 1980, when liberals challenged his suspension of Hans Küng, the pope responded by a spirited defence of his action, and strongly reaffirmed the dogma of papal infallibility. In a letter to the German bishops, he presented the Vatican's justification for Küng's suspension: 'Has a theologian who does not accept the integral doctrine of the Church the right to teach in the name of the Church and on the basis of a special mission received from the Church?'[17] The pope thought not, and did not hesitate to say so.

When John Paul learned that the Russians were considering ordering the Polish regime to purge the Solidarity leadership or face military intervention, he personally assumed the direction of Vatican-Polish relations and Vatican-Soviet affairs. He warned President Leonid Brezhnev that should a Soviet invasion materialize, he would relinquish the throne of St Peter and stand at the barricades with his fellow Poles. There was no recourse to impartiality, conciliation or silence on this pope's part. Some think that the threat helped to broker the eventual agreement that was reached between Solidarity and the Polish regime, precluding the prospect of a Russian intervention.[18] Others believe it prompted the assassination attempt on the pope's life on 13 May 1981, when Mehmet Ali Agca shot John Paul in the stomach, the right arm and right hand in St Peter's Square. Vatican circles were convinced that the Kremlin masterminds had ordered the assassination, considering the Pope a destabilizing factor in Eastern Europe.

In September 1981, while still convalescing, he issued the encyclical *Laborem exercens* ('By Means of Labour', but commonly called 'On Human Work'), commemorating the anniversary of Leo XIII's *Rerum novarum*. Defending the workers' right to organize, John Paul called for a new economic order that avoided the excesses of unrestrained capitalism and ideological Marxism, while recognizing the rights and dignity of labour. Although traditional in its approach to women's work, the encyclical argued that women should not be discriminated against in employment because of their gender or family responsibilities.[19] By 1982 the pope resumed his political and global commitments, and in Poland opened a dialogue with Warsaw and the Kremlin.

On 7 June 1982 John Paul II met President Ronald Reagan, who like the pope had escaped an assassination attempt, to discuss the consequences of Israel's invasion of Lebanon. Then on the second day they discussed Poland and the Soviet domination of Eastern Europe. According to Richard Allen, Reagan's first National Security adviser, the two plotted to 'hasten the dissolution of the Communist empire'.[20] It was within this framework that William Clark, Allen's successor, examined the prospect of the United States opening full diplomatic relations with the Holy See. According to accounts, the United States and the Vatican cooperated to keep the Solidarity Movement alive following the proclamation of martial law in December 1981, supplied and advised by a mechanism created under the auspices of President Ronald Reagan and Pope John Paul II. Drawing from a network that owed as much to the Vatican as the CIA, money and material was provided for the Poles, while all sorts of information was filtered to the West about the Polish regime and its relations with Moscow. The CIA director, William Casey, the principal architect of the American–Vatican cooperation on Solidarity and Poland, met various papal officials including Archbishop Achille Silvestrini, the Vatican's Deputy Secretary of State, and the apostolic delegate in Washington, Archbishop Pio Laghi.

Early in 1984 President Reagan announced that William A. Wilson of California, who had served as personal representative to the pope, would be appointed ambassador to the Holy See. By 1985, American–Vatican cooperation had frustrated the communist regime's campaign to suppress Solidarity, the first of a series of failures it had to endure.[21] That same year, following Mikhail Gorbachev's election to the post of General Secretary of the Central Committee of the Communist Party of the Soviet Union, he and President Reagan met at the first summit in Geneva, from 19–20 November 1985. Foreseeing the inevitable collapse of communism, the pope, in an encyclical of 1985, *Slavorum apostoli*, saluted ss Cyril and Methodius, who had evangelized Slavic Europe in the eleventh century. Meanwhile, the pope called for European unity with Christianity as its spiritual centre.[22] At the end of 1985 John Paul II convoked an extraordinary meeting of the World Synod of Bishops to mark the twentieth anniversary of the closing of the Second Vatican Council, whose decisions and reforms he continued to support.

In the interim the pope again met the Soviet foreign minister, Andrei Gromyko, on 27 February 1985, and following the accession of Gorbachev, immediately recognized that he brought new energy and initiatives into Soviet foreign policy. Gorbachev

favoured glasnost, a policy of 'openness', which paralleled John
xxiii's *aperturismo*, removing bureaucratic restrictions from the
flow of information, democratization and perestroika, a socio-
economic restructuring of Soviet society, rendering communism
more human and economically feasible. Gromyko's successor,
Eduard Shevardnadze, warned Gorbachev early on that much was
rotten in the Soviet Union and required change.[23] Perhaps this
played a part in Warsaw's pledge in 1987 to reopen dialogue with
the Catholic Church, which in turn encouraged President Reagan
to lift American sanctions against the Polish regime.

While supporting change in the Soviet Union, the pope was not
entirely pleased with developments in the United States. During the
course of his second visit he condemned the propensity of some
American Catholics for a cafeteria-style Catholicism, picking and
choosing to adhere to certain Church teachings while ignoring or
violating others. In his encyclical *Sollicitudo rei socialis* of 1987,
devoted to morality in economics, he revealed a critical attitude
towards liberalism and capitalism, as well as Marxist collectivism.
The pope, according to Archbishop Weakland of Milwaukee, was
'to the left' of most United States bishops and inspired them to focus
on international economic issues.[24]

In July 1988 Gorbachev ventured to Warsaw and in February
1989 the Soviets restored the cathedral of Vilnius to the Catholics,
and permitted expansion of the Catholic hierarchy. In return, the
pope gave his approval to have Polish bishops sit in a joint committee with communist delegates to outline a new Church–state
relationship. By April 1989 the government promised to legalize
Solidarity and called for open parliamentary elections in June. That
same month, the Vatican and Warsaw agreed to establish diplomatic relations with Jerzy Kugerski of the Central Party Committee,
appointed as the regime's ambassador to the Vatican, and Archbishop Józef Kowalczyk, named the pope's representative in Warsaw.
In July 1989 Poland was the first of the Eastern bloc nations to
establish diplomatic relations with the Holy See, facilitating the
dramatic changes that occurred between 1989 and 1992.

In July 1989 Gorbachev conveyed another positive signal to
John Paul, allowing him to appoint a Catholic bishop in Byelorussia

– the first in more than six decades.[25] In August President Bush's new ambassador to the Vatican, Thomas Patrick Melady, arrived in Rome.[26] In December Gorbachev went to Italy on a state visit, planning to meet the pope. That historic meeting occurred on 1 December 1989, during which the two discussed the plight of the 4 million or so Catholics in western Ukraine, whose hierarchy had been dissolved by Stalin and whose churches had been handed over to the Orthodox Church. The problem was not Gorbachev's hostility to religion or the Church, but his fear of alienating Russian Orthodoxy and stirring the nationalist fervour still linked with religion. The pope, even more clearly than Gorbachev, foresaw the revival of Christianity in the Soviet Union to fill the void left by the Soviets' experiment of expunging God from the human soul.[27]

At the end of 1990 Lech Wałęsa became president of Poland and the Russian hold on Eastern Europe was undermined. By 1991 the communist system in the Soviet Union was crumbling, as governments in the Russian republics refused to follow the directives of Moscow.[28] Towards the end of 1991 Pope John Paul II convoked a synod of European bishops, both from the East and West, to assess the situation presented by the political changes on the Continent and to promote a new evangelization of Europe. On 20 December 1991 President Boris N. Yeltsin of Russia visited the pope in Rome.[29] By Christmas 1991 the Holy See had witnessed the collapse of the Soviet Union, the end of Gorbachev's leadership and the transition to a 'commonwealth' of independent states. Subsequently, the ousted Soviet leader Gorbachev concluded that Pope John Paul II had played 'a major political role' in the undermining of communism in Eastern Europe.[30]

In 1991 John Paul II issued the encyclical *Centesimus annus* ('The Hundreth Year') to mark the 100th anniversary of Leo XIII's *Rerum novarum*. In it the pope warned capitalist countries that the collapse of communism should not blind them to the need to repair injustices in their own economic systems. In addition, he stressed the need for the world to find an alternative to military action to resolve problems and difficulties while examining the lessons that recent events provided for developing nations.[31] Rejecting the attempt to achieve 'an impossible compromise between Marxism and Christianity', thus condemning the excesses of Liberation Theology, he was likewise critical of the exploitation, neglect and quasi-servitude found in large parts of the globe and particularly in the developing world. 'The Marxist solution had failed, but the realities of marginalization and exploitation continued in the world, especially the third world', the pope wrote. 'Against these phenomena the Church strongly raises her voice.'[32]

During the course of his ten-day visit to Brazil in October 1991, John Paul did not hesitate to criticize both militant priests and conservative authorities. He denounced the political practices that favoured the large landowners at the expense of impoverished peasants and urged President Fernando Collor de Mello to resolve the 'enormous social and economic problems' of the country. John Paul decried the contrast between the two Brazils, the one highly developed, marching towards progress and riches, while the second was mired in untold poverty, suffering, illiteracy and marginalization. Throughout the course of his second trip to this country of 120 million Catholics, the pope denounced the stark disparities that persisted. Offering atonement to Brazil's dwindling native population for the defects of some missionaries during the centuries of conversion, he called for justice and land rights for them. The Church, he insisted, was the Church of the poor, reminding the slum dwellers of the *favela* Vidigal, the poorest quarter of Rio de Janeiro, that those in poverty are particularly close to God and his kingdom.[33]

In addressing the themes of poverty and inequality, the pope appeared to veer towards the Liberation Theology of some Brazilian bishops, who sought to combine the Marxist notion of class struggle with the Christian conception of championing the poor and defenseless. Distressed by the restrictive landowning system, the pope nonetheless discouraged the practice of squatting on untended land, fostered by some of the clergy. The interests of the poor were to be championed by Christian conscience and authentic evangelization, removed from the Marxist analysis of class struggle. The role of the Church was to be a witness to the truth. Whenever and wherever possible the pope counselled cooperation rather than confrontation.[34] Indeed, protracted Vatican negotiations with Mexico ended more than 70 years of hostility between the two.[35] In 1992 Mexico and the Vatican established diplomatic relations, and in August 1993 John Paul II ventured to Mexico once again, where he was greeted warmly by President Carlos Salinas de Gortari.

Likewise, when Yugoslavia disintegrated into its components the pope urged negotiation rather than war to resolve differences. During the course of his five-day visit to Hungary in August 1991, the pope received a group of Croatian pilgrims. Supportive of their 'legitimate aspirations', John Paul suggested that they achieve their goals through international mediation rather than warfare. The next day, federal army tanks crossed the border into Croatian territory, while their airforce bombed Stara Gradiška on the border with the republic of Bosnia–Herzegovina.[36] Appalled by the Serb destruction of churches and hospitals, in mid-January 1992 the Vatican unilaterally recognized the independence of both Croatia and Slovenia, underscoring its support for these two predominantly Catholic republics.[37]

There were also differences between the Vatican and the United States on the Gulf War, since the pope pleaded with President Bush not to resort to arms to redress Iraq's movement into Kuwait. On 13 January 1991 John Paul II had called for an Iraqi withdrawal from Kuwait and the convocation of a peace conference on the Middle East. Condemning the Iraqi invasion, and the scandalous arms trade, the pope believed that recourse to war would represent a 'decline' for the whole of humanity. He feared that the use of military force might trigger a broader regional conflict, considering war 'an adventure with no return'. Once the war started, articles in *La Civiltà Cattolica* and *L'Osservatore Romano* criticized the American action. Only at war's end, when the Vatican was informed that the United States and the Soviet Union were prepared to co-sponsor a peace initiative in Madrid, were relations improved between the Vatican and the United States.[38]

Whatever coldness had existed between Rome and Washington was dissipated during the course of President Bush's hour-long talk with Pope John Paul II in November 1991. Differences remained, including their attitude towards Israel, which the Vatican still did

not officially recognize early in the 1990s, fearing that either Arab
or Jewish domination would prove detrimental to Christian interests in the area. It also expressed concern about the status of
Jerusalem and sharing control of that Holy City and its shrines with
Jewish and Muslim religious leaders. Thus after Vatican II the major
obstacles in Jewish–Vatican relations remained political rather than
religious in their nature, since the Holy See was a major force in the
campaign against racism and anti-Semitism. The pope, who had
helped protect Jews in Poland during the German occupation,
continued to denounce the outbursts of xenophobia in Europe,
expressing his solidarity with the Jews.[39]

The Madrid Conference had an important impact on the Holy
See's attitude towards Israel; Rome hoped that it would signal the
start of new and improved relations between Israel and her Arab
neighbours and thus facilitate the normalization of relations
between the Holy See and Israel. Early in 1992 Cardinal John
O'Connor visited the Middle East and met both King Hussein of
Jordan and Yitzhak Shamir, prime minister of Israel. By this time
the Vatican no longer demanded the internationalization of
Jerusalem, asking only for international guarantees of access to the
holy sites. This was confirmed in the summer of 1992, when the
Holy See began talks with Israeli officials for the creation of a joint
commission to study the issue of full diplomatic relations, which
were established at the end of 1993 on the basis of a fifteen-point
agreement. Israel and the Vatican exchanged 'special representatives', to be followed by the exchange of full ambassadors. To
reassure Arab countries with Christian minorities, the Vatican indicated that a similar accord with Jordan would soon be approved. In
the interim, John Paul had a historic meeting with the chief rabbi of
Israel, who was, like the pope, a Pole.[40]

During the years from 1992 to 1995 Pope John Paul II resumed
his hectic travel schedule, targeting the developing world, which
housed more than half the world's Catholics. He made these jour-
neys in fulfilment of his apostolic ministry, explaining that the
practice had been begun by two of his great predecessors, the popes
of Vatican II, John XXIII and especially Paul VI. John Paul II saw the
need to continue its implementation.[41] In 1992 he ventured twice to

Africa, visiting Senegal in February and Angola in June, with the latter trip marking his 55th voyage outside Italy since he had assumed the papacy in 1978. In May he pleaded for peace in the Sudan, decrying the conflict between the Muslim and Arab-dominated government in the north, and the black, and Christian, south. The pope warned the Sudan's military leader that his Muslim fundamentalist government had the duty to protect the right of Christians to practise their faith.[42]

In 1992 the pope visited Santo Domingo to celebrate the 500th anniversary of Columbus landing in the New World and to open the Fourth Latin American Bishops' Conference. Although the pope reiterated the Church's 'preferential option for the poor', as called for by the Latin American bishops at their meetings in Medellín, Colombia, and Puebla, Mexico, Liberation theologians such as Enrique Dussel were not invited to the conference, and the pope cautioned the Latin American clergy not to forget their spiritual mission while battling economic, social and political injustices.[43] Later, the Vatican imposed a year's silence on Leonardo Boff, a leading Liberation theologian.

In March 1992 the German Catholic theologian Eugen Drewermann, who had earlier been forbidden to teach at Paderborn University, was suspended for questioning the Vatican's stance on contraception and priestly celibacy, as well as whether Jesus physically rose from the dead and whether Mary was a virgin. It should have provided an example for dissenting clergy, but did not deter the bishop of Evreux in Normandy, Jacques Gaillot, from adhering to similar views. Subsequently, the Vatican removed Gaillot for challenging the Catholic Church's position on homosexuality, abortion and other social issues. The bishop, who endorsed the controversial French-made abortion pill, advocated the use of condoms and favoured the marriage of priests, was allowed to retain his title, but all churches were removed from his jurisdiction.

Meanwhile, Father Charles Curran was prohibited from teaching theology at the Catholic University of America in Washington, DC, while the Vatican refused permission to publish the proceedings of an episcopal conference of 1988 that challenged the Church's ban on artificial contraception. Archbishop Raymond

G. Hunthausen of Seattle, chastised by the Vatican for his liberal policies involving marriage annulments, liturgy, sterilizations at Catholic hospitals, matters involving homosexual groups and clerical education, found his authority in these areas transferred to his auxiliary, Bishop Wuerl.[44] John Paul ordered the four Nicaraguan priests who participated in the Marxist Sandinista government to withdraw after a transition period. When they refused to do so, he had them defrocked. The pope was supported in this conservative course by Cardinal Joseph Ratzinger (the future Benedict XVI), named Prefect of the Congregation of the Doctrine of the Faith, and the equally traditional Jean Jérôme Hamer, Prefect of the Congregation for Institutes of Consecrated Life and Societies of Apostolic Life.

In the summer of 1993 the pope travelled to Denver in Colorado for the celebration of World Youth Day, following such gatherings in Spain in 1989, and Poland in 1991. In Denver the pope adhered to his traditionalist theological outlook, refusing to have Church doctrines determined by public opinion polls and disdainful of the penchant of some Americans for a pick-and-choose Catholicism. With President Clinton standing stiffly and impassively by his side, John Paul resolutely condemned abortion rights, which the American president supported. The president took the talk gamely, pronouncing the speech 'great' and retreating with the pope for a private discussion.

In August the Vatican found the American Church too lax in granting annulments. In September 1993, following his visit to the United States, the pope returned to the issues of sexual ethics and moral relativism, which he perceived as a great threat to Western civilization, in his long encyclical *Veritatis splendor*. In the 179-page document, which contains more than 180 notes, the pope rejected the idea that human freedom and human reason create values on their own, rather than discovering them in the order of the universe created by God. Arguing that good is distinct from evil and that morality cannot be situational, he rejected not only abortion and euthanasia but also contraception, artificial insemination, homosexual conduct, masturbation and premarital sex. While John Paul defended freedom of conscience and religion, at the same time the

pope fiercely defended priestly celibacy, while insisting that the way
to salvation was through obedience to the Church's magisterial
teachings. The media, he warned, have conditioned society to listen
to what it wants to hear and, worse still, some moralists actually ally
themselves with their message. The Church must not, and cannot,
court popularity, the pope insisted, but must teach what humanity
needs to do to gain eternal life and avoid eternal perdition. The
encyclical caused considerable controversy among those American
Catholics who adhered to a more liberal position on birth control.[45]
Subsequently, the pope cited television as a major threat to family
life, denouncing its glorification of sex and violence and its
spreading of false and degrading values.[46]

During the course of 1993, Pope John Paul II apologized for the
Catholic Church's collaboration in the enslavement of African men,
women and children, following the Vatican's belated vindication of
Galileo, but he did not budge on what he deemed moral and theological issues. He assailed the resolution of the European Parliament which proposed that homosexual couples should be allowed
to marry and adopt children, claiming such a move would legitimize 'moral disorder'.[47] In a week-long trip to the Baltic region in
September 1993, while pleading for ethnic reconciliation, the pope
did not hesitate to denounce atheism's immoral products such as
pornography. In Riga he presented Church doctrine as a *via media*
between the failure of communism and capitalism's excesses, including their inability to satisfy the needs of the weak. While accepting
the legitimacy of private property, he also referred to 'the dignity of
the human subject who performs it, who can never be reduced to a
commodity or a mere cog in the machinery of production';[48] words
that were not received kindly in the capitalist West.

In June 1994 the American pro-choice president met the pro-
life pope to discuss the draft for the International Conference on
Population and Development to be held in Cairo in September.
Disturbed that the first draft called for massive contraception
programmes worldwide, the pope warned the heads of state that the
conference could mean a setback for humanity as a whole. In
response, the Vatican issued a long document criticizing the
'contraceptive imperialism' of the modernized world vis-à-vis the

developing world. With Vice-President Gore leading the American delegation to the conference, the pope feared that it would endorse a programme to curb population by family planning. Some saw the impending clash between the Vatican and the United States at the Cairo conference as the greatest since the dropping of the atomic bomb on Japan in 1945, which the Vatican had opposed. On 2 June 1994, when President Clinton met the pope, he found that he and the pontiff faced irreconcilable differences on issues such as birth control and abortion. The pope expressed 'his concern that the world community in general and the United States in particular, not be insensitive to the value of life'.[49]

Conservative Muslims attacked the United Nations' plan to slow population growth and lambasted the UN document for encouraging extra-marital sex and undermining spiritual teachings. Many in the developing world shared the Vatican's perception that the plan reflected an attempt by wealthy Western industrial states to dictate policy to the poorer nations, rather than curb their squandering of precious resources. Vatican diplomacy played a crucial role in shifting the conference's focus from controlling population through artificial contraception to an emphasis on increased education, job opportunities and full civil rights for women.[50] Some were convinced that the strong role played by the Vatican at the United Nations Conference on Population and Development in Cairo marked a turning point in the role of religious groups in such international gatherings. At Cairo, Catholics and Muslims found themselves in agreement on a number of issues and played a part in revising the 98-page 'Program of Action' dealing with abortion, contraception and homo-sexual unions. In a shrewd new tack in international diplomacy, the Vatican for the first time selected a woman to head its delegation to a major world conference, the Fourth World Conference on Women held in Beijing.[51]

In December 1994 Pope John Paul II was selected as *Time* magazine's Man of the Year, for the Vatican's presence in Cairo, among other things, receiving an award that had been bestowed on Pope John XIII in 1962, the year he opened the Second Vatican Council. Contraception he held always and forever wrong, while insisting that the Church did not have the authority to bestow priestly ordination on women. During his talk to the Synod on religious life, the pope made it clear that the synod should not address the issue of female ordination. Abortion, he insisted, was a grave sin, holding that not even rape justified what was intrinsically evil. Sex outside marriage was wrong.[52] It was believed that the pope would venture to New York in October 1994 to address the General Assembly for a second time, during the International Year of the Family. Prospects for that trip were dimmed following the pope's fall in his bathtub that April, his second fall in six months since November. Early in the autumn the Vatican announced cancellation of the pope's visit to the United States.[53]

The accident also prevented John Paul from attending the ending of the month-long Synod of African Bishops in Rome during May 1994, to set the course for Africa's 95 million Catholics in the coming century. At its opening on 10 April, during which the marchers danced down the aisles of St Peter's to the music of drums, while worshippers carried the offertory gifts on their heads, the pope praised the African people's love of life and seconded their cry for an end to the slaughter in Rwanda. On African issues the Vatican sought inculturation, attempting to blend traditional African values with Catholic dogma, without diluting its central moral strictures.[54] 'Catholicism will be more universalized, with a different approach to the ancient cultures of non-European peoples', the pope had earlier said, adding: 'it must be de-westernized'.[55]

In a consistory in the autumn of 1994, the pope appointed 30 new cardinals, indicating that they would be confirmed at the end of November. In keeping with his vision of a universal Church, the new cardinals hailed from 24 countries, including two from the United States: William Henry Keeler, Archbishop of Baltimore, and Adam Joseph Maida, Archbishop of Detroit. There were candidates from countries where Catholics live under communist rule, such as Monsignor Jaime Lucas Ortega y Alamino from Cuba and Paul Joseph Pham Dinh Tung from Vietnam, while his selection of the archbishop of Sarajevo, Monsignor Vinko Puljić, underlined the pope's quest for peace in the Balkans. Additional cardinals were appointed from Lebanon, the Czech Republic, Italy, Japan, Chile, Scotland, Mexico, Indonesia, Belgium, France, Switzerland, Uganda,

Canada, Peru, Spain, Madagascar, Ecuador, Belarus, Albania and
Germany. The Italians, once the dominant element in the college,
had been whittled down to 20 out of 120 cardinal electors.[56]

In January 1995 the pope left for the Philippines for the International Youth Forum and an eleven-day tour of Asia that would
bring him to New Guinea, Australia and Sri Lanka. Although there
were reports of terrorist plots to kill the pope during the visit, John
Paul received a warm welcome in Manila, where an estimated 3.5
million people turned out to see him amid shouts of '*Viva il Papa!*'
During his final Mass in the Philippines, it is estimated that some
4–5 million Filippinos gathered to greet the pope, who was joined
in prayer by members of China's state-sponsored supervised
Church, the Chinese Patriotic Association, which since 1949 had
elected its own bishops without the approval of the Vatican. The
pope, in a message of 14 January 1995 broadcast to the estimated 10
million Roman Catholics in China, called for reconciliation and
unity in the Chinese Catholic Church.[57]

From the Philippines the pope travelled to New Guinea for the
beatification of Peter To Rot, a catechist ordered to halt his work by
the Japanese occupation forces during the Second World War, in
the process naming some 600 personages 'blessed' from the beginning of his pontificate, more than any other modern pope. Likewise
in Australia the pope presided over the beatification ceremonies for
Mother Mary MacKillop, the nineteenth-century foundress of the
Josephite order of nuns, who fought the male-dominated Aus-
tralian hierarchy to do so. While John Paul pronounced that 'the
Church stands firmly against every form of discrimination which in
any way compromises the equal dignity of women and men', he did
not budge from his ban on the ordination of women.[58] He proved
more conciliatory in Sri Lanka, where angry Buddhists were livid
about his remarks about their faith made in his book *Crossing the
Threshold of Hope*, in which he described Buddhism as an 'atheistic
system', while criticizing its indifference to the world.[59]

His encyclical *Evangelium vitae* ('The Gospel of Life', 25 March
1995), on the value and inviolability of human life, defended life
and the onslaught against it. Here the pope restated the Church's
opposition to contraception, abortion, euthanasia and capital

punishment, insisting that there was no obligation in conscience to obey such laws. He warned that 'each individual in fact has moral responsibility for the acts which she personally performs; no one can be exempted from this responsibility, and on the basis of it everyone will be judged by God himself'.[60] Some Jewish and Muslim as well as Catholic leaders applauded the pope's courage in denouncing the 'culture of death' and defending the sanctity of life. Not all agreed with him, even within his own Church. Nonetheless, there is a wide consensus that the pope's convictions provide a world view of a depth and consistency matched by no other world leader, assuring him a moral authority enjoyed by few others.[61]

The policies of John Paul have inspired both ardent support and bitter criticism. There is a broad consensus that the pope who preached that 'politics' was not the business of the Church practised it quite successfully. A number of writers have claimed that Pope John Paul II not only worked with President Ronald Reagan to keep the banned Solidarity union alive, but in the process played a crucial role in breaking the communist grip on Poland. 'Nobody believed the collapse of Communism would happen this fast or on this timetable', one of the pope's closest advisers confided, 'But in their first meeting, the Holy Father and the President committed them-selves and the institutions of the Church and America to such a goal.'[62] Other tours emboldened the opposition to a broad array of oppressive rulers, including João Baptista Figueiredo of Brazil, Ferdinand Marcos of the Philippines, Augusto Pinochet of Chile and the Argentine junta and South Korean generals, among others.[63]

Michael Novak has ranked John Paul II among the greatest popes in the long history of the papacy, 'easily in the top 10 and maybe even higher'.[64] His opinion was not shared by Sinead O'Connor, who tore a picture of the pontiff on national American television, or by one of his doctors, who pronounced him 'psychologically unbalanced'.[65] Equally critical were the more than 400 Catholic theologians who signed the 'Cologne Declaration' of 1989, which charged that in requiring blind obedience from the bishops, clergy and theologians, this pope was denying the Church's historical practice of constructive questioning, overstepping papal competence.

XII

Benedict XVI: Conflict and Conciliation with the Contemporary Age

We are accustomed to a period of mourning at the close of a pope's tenure because it is typically his death and not his own deliberations that ends it. Although the old Roman counsel – 'de nihil bonum mortius' ('of the dead speak nothing but good') – seems less and less to be practiced, it is still the custom to remember the life and accomplishments of a deceased pontiff in a more positive light – at least until after the next election. We can only hope that our Holy Father will receive such courtesy.

'The Pope Resigns', *The Tablet* (16 February 2013)

DEEP DIVISIONS REMAINED IN THE CHURCH OVER THE NEED for reform versus preservation, and especially over the impact and influence of the role of the Council half a century after its closure. For many, Joseph Ratzinger seemed an ideal choice for the task of conciliating conservatism and the Council. This brilliant theologian had attended all four Council sessions as a theological adviser to Cardinal Frings, Archbishop of Cologne, and would become one of John Paul II's closest confidants and collaborators. John Paul II trusted him to protect and preserve the principles and practices of the Church by naming him Prefect of the Congregation for the Doctrine of the Faith – the former Inquisition.

In the Congregation Ratzinger proceeded to defend and re-affirm Catholic doctrine, values and traditions on such issues as the celibacy of clergy, opposition to female ordination, homosexuality, birth control and abortion, among other practices and principles. This agenda and critique pleased traditionalists but alienated liberals, while his positive evaluation of the Council placated liberals but generally displeased conservatives. Although a confirmed traditionalist, as a theologian and cleric Ratzinger sought to strike a balance between the opposite extremes in the Church, Curia and Council. Though he later pursued a more conservative course, it must not be forgotten that Ratzinger was a founding member of the progressive theological journal *Concilium*.

Despite his later conservative reputation, Ratzinger adhered to a series of progressive beliefs throughout the greater part of the 1960s, and in 1968 joined liberals and progressives such as Hans Küng, Karl Rahner, Edward Schillebeeckx, Yves Congar, J. B. Metz and Roland Murphy, and signed a declaration supporting the right of theologians to seek and speak the truth. It read that a pope or bishop 'cannot and must not supersede, hamper and impede the teaching task of theologians and scholars'. The declaration, which Ratzinger readily endorsed, went on to conclude that the signers expected the pope and bishops to support them as theologians for the welfare and well-being of all of humanity and society, in the Church and in the world. Furthermore, the theologians asserted:

> We would like to fulfill our duty which is to seek the truth and speak the truth without being hampered by administrative measures and sanctions. We expect our freedom to be respected whenever we pronounce or publish, to the best of our knowledge and in conscience, our well-founded theological convictions.[1]

Ratzinger also proved supportive of the efforts of the Vatican Council to reform the Church and the Curia. Thus he deemed crucial the conciliar effort to explore the relationship between the Church and the modern world in *Gaudium et spes*, the Pastoral Constitution on the Church in the Modern World. Although considered one of the most important and best-known documents of the Council, Ratzinger found it somewhat inadequate for its failure to outline clearly the features of the modern era. In retrospect, Ratzinger recalled the great expectation that he, like many others, felt at the opening of the Council, but later acknowledged that many of their hopes were not fulfilled.[2] Although over the years Ratzinger had become somewhat more conservative, as well as a more pronounced traditionalist, his recollection of the Council proved more positive than negative. His assessment also proved more balanced than most of the Council's critics to the Left and Right.

During the Council he confounded critics who were convinced that he would denounce the 'Declaration on Religious Liberty' requested and drafted by the American bishops, which a series of popes had earlier denounced as indifferentism. Conservatives were shocked that during the Council Ratzinger had supported it and later listed it as one of the Council's major achievements. Conservatives were less than pleased with Ratzinger's approval of the related *Nostra aetate*, the Council's declaration that the 'spiritual, moral and socio-cultural values' of non-Christian religions were to be 'respected, protected and encouraged'.[3] Ratzinger's approval of this long-sought liberal objective pleased the liberal camp, but disturbed conservatives, who found this smacked of the indifferentism denounced by Popes Gregory XVI, Pius IX and Pius X.

Nostra aetate represented an important first step in improving Catholic–Jewish relations following the horror of the Nazi genocide. More needed to be done in this and other matters, but Ratzinger resented the distortions of the Council's aims and efforts by part of the press, along with ideologically committed partisans of the Left and the Right, who criticized all the decisions that did not conform to their narrow vision and political programme.[4] Early on he recognized that neither the radical left nor the conservative right was satisfied with the Council and almost immediately called for, indeed demanded, change. It was not the first challenge he confronted.

Joseph Ratzinger was born in Marktl am Inn, in lower Bavaria in the troubled Weimar Republic, on 16 April 1927 to a devout Catholic family of farmers of modest means. Josef and Maria had their younger son, Joseph, baptized on the day of his birth. This was generally done by parents who worried about the survival of a child, and especially his salvation. Having survived infancy, his parents – and particularly his mother – encouraged their sons' religious inclina-tions. This helps to explain why her two sons, early in childhood, determined to become priests. Joseph entered the minor seminary in 1939, at the age of twelve. Some believe that brutal Nazi violence and persecution sparked and fuelled his vocation. Unfortunately, that was also the year that the Second World War broke out; his seminary was slammed shut by the Nazi regime, and when Joseph reached sixteen he was drafted into an anti-aircraft unit, in which he served from August 1943 to September 1944, and was subsequently placed in the infantry, from which he deserted in May 1945.

Captured by the Americans, he did a short stint as an American prisoner of war. Although he had been conscripted and constrained to serve, some denounced him as a 'Wehrmacht warrior'. This was but one of the numerous and unfair charges launched against the intellectually inclined and religiously inspired young man who considered militarism a crime. Embroiled in a dangerous situation and destructive war, he survived by dreaming of returning home to his family, continuing his studies, gaining admission into the priesthood and teaching theology, religious study and philosophy at university level.

Only at war's end was he able to return to his goals, resuming the theological and philosophical studies he enjoyed. His studies at the seminary associated with the University of Munich from 1947 to 1951 went well, and he, along with his older brother Georg, was ordained to the priesthood in 1951. Following the death of Pius XII in 1958, he participated in the Second Vatican Council convoked by Pope John XXIII in 1961 and opened in 1962. Despite some dissatisfaction with aspects of the conciliar efforts, Ratzinger almost always supported its aims, even when he challenged the manner in which they were implemented. This remained true after he moved towards a more conservative stance, when he witnessed and experienced the violence of student demonstrations in German colleges and universities in 1968. The students' recourse to violence apparently brought back bitter memories of the Reich's Nazi past and his childhood under Hitler's regime, which continued to haunt him. He achieved a degree of tranquillity by concentrating on his theological studies and assuming a more conservative outlook.

Rather than seeking a pastoral position, in 1953 Ratzinger determined to continue his education and obtained a doctorate in theology with a thesis focused on 'People and the House of God in St Augustine's Doctrine of the Church' under the direction of the renowned professor of fundamental theology Gottlieb Söhngen. Subsequently, he qualified for university teaching with a dissertation on 'The Theology of History in St Bonaventure'. From 1959 to 1963 he taught at Bonn, at Münster from 1963 to 1966, and at Tübingen from 1966 to 1969. During the last year he held the chair of dogmatics and history at the University of Regensburg. His first book, *Introduction to Christianity*, published in 1968, was a bestseller that was translated into seventeen languages. During these decades – among the happiest in his life – he taught theology at various German schools, institutes and universities, engaged in research and writing as well as teaching, and was recognized and respected as a profound intellect and excellent teacher by almost all adversaries as well as allies. Few were surprised by the recognition he received, and few questioned or challenged his scholarly success, or his becoming a full professor of theology by 1958.

Ratzinger had happily returned to teaching and writing at the close of the Council, but his tranquil campus life was threatened by two factors: the student riots of 1968 and a series of assignments from Rome, which combined to keep him from pursuing the scholarly issues that most interested him. Despite his limited pastoral experience, in 1977 Pope Paul VI made him archbishop of Munich and named him a cardinal. He took as his episcopal motto 'Fellow Worker in the Truth' and found considerable tasks placed on his shoulders. Other honours and more burdensome posts and responsibilities were in store. Following Paul's death and the month-long pontificate of John Paul I, the new pope, John Paul II, was impressed with the learning of the German cardinal. Ratzinger formed a close intellectual bond with the extremely popular Polish pope, whom he met several times a week to discuss practical matters as well as theoretical issues. Very quickly Ratzinger emerged as one of John Paul II's closest confidants and collaborators, and played a central role in drafting this pope's encyclicals.

John Paul II reciprocated by nominating him to a series of important posts and named him president of the Pontifical Commission. In 1981 the pope appointed Ratzinger Prefect of the

Congregation for the Doctrine of the Faith – the former Inquisition. Presiding over this congregation, his decisions, articles and
books were in large part defensive, reflecting traditional Catholic
values and opinions. In this post Ratzinger was seen to voice suspicion of the implementation of innovation, and the transformation
of Church, state and society. In the eyes of many, this new office
moved Ratzinger further to the right as he confronted the problems
faced by the Church in Latin America, which had to deal with the
problems and philosophy of Liberation Theology. Ratzinger
determined to defend the priority of the universal Church over the
local Church.

Early in the new millennium Cardinal Ratzinger wrote
*Dominus Iesus: On the Unicity and Salvific Universality of Jesus
Christ and the Church*, which to many appeared to contradict his
earlier support for religious liberty. He now appeared to claim that
salvation would only be attained in the Catholic Church and
seemed to brand the non-Christian faiths as 'gravely deficient',
while describing Protestant houses of worship as something less
than true churches.[5] Later he ordered the bishops to refrain from
referring to the Orthodox, Anglican and Protestant churches as
'sister churches'.[6] This work not only moved the papacy and the
Church away from ecumenism, but also placed them both on a
more conservative course.

Ratzinger did not hide the fact that he favoured adherence to
traditional Catholic beliefs, liturgy and doctrine. This was reflected
in the judgements he made and his pronouncements on clerical
celibacy, female ordination and birth control, which did not endear
him to liberals nor even some moderates, but apparently approved
by the pope. His role as watchdog preserving the faith led him to
oppose a string of innovations, reinforcing his conservative image.
In retaliation, he was branded Hitler's Cardinal, John Paul's
Rasputin, Rome's Darth Vader, God's Rottweiler, the Grand
Inquisitor, the Heresy Hunter and the *Panzerkardinal*, among other
less than flattering names, and depicted by some as a fat rat. On the
other hand, John Paul appreciated the contribution of his friend
and colleague and apparently made it clear to most of the cardinals
he had appointed during his long pontificate that Ratzinger would

make a splendid successor. Some agreed, but others found him too traditional and conservative for the papacy of the third millennium. Other considerations, however, favoured Ratzinger's election as pope, including the fact that he was not particularly anxious to assume the post over a Church that had more than a billion followers across the world. He recognized that the office would impose massive responsibilities that would inevitably restrict his research, writing and teaching – which had long been his first love.

Nonetheless, John Paul II believed that he could persuade the cardinals, most of whom he had named, to support Ratzinger's selection to become the 265th successor of St Peter and the first German pope since Victor II (1055–7). Friend and foe alike acknowledged that although controversial, he was one of the most influential and persuasive members of the College of Cardinals and his knowledge of theology was unsurpassed. He proved able to communicate with millions of the faithful because he was reportedly able to read and speak ten languages and was fluent in Italian, French, Spanish and English, as well as German. For others in the conclave of 2005, the most important factor in John Paul's apparent choice was Ratzinger's age – he was 78 in 2005 – and word had spread of his heart failure and other health problems he had endured throughout the 1980s.

In September 1991 he had suffered a cerebral stroke that adversely affected his left field of vision. The following year he was hospitalized following a fall, which inflicted a serious cut to his head. Plagued by congestive heart failure, he had a pacemaker installed while he presided over the Congregation for the Preservation of the Faith, and at the beginning of 2013 had surgery to have its batteries replaced.[7] Thus even many of those cardinals who would have preferred to select another candidate were prepared to accept Ratzinger as an interim pontiff – which they believed he would be. This factor, the backing of John Paul II, the profound theological knowledge he possessed, his role as dean of the College of Cardinals and the desire to continue to block the Italian hold on the papacy combined to make Ratzinger the most serious candidate. In this instance the Roman adage that the cardinal who enters the conclave as the favourite to become the next pope leaves the conclave a cardinal did not hold. On 19 April 2005 Ratzinger was elected pope by a large majority on the fourth ballot of a short, two-day conclave. He assumed the name Benedict XVI.

Ratzinger's election as pope in 2005 did not please his 81-year-old brother, Georg Ratzinger, also a priest. Some saw this as sibling rivalry and jealousy on Georg's part. There is no evidence to suggest this, but there is considerable evidence that Georg knew of his brother's health problems and advanced age, and worried about his 'younger brother'. For these and other reasons, when Joseph was elected pope Georg concluded and confided that the responsibilities of the office were too great for his younger, but still almost 80-year-old brother. Although Benedict felt he could not avoid the burdensome duties of the papacy, he did not forget Georg's warning and fear, which probably led Benedict to conclude that working too hard is never a good thing, even for those involved in the governance of the Church.[8] He needed to show others, however, as well as prove to himself, that he could fulfil the papal role worldwide, and following Paul VI and John Paul II – two of the most travelled popes – travelled and emphasized the transnational position of the papacy.

Benedict prepared to make a series of trips that would make him the third most travelled pope and one of the few German leaders who proved capable of exercising this global mission. In doing so Benedict kept his brother's warning in mind – and some later believed that poor health may have been the chief factor that made him 'a man driven by fear'. Those who portrayed him as 'fear-ridden' were almost always also convinced that he 'lusted for power', which accounted for his preoccupation with his office and their conclusion that he lacked a sense of humour. In an interview in 1997 by Bavarian television, when he was asked point-blank about the role of fear in his life and career, his quick-witted response was, 'I'm only afraid of the dentist'![9] This was confirmed by those who knew him well. In light of his health and age, liberals believed that his pontificate would be short, while conservatives hoped it would be long enough to secure the election of another conservative and younger cardinal to follow as pope. Benedict, who did not seek the post, indicated after his election that he had no programme of his own, and sought only to implement the policies and texts of John XXIII, Paul VI and John Paul II, and the work of the Council.[10]

This alienated the more conservative clerics, while his homily at John Paul's funeral Mass aroused the suspicion of some liberals. Neither group went successfully against the determined stance of the popular Polish pope, who had appointed most of them into the College of Cardinals and the conclave to select his successor. In fact, Ratzinger appreciated John's call for *aggiornamento* or the updating of the Church and papacy, and dedicated a good part of his time in attempting to shape the Church's understanding and implementation of the decisions taken by that Council. Benedict was increasingly upset by the widespread distortions of its teachings and particularly decried much of the coverage of the press, which perceived and reported what transpired in its four sessions as an ideological and political struggle. He praised God, and the power of the Holy Spirit, that the true goal of the Council and its reformism was emerging not as a radical break with the past but as its logical development.[11]

A central belief and theme of his tenure was the strong defence of core Christian values and traditional doctrine, and opposition to the secularization and immorality he believed was sweeping over much of Europe. He hoped to combat this unfortunate development by the intervention of 'Catholics in the Americas', whom he deemed 'joyful missionaries, well-catechized and faithful to the teachings of the Church'.[12] Among other suggestions, he made a number of pronouncements on clerical celibacy, female ordination, homosexuality and birth control that did not endear him to liberals and some moderates. Liberals resented the note he sent regarding the absolute obligation of Catholics to reject and vote against all legislation supporting abortion.

Ignoring the criticism, Benedict took steps, and proposed means, to promote traditional values. He elevated the Tridentine Mass to a more prominent position, promoted the greater use of Latin in the liturgy and personally had recourse to traditional papal garments. Critics who transgressed traditional beliefs were censured and warned to desist holding or publishing these 'erroneous beliefs'. Not all Benedict's conclusions were critical. This agenda and critique pleased conservatives but alienated liberals, while his positive evaluation of the Council placated liberals but generally displeased conservatives.[13]

In 1986, while still Prefect of the Congregation for the Doctrine of the Faith, he issued the 'Letter to the Bishops on the Pastoral Care of Homosexual Persons', also known by its opening words *Homosexualitatis problema*, or disparagingly by some as 'the Halloween Letter'. It was delivered to the bishops of the Church in Rome on 1 October. The letter provided instructions on how the clergy should deal with and respond to lesbian, gay and bisexual people. Pope John Paul II approved the letter and ordered its publication. It was designed to correct misunderstandings and misinterpretations of a CDE letter of 1975, the 'Declaration on Certain Questions Concerning Sexual Ethics' (*Persona humana*).

Ratzinger clarified that the Church's teaching on the sinfulness of homosexual acts was more nuanced than is generally believed by the media and even by some Catholics:

It had been argued that the homosexual orientation in certain cases was not the result of deliberate choice, and so the homosexual person would then have no choice but to behave in a homosexual fashion. Lacking freedom, such a person, even if engaged in homosexual activity, would not be culpable. Here, he argued, the Church's wise moral tradition is necessary since it warns against generalizations in judging individual cases. In fact, circumstances may exist, or may have existed in the past, that would reduce or remove the culpability of the individual in a given instance, or other circumstances might increase it. What is at all costs avoided is the unfounded and demeaning assumption that the sexual behaviour of homosexual persons is always and totally compulsive and therefore inculpable.

Although much of this represented compromise, it was a compromise and solution that did not totally please either conservatives or liberals.

Since the new pope had ties to both the liberal and conservative camps, it was hoped that he could bring about a reconciliation

between the two. No easy task – even for a brilliant theologian and university professor of dogma who had published a series of scholarly and important works and hoped to do more. As Cardinal Prefect of the Congregation for the Doctrine of the Faith, and later as pope, Ratzinger also placed great emphasis on the relationship between faith and reason.

In 1994 Ratzinger assumed a conservative stance in his 'Letter to Bishops Regarding the Reception of Holy Communion by Divorced and Remarried Members of the Faithful'. Here he affirmed that those who are divorced and remarried should not be allowed to receive Communion. Subsequently, in 2003, he released 'Considerations Regarding Proposals to Give Legal Recognition to Unions Between Homosexual Persons'. While he called for compassion towards homosexuals as provided by the teaching of the Church, he opposed legal recognition of homosexual unions. Likewise in 2003 he released a 'Doctrinal Note on the Participation of Catholics in Political Life', which announced that individual Catholics could choose between legitimate parties and programmes, but this freedom did not allow them to support either abortion or euthanasia.[14]

A theologian, not a diplomat, a professor rather than politician, he addressed issues honestly but not always diplomatically or consistently, and in a number of cases his conclusions went counter to parts of his other claims. Theoretically, he favoured ecumenism, but first as prefect and later as pope he assumed positions that hindered its development. During the Council he favoured religious liberty, but following his appointment as Prefect for the Congregation of the Faith he assumed a more traditionalist and conservative stance. This confused liberals and conservatives, friends and foes alike, who wondered and asked 'Quo Vadis Benedict XVI?'

Although a confirmed traditionalist, as both cardinal and pope Ratzinger sought to strike a balance between the opposite extremes in the Church, Curia and Council. Thus he deemed crucial the conciliar efforts to explore the relationship between the Church and the modern world in *Gaudium et spes*, the Pastoral Constitution on the Church in the Modern World. Although considered one of the most important and best-known documents of the Council, Benedict found it inadequate for its failure to outline clearly the features of

the modern era.[15] During the first weeks of his pontificate he softened the hardliner image that had prevailed during his tenure at the
Congregation for the Preservation of the Faith.[16] Although he
called for obedience to the hierarchy, at the same time he proved
supportive of an enhanced role for the laity. This contradictory
course confused his critics, as did his emphasis on God's redemptive love. Some were also surprised that all three encyclicals this
pope wrote focussed on God's love rather than his retribution. His
first, *Deus Caritas Est* or 'God Is Love' (2005); his second, *Spe salvi*
or 'Saved in Hope' (2007); and his third, *Caritas in veritate* or 'Love
in Truth' (2009). In his first he concentrated on God's love rather
than his wrath and vengeance.

During his pontificate Pope Benedict attempted a synthesis of
sorts, between continuity and tradition on the one hand and change
and innovation on the other. He also sought to show that faith and
reason are not contradictory but complement each other. The
papacy had tackled these issues for centuries, so it was questionable
whether Ratzinger, elected pope at the advanced age of 78, would
have the energy or time to bring about such a resolution. Also questionable was Benedict's ability to finish and publish on time his
encyclical on faith – if he published it after his departure it would
not be considered a papal encyclical.[17] Throughout the years of his
pontificate he willingly assumed other tasks and burdensome
responsibilities without complaint, despite his advanced age and
deteriorating health, which made it increasingly difficult to fulfil his
papal responsibilities as he saw fit.

Since Benedict did not complain publicly about his difficulties,
and few popes have resigned voluntarily, his announcement on 11
February 2013 that he would resign on 28 February stunned
Catholics and non-Catholics alike.[18] There had not been a papal
resignation for over 500 years.[19] Benedict explained his decision by
asserting that 'both strength of mind and body are necessary' to
carry out the papal ministry in the modern world, implying that he
could no longer do so.[20]

Almost immediately all sorts of rumours were spread following
Benedict's decision. Some suggested that since he had been stationed
in Rome for more than 30 years and missed home, he resigned so

that he could return to Bavaria. This rumour was shown to be groundless when the Vatican reported that the retired pope – who had Vatican City as well as German citizenship – would move temporarily to the papal villa at Castel Gandalfo until remodelling work on the Mater Ecclesiae monastery in the Vatican Gardens was completed, which would then become his permanent residence.[21]

Other rumours surfaced about Benedict's resignation, including the 'bombshell charge' that the pope did not want to contend with the extortion attempt by gay laymen against hundreds of priests 'with whom they had relationships of a "worldly manner"'.[22] That such sexual abuses existed in the Curia as well as among the clergy has been shown, as well as the fact that Ratzinger was not always the first to respond publicly. He did come to appreciate the gravity of the situation, however, and took a series of steps to correct the abuse.[23] While Ratzinger was suspicious of the motives of those who harped upon the reported homosexuality of the clergy, and believed some used it to discredit the Church, he did not ignore the problem.[24] Specific instructions were dispatched by the Vatican to the entire hierarchy to bar men 'with homosexual tendencies' from being rectors or teachers at seminaries.[25]

The impact of these abuses upon Pope Benedict's resignation, however, remains questionable. In the words of the Jesuit father Federico Lombardi, director of the Vatican Press Office, 'If one wants to receive correct information, one must limit oneself to what the Pope has said about his renunciation.'[26] If Lombardi meant that only the pope knew why he had resigned, so only he could accurately relate why he had done so, then his response has some validity. Very few disputes, however, can be objectively resolved on the input of only one participant. Usually there is more than one side or cause for every story.

A sound historical approach requires that all the pertinent facts be gathered and assessed. Following the announcement of his resignation, Pope Benedict lamented that his age and health did not allow him to fulfil the responsibilities of his office. His German biographer, Peter Seewald, who wrote the 2010 bestseller *Light of the World*, before the exposé in the press of the gay clergy scandal, found the pope exhausted, disheartened and drained of energy.

When Seewald, working on yet another book on Benedict, asked him what he was doing, the pope responded: 'Not much now. I'm an old man and I have lost my strength.'[27] Benedict's exhaustion was confirmed by his close friend Rabbi Arthur Shneier, who wrote: 'When I saw him in November, it was apparent he was frail and burdened by the awesome responsibilities of his high office.'[28] Without mentioning his resignation or health problems the pope indicated that he was going through an unusual time and asked a group of Spanish visitors to continue to pray for him.[29]

As Benedict prepared for his departure by resignation – an extraordinarily rare event in the history of the papacy, which has witnessed only four such resignations – it is not surprising that all sorts of conjecture emerged. Unusual events very often prompt unwarranted conclusions. In the nineteenth century the unexpected death of Pope Pius VIII after a short pontificate (1830–31) led to the assertion that he had been poisoned. A secret autopsy proved that he died from a bout of asthma.[30] In the twentieth century the pontificate of Pope John Paul I was even shorter, lasting a scant 33 days (August–September 1978), and once again the word circulated that he was murdered – a charge that was difficult to prove or refute because papal law prohibits autopsies.

The reaction to Benedict's announcement has to be seen within historical perspective. His age, health and desire to devote his remaining time to other matters, as well as his earlier public statements, all indicate that it was not the sex abuse scandal – which sells newspapers and magazines – but a series of other more personal factors that prompted the resignation. Equally untrue was the story that he was abandoning the Church and retreating into isolation. On Sunday 24 February 2013 he told a huge crowd in St Peter's Square, estimated at a quarter of a million people, that his upcoming retirement did not mean that he was abandoning the Church but that he would be 'serving it in a new way, through prayer and meditation'. He went on to say that 'prayer doesn't mean isolating one's self from the world and its contradictions' but rather 'leads one back to the path of action'.[31] Long devoted to scholarship and academic affairs, it is understandable that the retired pope chose to be called Pope Emeritus.

Conclusion: The Papacy Past and Present

There is bound to be formed a solid right that is determined to live in a world that no longer exists. There is bound to be formed a scattered left captivated by now this now that new development, exploring now this, and now that new possibility.
Bernard Lonergan (1904–1984), 'Modern Control'

ALTHOUGH THE ROLE OF THE PAPACY HAS VARIED OVER TIME and place, it has long been, and remains, one of the most important offices in the world. Over the centuries it has fulfilled a number of roles, functioning in a princely, priestly, educational and pastoral manner, while having recourse to political and social as well as religious means to achieve its objectives. In the centuries following the French Revolution, those who donned the papal tiara have functioned as universal pastors rather than Italian princes.

Despite these and other differences on the part of its leaders and changes in practices, its core values and basic convictions have been largely, some would say miraculously, preserved. Studies of the institution, however, have not always been objective and often have a restricted focus. The emphasis assumed by each pope depends not solely on doctrine but also on personality, education, training and advisers, as well as the events and developments prior and during his pontificate. In fact, a series of factors are considered during papal elections. While numerous attempts have been made to preserve secrecy during most conclaves, the veil has often been lifted, helping to reveal the rationale for the selection of one individual rather than another.

The reasons for election vary, although often, but not always, the cardinals in conclave tend to support candidates for the papacy who share and reflect their own views of the policies to be pursued. From time to time members of the conclave who are dissatisfied with the course of events in the Church, state and society stress the need for a change. Their call for reform is often countered by those who favour preservation or restoration. Small wonder that in light of diverse and often changing factors and circumstances the personalities and policies of the popes should vary. This is not a new phenomenon, for the papacy has been questioned by some and challenged by others over the centuries, long before the outbreak of the American and French revolutions, where this book begins.

In the more than two centuries from the French Revolution to the present, seventeen popes have had to confront difficult social, diplomatic, economic and ideological situations, as well as religious ones. Early on there were different notions about the policies the papacy should pursue to cope with these pressing problems. The different experiences and backgrounds of the candidates for Peter's chair in part helps explain the variation among the seventeen pontificates from the outbreak of the French Revolution in 1789 to the election of Jorge Mario Bergoglio in 2013 as Francis, the first pope with that name, the first Jesuit pope and the first pope from the Americas.

There are similarities and differences in the personalities and the policies pursued by the different popes. Some advocated accommodation with state and society: Pius VII (1800–23), Pius XII (1939–58) and Paul VI (1963–78); others called for confrontation: Gregory XVI (1831–46), Pius IX (1846–78) and Pius XI (1922–39); while still others sought an *aggiornamento* or updating of Church programmes to deal with contemporary problems: Leo XIII (1878–1903) and John XXIII (1958–63). Some were more pastoral than political, as was Pius X (1903–14), while others more diplomatic: Benedict XV (1914–22). In part, these differences reflected the problems prevailing in the various pontificates from Pius VI (1775–99) to Francis (2013–).

Pius VI had to deal with the French Revolution and died in French captivity. His defiance of the revolutionaries led observers to forget his frivolous past and focus on his courageous opposition later in life. His successor, Pius VII (1800–23), confronted Napoleon and like his predecessor was captured by the French. Restored to power by the 'Quadruple Alliance' of Russia, Prussia, Austria and Britain, many in the European world, both inside and outside the Church, questioned the need for the papacy's temporal power, to which the Curia clung tenaciously.

The series of revolutions that followed led others to question whether the papacy could preserve its state or continue to insist upon the union of Church and state. The Papal States survived the revolutions of 1820 with the assistance of the Habsburg military intervention – but proved unable to destroy the radical ideas that inspired the revolutionaries and led to the call for liberal change. Consequently, the future of the papacy's temporal power remained dubious. During the restoration period the reformist programme of Pius VII was largely outlined by his secretary of state, Cardinal Ercole Consalvi, who called for a reform of the papal state but not the Church. The conservative faction known as the Zelanti, however, sanctioned neither the one nor the other.

The Zelanti were largely responsible for the election of Leo XII (1823–9), who would follow a more conservative course than his predecessor. Leo found himself caught between the liberal and conservative powers, and the clash of the traditionalism of the Church and Curia with the liberalism and nationalism of those inspired by the American and French revolutions. His conservatism was partially overcome by the policies of the short pontificate of his successor, Pius VIII (1829–30), but there was a return to a more determined conservatism – some branded it reaction – during the pontificate of Gregory XVI (1831–46). This monkish pope opposed liberalism and nationalism as well as socialism and communism, and insisted on the union of Church and state under papal leadership.

The conservative Gregory XVI had to confront revolutionary disturbances and nationalist agitation in Italy and Europe, and desperately sought a solution. In doing so he looked backwards rather than ahead. To defeat his opponents he had recourse to spiritual as well as military force. He unleashed a series of papal condemnations and excommunications – most notably the *Mirari vos* of 1832 – which condemned the ideological framework of the emerging society and the new order liberals envisioned. This and his other denunciations failed to resolve the unrest in the Papal States and the problems this posed for the papacy. A new course was needed, but Gregory was not the pope to provide it.

Liberals as well as moderates, in the Papal States and throughout much of Italy, therefore welcomed the election of Giovanni Mastai-Ferretti, who assumed the tiara as Pius IX in 1846. His reformist course was perceived as a welcome change to the reactionary path paved by Pope Gregory, which had created more problems than it resolved. Pius IX (1846–78), the longest reigning pope to date, came to power with the notion that the papal state could, and should, be reformed to satisfy its population and avert revolution. His reformism even led some to assume that he might take the lead in uniting the peninsula. This was wishful thinking, for Pius never planned or favoured Italian unification and the absorption of the Papal States into a secular kingdom.

Nonetheless, when revolution erupted in much of Europe in 1848, including Italy and the Papal States, nationalists in Rome and Italy expected the pope to participate in the war of national liberation waged against Austria and her Italian allies. The papal decision not to accede to this demand led nationalists to turn against the pope they had earlier praised, and provoked a series of revolutionary outbursts. The spread of violence in Rome and other parts of his state led to the papal decision to flee the capital at the end of 1848. The pope and his secretary of state Cardinal Giacomo Antonelli sought and received refuge in the Kingdom of Naples. The papal flight led to the proclamation in 1849 of the Second Roman Republic, in what for centuries had been the Papal States and was now for many an anachronism. Restored by French, Austrian, Spanish and Neapolitan arms, Pio Nono's triumph over liberalism and nationalism proved transitory and unable to prevent the unification of Italy and the loss of the greater part of temporal power in 1860.

Despite the denunciations and condemnations of Pius IX, in 1861 the Kingdom of Italy that was proclaimed absorbed the greater part of the Papal States. Rome was preserved for the pope by

French forces. In September 1864, however, Pius learned that the French and Italians had concluded a convention calling for the withdrawal of the French military from Rome. In response, in December 1864 he issued an encyclical or letter titled *Quanta cura*, to which was appended a list of 80 'erroneous propositions' condemned by himself or one of his predecessors. Among other things, this 'Syllabus of Errors' denounced the notion that society should be constituted and governed 'as if God did not exist', and included an unequivocal condemnation of contemporary political movements, and the notion that the sovereignty of the people was supreme. Later Pius and Antonelli had papal infallibility proclaimed during the course of the First Vatican Council (1869–70). When the Italians seized Rome, Pius IX refused to accept or recognize the loss, closed himself in the Vatican, and waged war upon the Italian kingdom and the modern world.

Although the pope locked himself in the Vatican, Pius IX perceived himself a prisoner there, hoping to be rescued. No rescue was forthcoming. To complicate his life and his post, he became embroiled in the *Kulturkampf* with Germany; the counter-Risorgimento with Italy; alienated Republican France; and all but isolated the papacy, which had relations with only a handful of states. His support of the doctrine of papal infallibility further antagonized the powers of Europe, who broke diplomatic relations with the papacy. In his seclusion Pius apparently came to the realization that the papacy could, and would, survive the loss of the temporal power, which had become more of a burden than a blessing. Many of the cardinals had arrived at a similar conclusion, but hesitated in saying so. Although Pius IX had named most of the cardinals in the college during his long pontificate, its members decided that a less confrontational and more diplomatic policy was needed, and this led to the election of a very different pope in 1878.

Papal isolation was ended by Pius IX's successor, Leo XIII (1878–1903), who recognized the need for some accommodation with contemporary developments. His diplomatic finesse and international expertise allowed him to restore systematically Rome's diplomatic situation and the international prestige of the papacy. Under his guidance the Catholic Church rapidly expanded Catholicism outside Europe. This outreach cost money and, when combined with bank failures, created problems for the papacy. Furthermore, Leo censured Americanism and his attempted reconciliation with Anglicanism failed. On the other hand, he brought the *Kulturkampf* to an end and appealed to the masses by his focus on the need for social reform (*Rerum novarum*), which won support from workers worldwide.

Despite a series of successes in the social and diplomatic realm, some believed that Leo neglected religious issues, and following his death in 1903 a more pastoral pope was sought, contributing to the election of Giuseppe Melchiorre Sarto as Pius X (1903–14), who differed markedly from Pope Leo. A pastoral rather than a political pope, his opposition to modernism made him a retrograde in the eyes of some. He won support, however, for favouring an end to the Roman Question, focusing on the missions and fearing for the future of the Church in Europe, which he worried was on the brink of war. He is at present the only pope of the modern age to have been proclaimed a saint.

In 1914 the cardinals in conclave moved away from the pastoral Pius X and chose the more diplomatic Benedict XV (1914–22), who together with his secretary of state Pietro Gasparri revised and brought forward the notion of papal impartiality in order to be able better to mediate between the combatants in the destructive First World War. Although he proved unable to bring about peace, he provided funds to aid the victims of the conflict in both camps. Although Pope Benedict's peace proposal of 1917 was not accepted by the powers, it influenced the Fourteen Points of the American president Woodrow Wilson. He also became known as the 'Pope of the Missions' for his support of them.

In 1922 Achille Ratti succeeded as Pius XI (1922–39), and concurred with his predecessor that while the notion of impartiality might be useful in certain diplomatic and territorial conflicts, it could not be employed – indeed should not –when religious issues were involved. With the help of his secretary of state Gasparri, he signed the Lateran Accords of 1929, which resolved the Roman Question. The negotiations with the Soviet Union proved abortive, and later in 1933 he reluctantly signed an agreement with Nazi

Germany. Alarmed by the racism of its regime, he issued a series of public condemnations in his crusade against anti-Semitism, which he deemed absolutely incompatible with Catholicism. Since his new secretary of state, Eugenio Pacelli, who replaced Gasparri in 1930, favoured conciliation rather than confrontation, Pius XI secretly called upon the American Jesuit John LaFarge to draft an encyclical condemning the anti-Semitism of the Nazi regime. Pius XI died before he could issue it.

Pius XII (1939–58) thought that the publication of his predecessor's encyclical critical of Nazi anti-Semitism would do more harm than good, and decided to shelve it. He had to confront the Second World War, and during the conflict pursued a policy of impartiality, refusing to differentiate between the aggressor and the aggrieved – which provoked criticism. On a more positive note, he favoured the internationalization of the Church and brought to an end the Italian domination of the College of Cardinals. He is presently being considered for canonization.

John XXIII (1958–63), who followed Pius XII, is also being considered for sainthood. He sought the modernization and *aggiornamento* of the Church and its reconciliation with the modern world. To achieve these objectives he convoked the Second Vatican Council (1962–5), but died before he could effect the many changes he sought. Part of his programme was implemented by his friend and collaborator Giovanni Montini, who followed as Pope Paul VI (1963–78) and is likewise being considered for canonization. Many were dissatisfied, however, with his work in the Council. Reformers and radicals felt that he did not do enough, while conservatives complained he did too much, too soon! John Paul I, who followed, wanted to implement the aims of the Council, but his short pontificate of a little over a month in 1978 did not give him the opportunity to do so.

John Paul II's much longer pontificate (1978–2005) provided the opportunity for a wider range of reforms and actions, including a major role in the collapse of communism, the ending of the Cold War and the break-up of the Soviet Union. From the beginning of his pontificate, he assumed a diplomatic and political role far greater than any of his modern predecessors and virtually abandoned the impartiality invoked by Pius VII during the Napoleonic Wars and Benedict XV during the First World War, as well as that of Pius XII during the Second World War and the Nazi genocide.

The different policies and personalities of a series of popes have been assessed, as have their varied practices. Questions have been raised about the papal role not only in the two World Wars, but also in the First and Second Vatican Councils, including the role of Pius IX in the proclamation of papal infallibility in the first, and the respective contributions of John XXIII and Paul VI in the second. More than half a century following the close of the Second Vatican Council in 1965, those inside the Church as well as those outside remain divided in their assessment of the Council's accomplishments, its transformation of the liturgy and the health of the faith, as well as the role of the papacy therein, and its relationship to the modern world.[1]

In addition to the focus on the Council, others have claimed that the seven post-war popes from Pius XII to Francis increased the influence of the papacy, which assumed a political, diplomatic and social as well as religious role, and functioned as one of the leading transnational institutions of the contemporary age. Although some have contested this positive assessment, the position of the Vatican in the twentieth century was a far cry from the isolation of the papacy of Pius IX, following the seizure of the greater part of the Papal States in 1860 and the loss of Rome in 1870, which led to his self-imposed imprisonment in the Vatican. Pius IX would leave only in his coffin – and even then an attempt was made by angry Italians to hurl his body into the Tiber.

The modern animosity towards the papacy and the Church, traced back to the outbreak of the French Revolution in 1789, has persisted in certain quarters to the present. Indeed, the proclamation of papal infallibility in 1870 has been seen by some as a defensive reaction to the threat posed to the papacy by the nationalism of the Risorgimento in Italy; the liberalism of the *Kulturkampf* in Germany; and the socialism and secularism that accompanied industrialization in a number of places in Europe and abroad. Although Pius IX chose to remain a 'prisoner in the Vatican', his successor Leo XIII restored the political, diplomatic and social role of the papacy alongside its religious one. Some, however, complained that the price paid by the Church and the faith for this expanded papal political role was too high and achieved at the expense of its primary pastoral responsibility. At times, this has led to dissension between those who championed continuity and those who called for change in the Church, and to the papacy's role in the modern world.

Liberals, instead, complained that Paul VI had not fulfilled John's call for *aggiornamento* and renewal, while they deplored his conservative stance on a wide range of issues including the ordination of women, birth control and abortion, the celibacy of the clergy and papal infallibility. These divisions were reflected in society, in the Curia and in the College of Cardinals. The problems, divisions, enormous responsibilities and heavy burdens contributed to the early death and very short pontificate of 33 days of John Paul I.

The Polish-born Karol Wojtyla, who succeeded Albino Luciani as John Paul II, shared his determination to implement the proposals of the Council and encountered some of the same problems that had confronted his predecessor. This first non-Italian pope in centuries, however, was younger, more energetic and healthier than his predecessor. He quickly let it be known that his task would be to implement the teachings and innovations of the Vatican Council and further the new mentality it envisioned in the Church and its leadership. At the same time, this Polish pope assumed a stronger stance against the Soviet Union and its domination of Eastern Europe. While at home he had been one of the chief supporters of the strikes of 1976, which culminated in the creation of the student Solidarity committee in Kraków. As archbishop of Kraków, John Paul II maintained close contact with the city's Jewish community and cordial relations with its head.

In October 1978, only days after his election, John Paul held a press conference announcing his international goals and his desire for dialogue with all nations. His claim of modern-day universality for the papacy was repeated in his talk on 8 December 1978. From the beginning of his pontificate he assumed a diplomatic and political role far greater than most of his modern predecessors and virtually abandoned the impartiality invoked by Pius VII, Benedict XV and Pius XII. In fact, following the death of Jean Villot, John Paul named Agostino Casaroli, who orchestrated the Ostpolitik, as his secretary of state and established bonds with the regimes in Eastern Europe.

John Paul II reacted swiftly and strongly to the threat of a Soviet invasion of Poland, which many believe worked to broker the eventual agreement that was reached between Solidarity and the Polish regime, avoiding Soviet intervention.[2] Others are convinced it prompted the assassination attempt on the pope's life on 13 May 1981, when Mehmet Ali Agca shot him in St Peter's Square. This did not stop or even lessen John Paul's aim and determination to liberate his homeland from Russian domination. For this and other reasons, he met the American president, Ronald Reagan. Thus the papacy played a part in 'hastening the dissolution of the Communist empire',[3] and called for European unity, with Christianity as its spiritual centre, to replace Russian control and domination.[4] Apparently, this interventionism was approved by the Curia, the Vatican establishment and the College of Cardinals, all of whom supported John Paul II's close collaborator and choice, Joseph Ratzinger, to succeed as Pope Benedict XVI. Ratzinger's unexpected resignation at the end of February 2013 was praised as courageous by some and denounced as cowardly and as a ploy by others.[5] How the retired and new pope would interact troubled some, and worried others as they awaited his successor, to be chosen by a conclave on 13 March 2013.

Benedict's unexpected resignation led to the election of the first Jesuit, Jorge Mario Bergoglio as Pope Francis – the third non-Italian in a row to preside over the world's 1.2 billion Catholics.[6] Some believe this represents an attempt by the Church to transcend the home continent and make it universal and transnational, in fact as well as theory. The pontificate of Francis faced a host of problems, including the persistent sex abuse scandal among the clergy; a Curia or Church bureaucracy in Rome bent on preserving its privileged position; a fiscal crisis; an increasingly divided flock, including the division between those who sought a liberalization of the Church and those who favoured a restoration; the division developing between the Church in the European and North American secular world and the growing and more traditional Church in the developing world. Bergoglio as priest, bishop, cardinal and now pope had long sympathized with the plight of the poor – hence his selection of the name Francis (another first) in honour of Francis of Assisi (*d.* 1226).

A number of serious problems and difficulties, however, awaited the 76-year-old pope, who had lost a lung and whose health was far from perfect. On the other hand, it must be recalled that the papacy and the Church have faced serious problems in the past and have successfully confronted a number of challenges in the modern age, including the threats posed by Napoleon, Mussolini, Hitler and Stalin. First Napoleon and later Stalin were initially dismissive. They later learned that their influence flowed from the support of the broader society rather than the military. Having only an honour guard and viewed as moribund by some, with the support of the faithful the papacy managed to overcome the ideologies of fascism, Nazism and communism and has survived for some two millennia. When confronted with stagnation, individuals who favoured change came to the fore, and in the centuries following the American and French revolutions the popes have been transformed from Italian princes to universal pastors. The last three popes have been neither Roman nor Italian but Polish, German and Argentinian. Predictions of the papacy's collapse, both past and present, have proved premature.

TIMELINE

1799   Pius VI dies in exile

1799–1804   The Consulate in France

1800   Cardinal Luigi Barnabà Chiaramonte elected pope: Pius VII

1800–23: PONTIFICATE OF PIUS VII

1801   Concordat signed with France – Napoleon violates it

1808   French invade and annex most of the Papal States; drag pope
            out of Rome

1809   Pius excommunicates French who took his state; carried off by
            French

1812   French invasion of Russia ends in disaster

1814   Treaty of Chaumont pits Britain, Austria, Prussia and Russia
            against France; facing defeat, Napoleon releases and restores
            Pius VII as ruler of the Papal States

1814–15   Congress of Vienna; Consalvi, the papal secretary of state,
            secures return of most of the Papal States for papacy

1816   Pius VII and Consalvi introduce a series of reforms in their state

1816–23   Conservative faction in Rome, the *Zelanti,* criticize reformism

1820   A series of revolutions in Italy; Papal States spared

1823   Death of Pius VII and Consalvi; conservative Cardinal della
            Genga elected pope and takes name Leo XII

1823–9: PONTIFICATE OF LEO XII

1824   *Ubi primum*, Leo's first encyclical, condemns liberalism and
            religious toleration

1825–9   Leo assumes a more balanced policy in foreign affairs

1829–30: PONTIFICATE OF PIUS VIII

1830   Revolution in Italy and the Papal States crushed by Austria

1831   Powers call for reform of the Papal States; Pius favoured limited
            change, but his pontificate proved too short to implement much;
            the monk Bartolomeo Alberto Cappellari elected pope

1831–46: PONTIFICATE OF GREGORY XVI

1831–2	Gregory confronts revolution in Papal States; relies on Austrian intervention
1832	By his encyclical *Mirari vos*, Pope Gregory condemns liberalism and the *Avenir* movement; he also denounces economic liberalism
1834	Pope Gregory's *Singulari vos* condemns Lammenais
1839	Gregory XVI condemns the slave trade
1846	Giovanni Maria Cardinal Mastai-Ferretti elected pope; takes name Pius IX

1846–78: PONTIFICATE OF PIUS IX

1846–8	Reformist phase of Pius IX's pontificate
1846	Grants amnesty; wins popular support
1847	Pius IX introduces a national consultative assembly
1848	Outbreak of revolution in Italy and Papal States; Pius flees Rome
1849	Pius deposed; proclamation of Second Roman Republic
1849	Austria, France, Spain and Naples overturn Republic; restore Papal States
1850	Pius returns to Rome; Piedmont passes Siccardi laws which restricts the Church in Piedmont
1850–70	Pius IX launches the counter-Risorgimento
1853	Re-establishment of Catholic hierarchy in the Netherlands
1854	Proclamation of dogma of the Immaculate Conception of the Virgin Mary
1855	Pius concludes concordat with Austria; Cavour joins Britain and France in Crimean War; Cavour sends the Contessa di Castiglione to Paris to seduce Napoleon III and make him support Italian unification
1858	Cavour and Napoleon III meet at Plombières to plot war against Austria and to liberate northern Italy
1859	In Franco-Austrian War, Cavour supports revolt in Papal States as national liberation

1860	Piedmontese forces seize most of the Papal States; Garibaldi overturns the Kingdom of Naples
1860	Pius IX excommunicates those who 'stole' his state
1861	Proclamation of Kingdom of Italy – French troops protect pope's position in Rome – but Cavour insists that eventually it will be the capital of the new Italian kingdom
1864	September Convention provides for French to leave Rome; Italians promise not to take Rome by force
1864	Pius IX's encyclical *Quata cura* and attached Syllabus of Errors attacks indifferentism
1869–70	First Vatican Council
1870	Council proclaims dogma of Papal Infallibility; Italian offers Law of Papal Guarantees, Pius rejects it – proclaims himself 'a prisoner in the Vatican'
1871	German empire proclaimed
1872–7	Bismarck and German liberals wage *Kulturkampf* against Church

1878–1903: PONTIFICATE OF LEO XIII

1891	Leo's *Rerum Novarum* on the condition of workers
1898	Opening of Boer War
1899	Leo condemns Americanism, which supposedly wanted to remake the Church in an American image
1901	Leo's *Graves de communi re* on Christian Democracy; Queen Victoria dies
1902	Lenin publishes *What Is To Be Done?*

1903–14: PONTIFICATE OF PIUS X

1903–14	Pius X and political Catholics work closely with Giovanni Giolitti's liberalism
1904	Russo-Japanese War begins; Britain and France conclude Entente Cordiale
1907	Decree *Lamentabili* condemns modernism, as does the encyclical *Pascendi* issued in the same year

| 1907–13 | Pope improves Vatican's relationship with Italy |

1913   Gentiloni pact

1913–14   Pope fears outbreak of catastrophic war

1914–22: PONTIFICATE OF BENEDICT XV

1914   Outbreak of First World War

1915   Treaty of London promises Italians that the papacy will not be invited to Peace Conference; Italy signs Treaty of London; enters war on side of Allies

1917   Benedict's Peace Proposal ignored by the powers

1918   President Wilson's Fourteen Points form the basis of the armistice but are violated

1919–20   Peace of Versailles and other treaties at end of First World War create more problems than they resolve

1922–39: PONTIFICATE OF PIUS XI

1922   Mussolini achieves power in Italy; Achille Ratti elected pope and takes name Pius XI

1929   Pius signs Lateran Accords with fascist Italy: ends Roman Question and recognizes Vatican as sovereign state

1929   Pius issues encyclical *Non abbiamo bisogno* critical of fascist abuses and totalitarian ambitions

1930   Pope fires Cardinal Gasparri, and makes Eugenio Pacelli his new secretary of state

1930–39   Worldwide economic depression

1933   Hitler comes to power in Germany; Vatican concludes concordat with Nazi Germany; Pius XI critical of Nazism's anti-Semitism

1935   Nuremburg racial laws

1936   Axis, formation of Rome–Berlin

1937   Pius XI issues *Mit brennender sorge* critical of Nazi abuse

1938   Mussolini adopts the Nazi racial policies; Pius XI commissions John LaFarge, SJ to draft an encyclical condemning racism; head of Jesuits seeks to moderate *Humni generis unitas*

1939   Death of Pius XI

1939–58: PONTIFICATE OF PIUS XII

1939   Outbreak of Second World War; Vatican proclaims impartiality

1940   Vatican fails to keep Italy out of war; German foreign minister
          visits pope

1941   Japan attacks Pear Harbor; u.s. declares war on Japan

1942   Wannasee Conference plans extermination of the Jews

1943   Pius XII opposes the policy of unconditional surrender adopted
          at Casablanca Conference; Allies take control of Sicily; Italy
          surrenders; Nazis push into Italy

1944   Rome liberated

1945   Germany surrenders

1950   President Truman approves development of H-Bomb

1950–55   Pius opposes Soviet domination of Eastern Europe; initiates
          Cold War

1958–63: PONTIFICATE OF JOHN XXIII

1958   John announces intention of modernizing and opening the
          Church

1958–9   Develops a threefold programme: 1) Establish diocesan synod
          for Rome; 2) call a council for the universal Church; 3) revise
          canon law

1959   Convokes Second Vatican Council

1962   First session of Council

1963   John XXIII dies; Giovanni Montini elected pope

1963–78: PONTIFICATE OF PAUL VI

1963–5   Presides over Second Vatican Council

1963   Second session of Council

1964   Third session of Council

1965   Fourth session of Council

1965–78   Paul VI attempts to implement Council's decisions

1978: PONTIFICATE OF JOHN PAUL I

1978   Pope for only one month

1978–2005: PONTIFICATE OF JOHN PAUL II

1980s–90s   Helps bring about collapse of communism

1990s–2005   Works closely with Joseph Ratzinger; favours him to succeed
             as pope

2005–13: PONTIFICATE OF BENEDICT XVI

2005   Ratzinger elected pope

2005–10   Attempts to steer middle course between reform and restoration

2013   Surprise resignation of Benedict

2013–: PONTIFICATE OF FRANCIS

2013   First Jesuit pope, first pope from the Americas, third non-Italian
             pope in a row (Polish, German, Argentinian)

REFERENCES

Introduction: Harmony and Hostility between the Papacy and the Powers

1 The apparent reason for the voyage was the papal consecration of the church of the Sagrada Familia in Barcelona, but the pope also hoped to curtail secularization and anti-clericalism in a state where Catholicism had once prevailed.

2 'Meeting of His Holiness Benedict XVI with Journalists during the Flight to Spain' (Papal Flight, 6 November 2010), in Supreme Pontifs: Benedict XVI: Speeches, at www.vatican.va.

3 With the election of Jorge Mario Bergoglio as Pope Francis, there have been 266 popes in the history of the Catholic Church.

4 'Papacy', in *New Catholic Encyclopedia*, 2nd edn (Farmington Hills, MI, 2003), vol. x, pp. 829, 854.

5 The books I have published on the modern papacy include: *Pope Pius IX: Crusader in a Secular Age* (1979), *Cardinal Giacomo Antonelli and Papal Politics in European Affairs* (1990), *The Modern Papacy since 1789* (1998), *The Papacy Confronts the Modern World* (2003), *The Papacy, the Jews and the Holocaust* (2006), *Politics and the Papacy in the Modern World* (2008), *The Policies and Politics of Pope Pius XII* (2011) and *The Life and Pontificate of Pope Pius XXIIII: Between History and Controversy* (2013).

6 John B. Wolf, *Early Modern Europe, 1500–1789* (London, 1972), pp. 1, 11.

7 The seventeen popes of the modern and contemporary age are: Pius VI (1775–99), Pius VII (1800–23), Leo XII (1823–9), Pius VIII (1829–30), Gregory XVI (1831–46), Blessed Pius IX (1846–78), Leo XIII (1878–1903), St Pius X (1903–14), Benedict XV (1914–22), Pius XI (1922–39), Pius XII (1939–58), Blessed John XXIII (1958–63), Paul VI (1963–78), John Paul I (1978), John Paul II (1978–2005), Benedict XVI (2005–13) and Francis (2013–).

8 Cindy Wooden, 'Fourth Century Emperor's Ruling on Religious Liberty Still Relevant Today', *The Tablet* [Brooklyn] (28 April 2012), p. 24.

9 The primacy of the papacy was perhaps most clearly expressed in *Unam*

sanctam, the bull of Pope Boniface VIII (1294–1303) promulgated in
1302. It declared that submission to the pope was essential for salvation
and worked to increased the division between critics and champions of
the papacy.

10   Friedrich Heyer, *The Catholic Church from 1648 to 1870*, trans. W. D. Shaw
      (London, 1969), pp. 13–14.

11   M. Vernon, *Italy from 1494 to 1790* (Cambridge, 1909), pp. 145–6.

12   Richard J. Kehoe, 'Gallicanism', in *Encyclopedia of the Vatican and Papacy*,
      ed. Frank J. Coppa (Westport, CT, 1999), pp. 170–71.

13   Ibid.

14   See Gemma Simmonds, 'Jansenism Versus Papal Absolutism', in *The
      Papacy since 1500: From Italian Prince to Universal Pastor*, ed. James
      Corkery and Thomas Worcester (Cambridge, 2010), pp. 90–106.

15   Peter Hanns Reill and Ellen Judy Wilson, *Encyclopedia of the Enlightenment*
      (New York, 1996), p. 220.

16   Heyer, *The Catholic Church from 1648 to 1870*, p. 45.

17   Sister Mary O' Callaghan, 'Febronianism', in *New Catholic Encyclopedia*,
      2nd edn, vol. v, pp. 657–9.

18   More limited regulations are usually termed agreements, accords, protocols
      or *modus vivendi*.

19   The Church was constrained to compromise in the Concordat of London
      of 1107 and the German Concordat of Worms of 1122, which followed.
      In both, the papacy was permitted to invest episcopal candidates with the
      symbols of spiritual office, but the rulers insisted on their right to bestow
      those of the bishop's temporal power. Two French concordats, that of
      1417 followed by that of 1516, sought to impose Gallican principles and
      restrictions upon the papacy. The agreement of 1516 between Pope Leo x
      (1513–21) and Francis I of France made the French king virtual head of
      the French Church, placing both the nominations for sees and the granting
      of benefices in his hands. The Pragmatic Sanction of Bourges of 1438,
      agreed upon by the papacy and the French monarchy, rendered the
      papacy subject to the rulings of a general council. The councils likewise
      at first failed to fulfil papal expectations. While the Council of Constance,
      which met from 1414 to 1418, resolved one problem by ending the
      conflict between contending candidates for the papal throne, it created
      another for the Holy See. Since the council had decided and determined
      who should be pope and who should not, it was perceived as being above
      the popes. Not surprisingly, it made a number of demands upon those
      who donned the tiara. Its canon *Sacrosanta* of 1415 rendered the pope
      subject to the council in matters of faith and reform of the Church, while
      its decree *Frequens* of 1417 established and imposed a schedule of council
      meetings upon the papacy – which Rome very much resented and from
      the first sought to evade. Future popes took exception to the impositions

of the councils and the constraints of the concordats, with some branding them a cure worse than the disease!

20 Frank J. Coppa, *The Papacy, the Jews and the Holocaust* (Washington, DC, 2006), pp. 8–13.

21 Heyer, *The Catholic Church from 1648 to 1870*, p. 29.

22 R. J. White, *Europe in the Eighteenth Century* (New York, 1965), p. 212.

23 Heyer, *The Catholic Church from 1648 to 1870*, p. 18.

24 Giuseppe Hergenröther, *Storia universale della Chiesa* (Florence, 1911), vol. VII, p. 210.

25 Ibid., vol. VII, pp. 196–7.

26 'Portugal to Suppress Two Religious Holidays', *The Tablet* [Brooklyn] (5 May 2012), p. 6.

27 Hergenröther, *Storia universale della Chiesa*, vol. VII, p. 218.

28 Solomon F. Bloom, *Europe and America* (New York, 1961), p. 48.

29 Leslie Lipson, 'European Responses to the American Revolution', *Annals of the American Academy of Political and Social Science*, 428 (1976), pp. 22–25.

30 Luigi Castiglioni, *Viaggio: Travels in the United States of North America, 1785–1787*, trans. Antonio Pace (Syracuse, NY, 1983), p. 3.

31 Frank J. Coppa, 'American Constitutionalism and the Separation of Church and State in Italy', in *The American Constitution as a Symbol and Reality for Italy*, ed. Emiliana P. Noether (Lewiston, NY, 1989), p. 140.

32 Martina Giacomo, *La Chiesa nell'età dell'assolutismo* (Brescia, 1970), pp. 43–7.

33 J. Derek Holmes, *The Triumph of the Holy See: A Short History of the Papacy in the Nineteenth Century* (London, 1978), p. 16.

34 Charles Burns, former prefect of the ASV, 'Secret Vatican Archives', in *Encyclopedia of the Vatican and Papacy*, pp. 361–3; 'The Not-So Secret-Archives', *The Tablet* [Brooklyn] (10 March 2012), p. 28.

35 Prior to the election of John Paul II in 1978, the last non-Italian pope was Hadrian VI of Utrecht (1522–3).

I: Revolution Turns the Papal World Upside Down

1 Lillian Browne Olf, *Their Name is Pius: Portraits of Five Great Modern Popes* (Milwaukee, WI, 1941).

2 M. E. Barlen, *The Foundations of Modern Europe, 1789–1871* (New York, 1968), pp. 57–60.

3 Olf, *Their Name is Pius*, p. 22.

4 Frank J. Coppa, *Politics and the Papacy in the Modern World* (Westport, CT, 2008), p. 13.

5 E.E.Y. Hales, *Revolution and Papacy, 1769–1846* (Notre Dame, IN, 1966), p. 70.

6 Leo A. Loubère, *Nineteenth Century Europe: The Revolution of Life* (Saddle River, NJ, 1994), p. 21.

7 Giuseppe Hergenröther, *Storia universale della Chiesa*, ed. G. P. Kirsch, trans. P. Enrico Rosa (Florence, 1911), vol. VII, p. 328.

8 Prince Richard Metternich-Winneburg, ed., *Memoirs of Prince Metternich, 1773–1815*, trans. Mrs A. Napier (New York, 1970), vol. I, p. 116.

9 Frank J. Coppa, *The Modern Papacy since 1789* (London and New York, 1998), pp. 20–21.

10 Barlen, *The Foundations of Modern Europe*, p. 65.

11 J. Derek Holmes, *The Triumph of the Holy See: A Short History of the Papacy in the Nineteenth Century* (London, 1978), p. 28.

12 Hergenröther, *Storia universale della Chiesa*, vol. VII, p. 333.

13 Olf, *Their Name is Pius*, p. 27.

14 Alec R. Vidler, *The Church in an Age of Revolution* (London, 1961), pp. 14–17.

15 Anne Freemantle, ed., *The Papal Encyclicals in their Historical Context* (New York, 1956), p. 117; *The Papal Encyclicals*, ed. Claudia Carlen (Ann Arbor, MI, 1981), vol. I, pp. 177–84.

16 Frank J. Coppa, *The Papacy Confronts the Modern World* (Malabar, FL, 2003), pp. 127–8.

17 Hergenröther, *Storia universale della Chiesa*, vol. VII, p. 338.

18 Alphonse Aulard, ed., *Recueil des actes du Comité de salut public* (Paris, 1889), vol. II, pp. 468–9.

19 'Ignotae Nemini', in *Tutte le encicliche dei sommi Pontefici*, ed. E. Momigliano (Milan, 1959), p. 128.

20 William L. Langer, ed., *An Encyclopedia of World History* (Boston, MA, 1948), p. 582.

21 It called for the dispatch of a nuncio to Paris to apologize for Bassville's murder, permission to place Republican symbols on the French consulate in the Holy City, the banishment of French emigrés, both lay and clerical, immediate punishment for the instigators of the riots of 12–13 January, indemnity for the victims of these riots, and finally the restoration of the French Art Academy by the Roman government.

22 Ludwig von Pastor, *The History of the Popes* (St Louis, 1953), vol. XL, pp. 295–6.

23 Olf, *Their Name is Pius*, p. 36.

24 Ibid., p. 37.

25 Holmes, *The Triumph of the Holy See*, pp. 24, 31; Owen Chadwick, *The Popes and European Revolution* (Oxford and New York, 1981), pp. 448, 462; Fremantle, ed., *The Papal Encyclicals in their Historical Context*, pp. 118–19.

26 Maurice Andrieux, *Rome* (New York, 1968), pp. 385–6; Olf, *Their Name is Pius*, pp. 37–41.

27 Olf, *Their Name is Pius*, p. 41.
28 Ibid., p. 47.

II: The Papacy between Transformation and Restoration

1 Alec R. Vidler, *The Church in an Age of Revolution* (London, 1961), p. 19.
2 The executives were reduced from five to three: Bonaparte, Sieyes and
   Ducos, who, in turn, introduced a tribunate to discuss and ponder
   legislation, a legislative corps to pass it and a senate to execute the
   measures approved.
3 Prince Richard Metternich-Winneburg, ed., *Memoirs of Prince Metternich,
   1773–1815*, trans. Mrs A. Napier (New York, 1970), vol. I, p. 78.
4 Jean Leflon, *Pie VII: Des abbayes benedictines à la Papaute* (Paris, 1958),
   vol. I, pp. 570–74.
5 J. Derek Holmes, *The Triumph of the Holy See: A Short History of the
   Papacy in the Nineteenth Century* (London, 1978), p. 41; Owen Chadwick,
   The Popes and European Revolution (Oxford, 1981), p. 455; E.E.Y. Hales,
   The Catholic Church in the Modern World (Garden City, NY, 1958), p. 54;
   Margaret M. O'Dwyer, *The Papacy in the Age of Napoleon and the
   Restoration: Pius VII, 1800–1823* (Lanham, MD, 1985), pp. 24–5;
   Vittorio E. Giuntella, 'Cristianesimo e democrazia in Italia al tramonto
   del Settecento', *Rassegna storica del Risorgimento*, XLII (1955), p. 291.
6 Robert B. Holtman, *The Napoleonic Revolution* (New York, 1967), p. 121.
7 *Documents diplomatique français* (Paris, 1931–9), vol. II, p. 156.
8 'Dius Satis', in *The Papal Encyclicals*, ed. Claudia Carlen (Ann Arbor, MI,
   1981), vol. I, pp. 189–93; Erasmo Pistolesi, *Vita del Somo Pontefice Pio VII*
   (Rome, 1824), vol. I, pp. 76–80; Giuseppe Hergenröther, *Storia universale
   della Chiesa*, ed. G. P. Kirsch, trans. P. Enrico Rosa (Florence, 1911), p. 362.
9 *Documents sur la negociation du Concordat et sur les autres rapports de la
   France avec le Saint-Siège en 1800 et 1801*, ed. A. Boulay de la Meurthe,
   6 vols (Paris, 1891–1905), vol. I, pp. 21–6, 273.
10 The developments leading to the conclusion of the concordat of July 1801
   and the final text can be found in ibid., and in the two volumes edited by
   J. Crétineau-Joly, *Mémoires du Cardinal Consalvi, secrétaire d'état du Pape
   Pie II, avec un introduction et des notes* (Paris, 1866).
11 William Roberts, 'Napoleon, the Concordat of 1801 and its Consequences',
   in *Controversial Concordats: The Vatican's Relations with Napoleon,
   Mussolini and Hitler*, ed. Frank J. Coppa (Washington, DC, 1999), pp. 44–5.
12 Maurice Andrieux, *Rome*, trans. L. Markmann (New York, 1968), p. 388.
13 Vidler, *The Church in an Age of Revolution*, pp. 19–20.
14 *Papal Pronouncements: A Guide, 1740–1798*, ed. Claudia Carlen
   (Ann Arbor, MI, 1900), vol. I, p. 19.
15 For a positive evaluation of the concordat from the papacy's perspective,

see P. Ferraris, 'Il Concordato Francese e il Card. Fesch', *La Civiltà Cattolica*, LXXXVII (1936), p. 497, while a less positive evaluation is provided in Luigi Sturzo, *Church and State* (Notre Dame, IN, 1962), vol. II, pp. 378–81.

16 Lillian Browne Olf, *Their Name is Pius: Portraits of Five Great Modern Popes* (Milwaukee, 1941), p. 77.

17 Frank J. Coppa, *The Papacy Confronts the Modern World* (Malabar, FL, 2003), p. 129.

18 'Convention between the French Government and Pius VII', in *The Encyclopedia of Religion and Ethics*, ed. J. Hastings (New York, 1911), vol. III, pp. 191–3.

19 Olf, *Their Name is Pius*, p. 79.

20 Hergenröther, *Storia universale della Chiesa*, p. 375; Cardinal Jean Caprara, *Concordat, et recueil des bulles et bres de N.S.P., le Pape Pie VII, sur les affaires actuelles de l'Eglise de France* (Liège, 1802), pp. 23–31.

21 Roberts, 'Napoleon, the Concordat of 1801 and its Consequences', p. 46.

22 Caprara, *Concordat*, pp. 2–15.

23 Olf, *Their Name is Pius*, p. 81.

24 Credineau-Joly, ed., *Mémoires du Cardinal Consalvi*, vol. II, p. 425.

25 Ibid., p. 89.

26 Project for a political treaty between the Holy See and the Emperor Napoleon: Archivio Segreto del Vaticano, Archivio Particolare Pio IX, oggetti vari, *n.* 909, *fascioli* 4–5.

27 Ibid.

28 Olf, *Their Name is Pius*, pp. 94–5.

29 Napoleon's decree of 2 April 1808: Archivio Segreto del Vaticano, Archivio Particolare Pio IX, oggetti vari, *n.* 909, *fascicolo* 1.

30 *Cum, memoranda illa die* was directed against the counsellors and executors of the spoliation of the dominion of St Peter, and was pasted on the walls of the basilicas in Rome.

31 Andrieux, *Rome*, p. 390.

32 In attendance were 95 French bishops, about half that number of Italians, as well as a sprinking of Germans.

33 Hergenröther, *Storia universale della Chiesa*, pp. 390–98; O'Dwyer, *The Papacy in the Age of Napoleon and the Restoration*, pp. 108–11; André Latreille, *L'Eglise catholique et la Revolution française* (Paris, 1950), vol. II, pp. 202–25.

34 John Tracy Ellis, *Cardinal Consalvi and Anglo-Papal Relations, 1814–1824* (Washington, DC, 1942), p. 18.

35 *An Encyclopedia of World History*, ed. William Langer (Boston, MA, 1940), p. 596.

36 Metternich-Winneburg, ed., *Memoirs of Prince Metternich*, vol. I, p. 141.

37 H. Daniel-Rops, *The Church in an Age of Revolution, 1789–1870* (London and New York, 1965), vol. I, p. 154.

38 Bartolomeo Pacca, *Historical Memoir*, trans. George Head (London, 1850), vol. II, pp. 233–83.

39 Metternich-Winneburg, ed., *Memoirs of Prince Metternich*, vol. I, p. 201; Hergenröther, *Storia universale della Chiesa*, pp. 401–2.

40 M. E. Barlen, *The Foundations of Modern Europe, 1789–1871* (New York, 1968), p. 151.

41 Angelo Filipuzzi, *Pio IX e la politica austriaca in Italia dal 1815 al 1848* (Florence, 1958), p. 10.

42 Luigi Rodelli, *La Repubblica Romana del 1849* (Pisa, 1955), p. 31.

43 John H. Brady, *Rome and the Neapolitan Revolution of 1820–1821* (New York, 1976), p. 15.

III: The Papacy in an Age of Liberalism and Nationalism, 1820–1846

1 *The Papal Encyclicals*, ed. Claudia Carlen (Ann Arbor, MI, 1981), vol. I, p. 236.

2 M. E. Barlen, *The Foundations of Modern Europe, 1789–1871* (New York, 1968), p. 169.

3 Alan J. Reinerman, 'Pius VII (1800–1823)', in *Great Popes Through History*, ed. Frank Coppa (Westport, CT, 2002), vol. II, p. 449.

4 Sheridan Gilley, 'The Papacy', in *The Cambridge History of World Christianities, 1815–1914*, ed. Sheridan Gilley and Brian Stanley (Cambridge, 2006), p. 14.

5 Maurice Andrieux, *Rome*, trans. L. Markmann (New York, 1968), p. 417.

6 Giuseppe Hergenröther, *Storia universale della Chiesa*, ed. G. P. Kirsch, trans. P. Enrico Rosa (Florence, 1911), vol. VII, p. 433.

7 John Julius Norwich, *Absolute Monarchs: A History of the Papacy* (New York, 2012), p. 389.

8 Andrieux, *Rome*, p. 418.

9 Ibid., p. 420.

10 Giovanni Maria Mastai's funeral oration for Leo XII, 21 February 1829: Archivio Segreto del Vatican, Fondo Particolare Pio IX, *cassetta IX, fascicolo 46*.

11 Frank J. Coppa, 'Italy: The Church and the Risorgimento', in *The Cambridge History of World Christianities*, p. 235.

12 Frank J. Coppa, *The Modern Papacy since 1789* (London, 1998), p. 65.

13 Fiorella Bartocinni, *Roma nell'Ottocento* (Bologna, 1985), p. 26.

14 Antonio Monti, *Pio IX nel Risorgimento Italiano con documenti inediti* (Bari, 1928), p. 38.

15 Pierre Fernessole, *Pie IX, pape* (Paris, 1960), vol. I, pp. 66–8; Monti, *Pio IX nel Risorgimento*, pp. 40–41.

16 Giovanni Maiolo, ed., *Pio IX da vescovo a pontefice: Lettere al card, Luigi*

Amat, agosto 1839–luglio 1848 (Modena, 1943), pp. 7–8.

17 Alexandre de Saint-Albin, *Pie ix* (Paris, 1860), p. 35.

18 Carlo Ghisalberti, 'Il Consiglio di Stato di Pio ix: nota storia giuridica', *Studi romani*, ii (1954), p. 56; Filipuzzi, *Pio ix*, p. 109; Edgar Quinet, *La Question romaine devant l'histoire, 1840–1867* (Paris, 1868), p. 16.

19 *Catechismo sulle rivoluzioni* (1832): Archivio Segreto del Vaticano, Fondo Particolare Pio ix, *cassetta* 5, *busta* 4.

20 *Cum Primum* (To the bishops of Poland: on civil obedience), 9 June 1832, in *Papal Pronouncements: A Guide, 1740–1798*, ed. Claudia Carlen (Ann Arbor, mi, 1900), vol. i, p. 25.

21 *Magnum Bullarium Romanum Continuatio, Gregory xvi*, vol. xix, pp. 117–19.

22 M. Patricia Dougherty, 'The Rise and Fall of *L'Ami de la réligion*: History, Purpose and Readership of a French Catholic Newspaper', *Catholic Historical Review*, lxxxvii/2 (January 1991), p. 31.

23 Eucardio Momigliano, ed., *Tutte le encicliche dei sommi pontefici* (Milan, 1959), p. 185.

24 Francesco Andreu, *Un aspetto inedito nel rapporto Ventura-Lamennais*, ed. Eugenio Guccione (Florence, 1991), vol. ii, pp. 635–6.

25 Ellen Evans, 'Joseph Gorres and Felicité de Lamennais: Early Catholic Politics', in *Consortium on Revolutionary Europe, 1750–1850: Proceedings, 1991*, ed. Karl A. Roider, Jr, and John C. Horgan (Tallahassee, fl, 1992), p. 197.

26 Carlen, ed., *Papal Pronouncements*, vol. i, pp. 25–6.

27 Hergenröther, *Storia universale della Chiesa*, pp. 450–57.

28 See *In supremo apostolatus*, 3 December 1839, in *Papal Pronouncements*, ed. Carlen, vol. i, p. 27.

29 See *Afflictas in Tunquino*, ibid., vol. i, p. 27.

30 Carlen, ed., *The Papal Encyclicals*, vol. i, p. 260.

31 Giacomo Antonelli to Filippo Antonelli, 7 September 1837: Archivio di Stato di Roma, Fondo Famiglia Antonelli, *busta* 1, *fascicolo* 125.

32 M. A. Klinkowstroem, ed., *Mémoires, documents et écrits divers laissés par le Prince de Metternich*, 8 vols (Paris, 1880–84), vol. vii, p. 246; *British and Foreign State Papers*, vol. xxxvi (1847–8), p. 1195.

IV: Pio Nono's Transition from Reform to Reaction

1 Pasquale de Franciscis, ed., *Discorsi del Sommo Pontifice Pio ix proniunziato in Vaticano ai fedeli di Roma e dell'orbe della, sua prigionia fino al presente* (Rome, 1872), vol. i, pp. 283–4.

2 Angelo Filipuzzi, *Pio ix e la politica austriaca in Italia* (Florence, 1958), pp. 100–105.

3 Giovanni Maioli, ed., *Pio ix da vescovo a pontefice: Lettere al card, Luigi*

Amat, agosto 1839–luglio 1848 (Modena, 1943), pp. 44–5.

4 Ibid.

5 Giuseppe Pasolini, *Memorie, 1815–1876* (Turin, 1887), p. 57.

6 Report on Central Italy: Archivio Segreto del Vaticano, Archivio
   Particolare Pio IX, oggetti vari, *n.* 412.

7 'Breve racconto degli avvenimenti successi in Roma dall'esaltazione al
   trono del glorioso Pontefice Papa Pio Nono, fino all'epoca in cui ebbe
   luogo l'interventi armato delle quattro potenze cattoliche': Archivio
   Segreto del Vaticano, Archivio Particolare Pio IX, oggetti vari, *n.* 515.

8 Report of Monsignor Corboli-Bussi to Pope Pius IX on the first session
   of the Congregation of State, 1 July 1846: Archivio Segreto del Vaticano,
   Archivio Particolare Pio IX, Stato Pontificio, *n.* 1.

9 'Amnistia accordata dalla Santità di nostro Signore Pio IX nella sua
   esaltazione al Pontificato', 16 July 1846, *Atti del Sommo Pontefice Pio IX,
   felicemente regnante* (Rome, 1857), vol. I, pp. 4–6.

10 'Breve racconto degli avvenimenti successi in Roma': Archivio Segreto
   del Vaticano, Archivio Particolare Pio IX, oggetti vari, *n.* 515.

11 Frank J. Coppa, 'Pessimism and Traditionalism in the Personality and
   Policies of Pio Nono', *Journal of Italian History*, II (Autumn 1979), p. 212.

12 *Acta Pio IX*, vol. I (1846–54), pp. 4–24.

13 'Pensieri relativi alla Amministrazione pubblica dello Stato Pontificio',
   in Alberto Serafini, *Pio Nono: Giovanni Maria Mastai Ferretti dalla
   giovinezza alla morte nei suoi scritti e discorsi editi e inediti* (Vatican City,
   1958), vol. I, pp. 1397–406.

14 'Amnistia accordata dalla Santità di nostro Signore Pio IX nella sua
   exaltazione al Ponificato', 16 July 1846, in *Atti del Sommo Pontefice Pio IX,
   felicemente regnante: parte seconda che comprende i Motu-proprii,
   chirografi editti, notificazioni, ec. per lo stato pontificio* (Rome, 1857),
   vol. II, pp. 4–6.

15 Ibid., vol. I, p. 15.

16 Ibid., vol. I, pp. 7, 12–13.

17 *British and Foreign State Papers*, XXXVII (1848–9), p. 918.

18 Domenico Demarco, *Pio IX e la rivoluzione del 1848: saggio di storia
   economica-sociale* (Modena, 1947), p. 42.

19 Ibid., pp. 47–8, 52–4, 68.

20 Romolo Quazza, *Pio IX e Massimo d'Azeglio nelle vicende romane del 1847*
   (Modena, 1954), vol. I, p. 168; vol. II, p. 5.

21 M. A. Klinkowstroem, ed., *Mémoires, documents et écrits divers laissés
   par le Prince de Metternich*, 8 vols (Paris, 1880–84), vol. VII, pp. 298–9.

22 *British and Foreign State Papers*, XXXVI (1847–8), p. 1195.

23 Klinkowstroem, ed., *Mémoires*, vol. VII, pp. 300, 572.

24 Luigi Rodelli, *La Repubblica Romana del 1849* (Pisa, 1955), p. 41.

25 Giacomo Martina, *Pio IX, 1846–1850* (Rome, 1974), p. 21.

26 'Statuto fondamentale del governo temporale degli Stati. S. Chiesa', *Atti del Sommo Pontefice Pio IX*, vol. I, p. 229.

27 Pius IX to Cardinal Fieschi, legate for Urbino and Pesaro, 26 February 1848: Archivio Segreto del Vaticano, Archivio Particolare Pio IX, Stato Pontificio, *n.* 6.

28 Pietro Plazzini, 'Spiritualità di Pio IX: il Papa della Croce', *Pio IX*, VI (January–April 1977), p. 11.

29 Martina, *Pio IX*, p. 237.

30 Maioli, ed., *Pio IX da vescovo a pontifice*, p. 117.

31 Pius to Corboli Bussi, 27 April 1848: Archivio Segreto del Vaticano, Archivio Particolare Pio IX, Stato Pontificio.

32 Frank J. Coppa, 'Cardinal Antonelli, the Papal States and the Counter-Risorgimento', *Journal of Church and State*, XVI (Autumn 1974), pp. 461–3; *British and Foreign State Papers*, XXXVII (1848–9), p. 1065.

33 Pio Nono to Monsignor Corboli-Bussi, 28 December 1848: Archivio Segreto del Vaticano, *Archivio Particolare Pio IX, Stato Pontificio, n.* 6.

34 'Protesta fatta in Gaeta da Sua Santità Pio PP. IX contro l'atto del sedicente assemblea consituente romana in data Febbrajo corrente', *Atti del Sommo Pontefice Pio IX*, vol. I, pp. 262–3.

35 See Mastai's speeches in the cathedral of Spoleto, 1827–32: Archivio Segreto del Vaticano, *Fondo Particolare Pio IX, cassetta* IX, *busta* 1, *nn.* 38ff.

36 Antonio Rosmini, *Della missione a Roma* (Turin, 1854), pp. 143–4; Gianfranco Radice, *Pio IX e Antonio Rosmini* (Vatican City, 1974), p. 80.

37 Pius to the archbishop of Bourges, 10 June 1849: Archivio Segreto del Vaticano, Archivio Particolare Pio IX, Francia, particolari, *n.* 8.

38 John T. Graham, *Donoso Cortés: Utopian Romanticist and Political Realist* (Columbia, MO, 1974), p. 293.

39 Raffaele De Cesare, *The Last Days of Papal Rome, 1850–1870* (London, 1909), pp. 261–2.

40 Battista Mondin, *The Popes of the Modern Ages: From Pius IX to John Paul II* (Rome, 2004), p. 31.

41 *Il Risorgimeto* (30 November 1848), p. 148.

42 Frank J. Coppa, *Pius IX: Crusader in a Secular Age* (Boston, MA, 1979), p. 110.

43 Frank J. Coppa, 'The Contessa di Castiglione: The Forgotten Figure of the Risorgimento', *Italian Quarterly* (Winter–Spring 2004), pp. 47–53.

44 Nicomede Bianchi, *Storia documentato della diplomazia in Italia dall'anno 1814 all'anno 1861* (Turin, 1872), vol. VII, p. 50.

45 Frank J. Coppa, '*Realpolitik* and Conviction in the Conflict between Piedmont and the Papacy during the *Risorgimento*', *Catholic Historical Review*, LIV/4 (January 1969), p. 609.

46 Coppa, *Pope Pius IX*, pp. 147–8.

47 Paolo Dalla Torre, *L'Anno di Mentana* (Milan, 1967), pp. 38–9.
48 Ernesto Vercesi, *Pio IX* (Milan, 1930), pp. 254–5.
49 Archivio Segreto del Vaticano, Archivio Particolare Pio IX, Francia, particolari, *n.* 183.
50 Noel Blakiston, ed., *The Roman Question: Extracts from the Despatches of Odo Russell from Rome, 1858–1870* (London, 1962), p. 307.
51 Johann von Dollinger, *Letters from Rome on the Council by Quirinus* (New York, 1973), vol. II, p. 713.
52 Frank J. Coppa, *Cardinal Giacomo Antonelli and Papal Politics in European Affairs* (Albany, NY, 1990), p. 129.
53 De Cesare, *The Last Days of Papal Rome*, p. 696.
54 *Dogmatic Canons and Decrees* (New York, 1912), pp. 256–7.
55 De Franciscis, ed., *Discorsi del Sommo Pontefice Pio IX*, vol. I, pp. 283–4.

V: Leo XIII: Conciliation with Modernity, Conflict with Italy

1 *Rerum novarum*, reprinted from *Principles for Peace: Selections from Papal Documents from Leo XIII to Pius XII*, ed. Harry C. Koenig (Washington, DC, 1943), pp. 52–81.
2 Revd Bernard O'Reilly, ed., *Life of Leo XIII: From an Authentic Memoir Furnished by his Order* (New York, 1903), p. 34.
3 Frank J. Coppa, *The Papacy Confronts the Modern World* (Malabar, FL, 2003), pp. 25–6.
4 Giuseppe Hergenröther, *Storia universale della Chiesa*, ed. G. P. Kirsch, trans. P. Enrico Rosa (Florence, 1911), vol. VII, p. 619.
5 Emiliana P. Noether, 'Leo XIII, 1878–1903: The Working Man's Pope', in *The Great Popes through History*, ed. F. J. Coppa (Westport, CT, 2002), vol. II, p. 464.
6 O'Reilly, ed., *Life of Leo XIII*, p. 316.
7 Hergenröther, *Storia universale della Chiesa*, vol. VII, p. 622.
8 O'Reilly, ed., *Life of Leo XIII*, p. 323.
9 Hergenröther, *Storia universale della Chiesa*, vol. VII, p. 620.
10 Claudia Carlen, ed., *Papal Pronouncements: A Guide, 1740–1978* (Ann Arbor, MI, 1990), vol. I, p. 43.
11 Ibid.
12 Ibid.
13 Thomas Massaro, 'The Social Question in the Papacy of Leo XIII', in *The Papacy since 1500: From Italian Prince to Universal Pastor*, ed. J. Corkery and T. Worcester (Cambridge, 2010), pp. 143–5.
14 Ibid., pp. 151, 159.
15 Frank J. Coppa, *Politics and the Papacy in the Modern World* (London, 2008), pp. 65–6.
16 Allocution *Etsi res* to the College of Cardinals, 15 January 1886, ibid., p. 35.

17 Loretta Devoy, 'Americanism', in *Encyclopedia of the Vatican and Papacy*, ed. F. J. Coppa (Westport, CT, 1999), pp. 21-2.

18 At Bismarck's prodding it was approved by a vote of 224 in its favour and 107 against.

19 Harry C. Koenig, ed., *Principles for Peace: Selections from Papal Documents from Leo XIII to Pius XII* (Washington, DC, 1943), pp. 23-5, 31-2.

20 Hergenröther, *Storia universale della Chiesa*, vol. VII, p. 624.

21 Carlen, ed., *Papal Pronouncements*, vol. I, p. 49.

22 Ibid., vol. I, p. 51.

23 O'Reilly, ed., *Life of Leo XIII*, p. 310.

24 Ibid., pp. 141, 244.

VI: Pius X: Confrontation with Modernity, Conciliation with Italy

1 *Pascendi domini gregis*, in *The Papal Encyclicals*, ed. Claudia Carlen (Ann Arbor, MI, 1981), vol. III, p. 71.

2 The conclave consisted of 62 cardinals, 98 per cent of whom were from Europe and 61 per cent from Italy.

3 Igino Giordani, *Pius X: A Country Priest*, trans. Thomas J. Tobin (Milwaukee, WI, 1954), p. 68.

4 Jan Olav Smit, *St Pius X, Pope* (Boston, MA, 1965), p. 99.

5 Owen Chadwick, *A History of the Popes, 1830–1914* (Oxford, 2003), p. 340.

6 Battista Modin, *The Popes of the Modern Age: From Pius X to John Paul II* (Vatican City, 2004), p. 58.

7 Claudia Carlen, ed., *Papal Pronouncements: A Guide, 1740–1978* (Ann Arbor, MI, 1990), vol. I, p. 65.

8 Ibid.

9 Frank J. Coppa, *Politics and the Papacy in the Modern World* (Westport, CT, 2008), p. 67.

10 Motu proprio *Tra le sollecitudini*, 22 November 1903, in *Papal Pronouncements*, ed. Carlen, vol. I, p. 66.

11 Andrew M. Canepa, 'Pius X and the Jews: A Reapparaisal', *Church History*, LXI/3 (September 1992), p. 369.

12 Apart from Gregory XVI, who had a middle-class background, Pius X was the only pope since Sergius IV (1009–12) not to hail from the aristocracy.

13 Chadwick, *A History of the Popes*, p. 341.

14 Giordani, *Pius X*, pp. 3-12.

15 William Roberts, 'Pius X, 1903–14: The Pope of the Curia', in *The Great Popes through History: An Encyclopedia*, ed. Frank J. Coppa (Westport, CT, 2002), vol. II, pp. 473-4.

16 Hans Küng, *Global Responsibility: In Search of a New World Ethic* (New York, 1996), p. 54.

17 Raymond Corrigan, *The Church and the Nineteenth Century* (Milwaukee, WI, 1938), p. 5.

18 Giacomo Martina, *La Chiesa nell'età del liberalismo* (Brescia, 1978), p. 103.

19 Speech of Pius IX to former employees, 2 July 1873, in *Discorsi del Sommo Pontefice Pio IX Pronunziati in Vaticano ai fedeli di Roma e dell'orbe dal principio della sua prigionia fino al presente*, ed. Pasquale de Franciscis (Rome, 1872), vol. II, p. 366.

20 'Search for Peace Marked his Reign', *New York Times* (9 October 1958), p. 23.

21 Giordani, *Pius X*, p. 73.

22 *Iucunda sane*, 12 March 1904, in *Papal Pronouncements*, ed. Carlen, vol. I, p. 67.

23 Carlen, ed., *Papal Pronouncements*, vol. I, pp. 68–9.

24 *Lacrimabili statu* of 7 January 1912, in ibid., vol. I, p. 76.

25 Chadwick, *A History of the Popes*, p. 345.

26 Smit, *St Pius X, Pope*, p. 106.

27 Andrew M. Canepa, 'Pius X, 1903–1914', in *Encyclopedia of the Vatican and Papacy*, ed. Frank J. Coppa (Westport, CT, 1999), pp. 336–8.

28 Modin, *The Popes of the Modern Age*, p. 59.

29 Carlen, ed., *Papal Pronouncements*, vol. I, p. 71.

30 Ibid., vol. I, p. 70.

31 Ibid., vol. I, p. 71.

32 Giuseppe Hergenröther, *Storia universale della Chiesa*, ed. G. P. Kirsch, trans. P. Enrico Rosa (Florence, 1911), p. 767; Giordani, *Pius X*, p. 154.

33 Carlen, ed., *Papal Pronouncements*, vol. I, p. 72.

34 Reprinted from *The Tablet* [London] (28 September 1907).

35 Chadwick, *A History of the Popes*, p. 357.

36 Carlen, ed., *Papal Pronouncements*, vol. I, p. 73.

37 Frank J. Coppa, *The Modern Papacy since 1789* (London, 1998), p. 146.

38 Frank J. Coppa, 'Giolitti and the Gentiloni Pact: Between Myth and Reality', *Catholic Historical Review*, LIII/2 (July 1967), p. 224.

39 Frank J. Coppa, *Planning, Protectionism and Politics in Liberal Italy: Economics and Politics in the Giolittian Era* (Washington, DC, 1971), p. 120.

40 Giovani Spadolini, *Giolitti e i Cattolici, 1901–1914* (Florence, 1960), p. 85.

41 Smit, *St Pius X, Pope*, p. 154.

VII: Benedict XV: The First World War, the League and the Missions

1 *Peace Action of Pope Benedict XV: A Summary by the History Committee of Friedrich Ritter von Lama's 'Die Friedensvermittlung papst Benedict XV'* (Washington, DC, n.d.), p. 10.

2 *Ad beatissimi* (1 November 1914), in *Acta Apostolicae Sedis* (25 November 1914), VI/19, pp. 585–99.

3 Walter H. Peters, *The Life of Benedict xv* (Milwaukee, WI, 1959), p. 75.
4 William A. Renzi, 'The Entente and the Vatican during the Period of Italian Neutrality', *Historical Journal*, XIII (1970), p. 491.
5 *Ubi primum* (8 September 1914), in *Papal Pronouncements: A Guide, 1740–1978*, ed. Claudia Carlen (Ann Arbor, MI, 1990), vol. I, p. 79.
6 Peters, *The Life of Benedict xv*, p. 96.
7 *Papal Pronouncements*, ed. Carlen, vol. I, p. 68.
8 *Qui siam a Sancto* (21 January 1907) and *In principibus catholicorum* (3 April 1908), in ibid., vol. I, pp. 72–3.
9 *Lacrimabili statu* (7 June 1912), in ibid., vol. I, p. 76.
10 Ibid., vol. I, p. 83.
11 *Ubi primum*, in ibid., vol. II, p. 79.
12 *Ad beatissimi*, in *Acta Apostolicae Sedis*, vol. VI, pp. 585–99
13 Peters, *The Life of Benedict xv*, p. 123.
14 Harry C. Koenig, ed., *Principles for Peace: Selections from Papal Documents from Leo XIII to Pius XII* (Washington, DC, 1943), p. 181.
15 'Pope Asks Wilson To Send Peace Appeals to Warring Parties', *New York Times* (3 September 1915).
16 'E pur troppo vero', in *Principles for Peace*, ed. Koenig, pp. 193–7.
17 Koenig, ed., *Principles for Peace*, p. 199.
18 'The Pope and the War', *The Times* [London] (6 September 1914).
19 'Pope Eager To Convince the World at Large of his "Absolute Impartiality" in the War', *New York Times* (24 July 1916).
20 Peters, *The Life of Benedict xv*, p. 113.
21 Ibid.
22 'Pope Hails Wilson's Efforts for Peace', *New York Times* (1 January 1917).
23 'Pope Lauds Wilson's Speech', *New York Times* (26 January 1917).
24 Ibid.
25 'To the Bellgerent and their Leaders' (1 August 1917), in *Principles for Peace*, ed. Koenig, pp. 229–32.
26 *Evening Post* (14 August 1917).
27 'Pope Endorses Wilson's Speech', *New York Times* (27 August 1917).
28 'The Fourteen Points' (8 January 1918), in *Documents in the Political History of the European Continent, 1815–1939*, ed. G. A. Kertesz (Oxford, 1968), pp. 347–9.
29 *New York Times* (17 January 1918).
30 On these matters, see his allocution of 16 December 1920 to the College of Cardinals and his letter of 24 January 1921 to Cardinal Gasparri on conditions in Austria, both in *Principles for Peace*, ed. Koenig, pp. 301–2, 304–6.
31 Pacelli to Gasparri, 18 April 1920: Archivio Segreto del Vaticano, *Archivio della Sacra Cogregazione per gli Affari Ecclesiastici Straordinari, Germania*, 891.

32 *La Civiltà Cattolica* (30 August 1919).
33 Koenig, ed., *Principles for Peace*, pp. 178–9, 220–21.
34 Ibid., p. 232.
35 Ibid., pp. 238–9.
36 *Pacem, Dei munus pulcherrimum* (23 May 1920), in *The Papal Encyclicals*, ed. Claudia Carlen (Ann Arbor, MI, 1981), vol. III, p. 174.
37 Anne O'Hare McCormick, *Vatican Journal, 1921–1954* (New York, 1957), pp. 20–21.
38 Telegram of Benedict XV to the League of Nations (September 1921), in *Principles for Peace*, ed. Koenig, p. 314.
39 Ibid., p. 176.

VIII: The Crusade of Pius XI against Anti-Semitism

1   The two Jesuits who worked with LaFarge were the Frenchman Gustave Desbuquois and the German Gustav Gundlach.
2   George Passelecq and Bernar Suchecky, *The Hidden Encyclical of Pius XI*, trans. Steven Rendall (New York, 1997), p. 246.
3   *Principles for Peace: Selections from Papal Documents from Leo XIII to Pius XII*, ed. Harry C. Koenig (Washington, DC, 1943), pp. 359–60.
4   Joseph A. Biesinger, 'The Reich Concordat of 1933: The Church Struggle against Nazi Germany', in *Controversial Concordats: The Vatican's Relations with Napoleon, Mussolini and Hitler*, ed. Frank J. Coppa (Washington, DC, 1999), pp. 120–81.
5   Frank J. Coppa, 'Mussolini and the Concordat of 1929', in *Controversial Concordats*, pp. 81–119.
6   John Cornwell, *Hitler's Pope: The Secret History of Pius XII* (New York, 1999), p. 99.
7   *Records and Documents of the Holy See Relating to the Second World War: The Holy See and the War in Europe, March 1939–August 1940* (Washington, DC, 1968), vol. I, pp. 5–6.
8   Cardinal Domenico Tardini, *Memories of Pio XII*, trans. Rosemary Goldie (Westminster, MD, 1961), p. 109.
9   Frank J. Coppa, 'The Vatican and the Dictators between Diplomacy and Morality', in *Catholics, the State and the European Radical Right, 1919–1945*, ed. Richard J. Wolff and Jörg K. Hoensch (New York, 1987), p. 199.
10 Anthony Rhodes, *The Vatican in the Age of Dictators, 1922–1945* (New York, 1973), p. 29; E.E.Y. Hales, *The Catholic Church in the Modern World* (Garden City, NY, 1958), p. 266; John P. McKnight, *The Papacy: A New Appraisal* (London, 1953), p. 141.
11 For an examination of fascist anti-Semitism, see Renzo de Felice, *Storia degli ebre sotto il fascismo* (Turin, 1961), and Luigi Preti, *Impero fascista, africani ed ebrei* (Milan, 1968).

12 Meir Michaelis, *Mussolini and the Jews: German–Italian Relations and the Jewish Question in Italy, 1922–1945* (Oxford, 1978), p. 240.

13 Susan Zuccotti, *The Italians and the Holocaust: Persecution, Rescue and Survival* (New York, 1987), p. 61.

14 Antonio Pellicani, *Il papa di tutti: La Chiesa Cattolica, il fascismo e il razzismo, 1929–1945* (Milan, 1964), p. 103.

15 Renato Moro, *La Chiesa e lo sterminio degli ebrei* (Bologna, 2002), p. 60.

16 Richard A. Webster, *The Cross and the Fasces* (Stanford, CA, 1960), p. 96.

17 Consistorial Allocution of 20 December 1926, in *Discorsi di Pio XI*, ed. Domenico Bertetto (Turin, 1959), vol. I, p. 647.

18 John M. Oesterreicher, *The New Encounter between Christians and Jews* (New York, 1985), p. 117.

19 'Cum Tertio' (17 September 1922), in *Principles for Peace*, ed. Koenig, p. 329.

20 Cardinal Gasparri to the Conference of Lausanne, 5 December 1922, ibid., p. 330.

21 Consistorial Allocution of 20 December 1926, in *Discorsi di Pio XI*, vol. I, p. 647.

22 Pinchas Lapide, *Three Popes and the Jews* (New York, 1967), pp. 98, 100.

23 Rhodes, *The Vatican in the Age of Dictators*, p. 166; Guenter Lewy, *The Catholic Church and Nazi Germany* (New York, 1964), pp. 10–11.

24 Edith Stein to Pius XI, 12 April 1933: Archivio Segreto del Vaticano, Segreteria di Stato, Archivio della Sacra Congregazione per gli Affari Ecclesiastici Straordinari, Germania, *posizione* 643, 1092/33.

25 Pacelli to Orsenigo, 4 April 1933: ibid., *posizione* 643, *fascicolo* 158.

26 Orsenigo to Pacelli, 28 April 1933: ibid., *posizione* 643, *fascicolo* 158, n. 1366/33; also see *posizione* 585, *fascicolo* 93.

27 Ibid., *posizione* 650, 194.

28 'Cronaca Contemporanea', 7–20 April 1933: *La Civiltà Cattolica*, anno 84 (1933), 2.301; John Jay Hughes, 'The Pope's Pact with Hitler: Betrayal or Self-Defense?', *Journal of Church and State*, XVII (Winter 1975), p. 64; Klaus Scholder, *The Churches and the Third Reich*, II: *The Year of Disillusionment, 1934* (Philadelphia, PA, 1988), p. 1.

29 Hughes, 'The Pope's Pact with Hitler', p. 64; Scholder, *The Churches and the Third Reich*, p. 1.

30 Mr Kirkpatrick (the Vatican) to Sir R. Vansittart, 19 August 1933, in *Documents on British Foreign Policy*, 2nd ser., v/342, pp. 524–5; *L'Osservatore Romano* (11–12 September 1933); 'Cronaca contemporanea', 7–26 September 1933: *La Civiltà Cattolica*, anno 84 (1933), p. 89.

31 Italian translation of the Reich Concordat of July 1933: Archivio Segreto del Vaticano, Segreteria di Stato, Archivio della Sacra Congregazione per gli Affari Ecclesiastici Straordinari, Germania, *posizione* 645, *fascicolo* 157.

32 Addenda to article XIII: ibid., *posizione* 645, *fascicolo* 164.

33 Gasparri to Pacelli, 24 July 1933: ibid., *posizione* 645, *fascicolo* 165.

34 *Anglo-Vatican Relations, 1914–1939: Confidential Reports of the British Minister to the Holy See*, ed. Thomas E. Hachey (Boston, MA, 1972), pp. 253–5; Camille M. Cianfarra, *The War and the Vatican* (London, 1945), p. 96.

35 Nathaniel Micklem, *National Socialism and the Roman Catholic Church* (London, 1939), p. 95; A. J. Ryder, *Twentieth-Century Germany: From Bismarck to Brandt* (New York, 1973), p. 377.

36 Luciani Martini, 'Chiesa cattolica ed ebrei', *Il ponte*, XXXIV (1978), pp. 1458–9; Igino Giordani, 'Ebrei, protestanti e cattolici', *Fides*, 4 (April 1933).

37 Michael Phayer, *The Catholic Church and the Holocaust, 1930–1965* (Bloomington, IN, 2000), p. 222.

38 'Ai superiori della Compagnia di Gesù', in *Discorsi di Pio XI*, vol. III, p. 383.

39 *Anglo-Vatican Relations, 1914–1939*, pp. 253–4; Camille M. Cianfarra, *The War and the Vatican* (London, 1945), p. 96; *Documents on German Foreign Policy*, series C, vol. IV, pp. 793–4.

40 Archivio Segreto del Vaticano, Segreteria di Stato, Archivio della Sacra Congregazione per gli Affari Ecclesiastici Straordinari, Germania, *posizioni* 641–3.

41 Speeches of 4 April 1934 and 29 April 1934 in *Discorsi di Pio XI*, vol. III, pp. 90–93, 114–15.

42 Edith Stein to Pius XI, 12 April 1933: Archivio Segreto del Vaticano, Segreteria di Stato, Archivio della Sacra Congregazione per gli Affari Ecclesiastici Straordinari, Germania, *posizione* 643, 1092/33.

43 Cesare Orsenigo to Pacelli, 11 April 1933: ibid., *posizione* 643, *fascicolo* 158, nn. 6953–6594.

44 Cesare Orsenigo to Pacelli, 6 April 1933: ibid., *posizione* 643, *fascicolo* 159.

45 *Jewish Chronicle of London* (1 September 1933): ibid., *posizione* 643, 2574/33.

46 Peter Godman, *Hitler and the Vatican: Inside the Secret Archives that Reveal the New Story of the Nazis and the Church* (New York, 2004), appendix II, p. 197.

47 Giovanni Miccoli, 'Santa sede e Chiesa Italiana di Fronte alle Leggi Antiebraiche del 1938', *Studi storici*, XXIX/4 (October–December 1988), p. 859.

48 Godman, *Hitler and the Vatican*, p. 108.

49 Archivio Segreto del Vaticano, Segreteria di Stato, Rapporti con gli stati, Archivo Storico, Archivio della Sacra Congregazione per gli Affari Ecclesiastici Straordinari, Germania, 1922–39, *posizione* 693–4, *fascicolo* 264, *n.* 226.

50 Francois Charles-Roux, *Huit ans au Vatican* (Paris, 1947), p. 106.

51 Michael Phayer, 'The Catholic Resistance Circle in Berlin and German

Catholic Bishops during the Holocaust', *Holocaust and Genocide Studies* (1993), VII/2, p. 226.

52 For English versions of *Mit brennender Sorge* of 14 March 1937, see Claudia Carlen, ed., *The Papal Encyclicals* (Ann Arbor, 1981), vol. III, pp. 525–35, and *Principles for Peace*, ed. Koenig, pp. 498–510. The original version may be found in *Acta Apostolicae Sedis: commentarium officiale*, vol. XXIX (Rome, 1937), pp. 145–67, followed by an Italian version, pp. 168ff.

53 'Lettera enciclica sulla situazione della Chiesa Cattolica nel Reich Germanico', in *Acta Apostolicae Sedis*, vol. XXIX, p. 168.

54 Archivio Segreto del Vaticano, Segreteria di Stato, Rapporti con gli stati, Archivo Storico, Archivio della Sacra Congregazione per gli Affari Ecclesiastici Straordinari, Germania, 1922–39, *posizione* 719, *fascicoli* 312–21.

55 *Acta Apostolicae Sedis*, vol. XXIX, p. 172.

56 Owen Chadwick, *Britain and the Vatican during the Second World War* (Cambridge, 1986), p. 20.

57 Rhodes, *The Vatican in the Age of Dictators*, pp. 228–9.

58 Amleto Cicognani to Pacelli, 24 April 1937: Archivio Segreto del Vaticano, Archivio della Sacra Congregazione per gli Affari Ecclesiastici Straordinari, Germania, 1937–8, *posizione* 720, *fascicolo* 329, *n.* 40.

59 Emma Fattorini, *Hitler, Mussolini and the Vatican: Pope Pius XI and the Speech that was Never Made* (Cambridge, 2011), p. 137.

60 *Documents on German Foreign Policy*, series D, vol. I, nn, pp. 665–9.

61 'La questione giudaica e l'apostalto cattolico', *La Civiltà Cattolica* (23 June 1937).

62 Allocution *Quod Iterum*, 13 December 1937, in *Discorsi di Pio XI*, vol. III, p. 671; 'Al Sacro Collegio e alla Prelatura Romana', ibid., vol. III, p. 679.

63 *Anglo-Vatican Relations, 1914–1939*, pp. 370, 379.

64 'Cronaca contemporanea', *La Civiltà Cattolica* (9–22 June 1938); Patricia M. Keefe, 'Popes Pius XI and Pius XII, the Catholic Church and the Nazi Persecution of the Jews', *British Journal of Holocaust Education*, II/1 (Summer 1993), p. 32.

65 'Dalla Germania: voci dell'episcopato', *L'Osservatore Romano* (8 June 1934); Orsenigo to Giuseppe Pizzardo on the new paganism in the Reich, 12 October 1934: Archivio Segreto del Vaticano, Segreteria di Stato, Rapporti con gli stati, Archivio della Sacra Congregazione per gli Affari Ecclesiastici Straordinari, Germania, *posizioni* 670–73, *fascicolo* 233.

66 'Il Santo Padre ha incominciato', 24 December 1937, in *Principles for Peace*, ed. Koenig, pp. 539–40; 'Le missioni e il nazionalismo', 21 August 1938, in ibid., p. 545; *Anglo-Vatican Relations, 1914–1939*, pp. 370, 379.

67 *Anglo-Vatican Relations, 1914–1939*, p. 52.

68 Hitler in Rome, 1938: Archivio Segreto del Vaticano, Segreteria di Stato, Rapporti con gli stati, Archivo Storico, Archivio della Sacra Congregazione

per gli Affari Ecclesiastici Straordinari, Germania, 1922–39, *posizione* 735, *fascicolo* 353.

69 Pacelli's minutes of audience of 9 September 1938: 'Fogli di udienza', in ibid., *posizione* 1054, *fascicolo* 727.

70 'Alle Suore di Nostra Signora del Cenacolo', 15 July 1938; in *Discorsi di Pio XI*, vol. III, pp. 766–72.

71 Robert A. Hecht, *An Unordinary Man: A Life of Father John LaFarge, s.j.* (Lanham, MD, 1996), pp. 114–15.

72 John LaFarge, SJ, *Interracial Justice: A Study of the Catholic Doctrine of Race Relations* (New York, 1937), pp. 12–15, 59–61, 75, 172–3.

73 Hecht, *An Unordinary Man*, pp. 114–15.

74 See John LaFarge, *The Manner is Ordinary* (New York, 1954), p. 273.

75 'Alle Suore di Nostra Signora del Cenaccolo', in *Discorsi di Pio XI*, vol. III, pp. 766–72.

76 LaFarge, *The Manner is Ordinary*, p. 273.

77 On 15 July, 28 July, 21 August and 6 September 1938, in *Discorsi di Pio XI*, vol. III, pp. 766–72, 777–90, 793–8, 869–72.

78 *La Civiltà Cattolica* (29 July 1938).

79 'Agli Alunni del Collegio di Propaganda Fide', 28 July 1938, in *Discorsi di Pio XI*, vol. III, pp. 777–81.

80 William M. Harrigan, 'Pius XII's Efforts to Effect a Detente in German-Vatican Relations, 1939', *Catholic Historical Review*, XLIX (July 1963), p. 177.

81 *Discorsi di Pio XI*, vol. III, p. 770.

82 Georges Passelecq and Bernard Suchecky, *L'Encyclique cachée de Pie XI* (Paris, 1995), p. 180.

83 'Appunti di Tardini', October 1938: Archivio Segreto del Vaticano, Archivio della Sacra Cogregazione per gli Affari, Stati Eccesiastici Straordinari, *posizione* 560, *fascicolo* 592.

84 'Jesuit Says Pius XI Asked for Draft', *National Catholic Reporter* (22 December 1972), p. 3.

85 Angelo Martini, 'L'ultima battaglia di Pio XI', in *Studi sulla questione romana e la conciliazione* (Rome, 1963), pp. 186–7.

86 Fattorini, *Hitler, Mussolini and the Vatican*, p. 214.

IX: Pius XII: The Second World War, the Holocaust and the Cold War

1 Carlo Falconi, *The Silence of Pius XII*, trans. Bernard Wall (Boston, MA, 1970), p. 238.

2 Some have used this belief to justify Pius XII's conciliatory course towards Nazi Germany, but cannot explain his confrontational policy towards the Soviet Union.

3 *Records and Documents of the Holy See Relating to the Second World War:*

The Holy See and the War in Europe, ed. Pierre Blett et al., trans. Gerard Noel (Cleveland, OH, 1968), pp, 1, 4; Oscar Halecki, *Eugenio Pacelli: Pope of Peace* (New York, 1951), p. 138.

4 Galeazzo Ciano, *The Ciano Diaries, 1939–1943*, ed. Hugh Gibson (Garden City, NY, 1946), pp. 45–7.

5 Galeazzo Ciano, *The Ciano Diaries, 1939–1943*, ed. Malcolm Muggeridge (London, 1947), p. 50.

6 Ibid., p. 91.

7 In this regard, see Patricia Marx Ellsberg, 'An Interview with Rolf Hochhuth', in *The Papacy and Totalitarianism between the Two World Wars*, ed. Charles F. Delzell (New York, 1974), pp. 109–24.

8 Falconi, *The Silence of Pius XII*, p. 238.

9 Peter Kent, 'A Tale of Two Popes', *Journal of Contemporary History*, XXIII/4 (October 1988); Emma Fattorini, *Pio XI, Hitler e Mussolini: la solitude di un papa* (Turin, 2007).

10 Cardinal Domenico Tardini, *Memories of Pius XII*, trans. Rosemary Goldie (Westminister, MD, 1961), p. 7

11 Fattorini, *Pio XI, Hitler e Mussolini*, p. 214.

12 *Records and Documents of the Holy See Relating to the Second World War*, p. 169.

13 In this regard, see *The Pius War: Responses to the Critics of Pius XII*, ed. Joseph Bottum and David G. Dalin (Lanham, MD, 2004).

14 Paul L. Murphy with Rene Arlington, *La Popessa* (New York, 1983), p. 197.

15 *Records and Documents of the Holy See Relating to the Second World War*, p. 423.

16 Ibid.

17 *Acta Apostolicae Sedis: commentarium officiale*, vol. XXXI (Rome, 1939), pp. 413–53.

18 *Principles for Peace: Selections from Papal Documents from Leo XIII to Pius XII*, ed. Harry C. Koenig (Washington, DC, 1943), p. 804.

19 Falconi, *The Silence of Pius XII*, p. 238.

20 *Die Briefe Pius XII an die deutschen Bischöfe, 1939–1944*, ed. Burkhart Schneider et al. (Mainz, 1966), p. 241; Karl Otmar von Aretin, *The Papacy and the Modern World*, trans. Roland Hill (New York, 1970), p. 213.

21 José M. Sánchez, 'The Popes and Nazi Germany: The View from Madrid', *Journal of Church and State*, XXXVIII (Spring 1996), p. 374.

22 Jan Olav Smit, *Angelic Shepherd: The Life of Pope Pius XII* (New York, 1950), pp. 224–5.

23 *Records and Documents of the Holy See Relating to the Second World War*, p. 423.

24 'Treaty between the Holy See and Italy' (11 February 1929), in Shepard Clough and Salvatore Saladino, *A History of Modern Italy* (New York, 1968), p. 477.

25 Harold H. Tittmann III, ed., *Inside the Vatican of Pius XII: The Memoir of an American Diplomat during World War II* (New York, 2004), pp. 124–5.

26 Angelo Giuseppe Roncalli, *La mia vita in Oriente: agende del delegato apostolico, 1940–1944*, ed. Valeria Martano (Bologna, 2008), pp. 290–91.

27 An article in *Catholic World News* on 14 January 2008 reported that the Pave the Way Foundation, an organization devoted to inter-religious understanding, had uncovered a large amount of evidence to rebut the charge that Pope Pius XII was indifferent to Jewish suffering during the Holocaust and that he had actually worked to save the lives of Jews. Gary Krupp, the group's president, reported that much of this evidence was already 'available publicly but simply not known'.

28 'Oggi, al compiersi', in *Papal Pronouncements: A Guide, 1740–1978*, ed. Claudia Carlen (Ann Arbor, MI, 1990), vol. I, p. 121.

29 Sandro Magister, *La politica vaticana e l'Italia, 1943–1978* (Rome, 1979), pp. 132–3; G. Alberigo, 'La condanna della collaborazione dei Cattolici con i partiti comunisti, 1949', *Concilium*, XI/7 (1975), pp. 145–58.

30 Richard J. Wolff, 'The Catholic Church and the Dictatorships in Slovakia and Croatia, 1939–1945', *Records of the American Catholic Historical Society of Philadelphia*, LXXXVIII/1–4 (1977), pp. 14–15.

31 Jörg K. Hoensch, 'Slovakia: "One God, One People, One Party"', in *Catholics, the State and the European Radical Right, 1919–1945*, ed. R. J. Wolff and J. Hoensch (New York, 1987), p. 177.

32 Letter of Cardinal Tisserant of 11 June 1940, found in *Bundesarchiv, Koblenz, Reichkanzlei/Frankreich*, R 43, Ii, 1440a, cited in Hansjakob Stehle, *Eastern Politics of the Vatican* (Athens, OH, 1981), p. 215.

33 Michael Feldkamp, 'Hochhuth Exposed', trans. John Jay Hughes, in Association of Contemporary Church Historians newsletter: *Arbeitsgemeinschaft kirchliche Zeitgeschichtler*, XIII/7–8 (July–August 2007).

34 *Journal of Church and State*, XXXVIII (Spring 1996), p. 376.

x: *Aggiornamento* and *Aperturismo*: The Second Vatican Council and Beyond

1 Frank J. Coppa, *The Papacy Confronts the Modern World* (Malabar, FL, 2003), p. 160.

2 English versions of Pope John's encyclicals can be found in *The Papal Encyclicals*, ed. Claudia Carlen (Ann Arbor, MI, 1981), vol. V, pp. 5–129.

3 His five other encyclicals: *Ad Petri Cathedram* (June 1959), *Sacerdotii nostri primordia* (August 1959), *Grata recordatio* (September 1959), *Aeterna dei sapientia* (November 1961) and *Paenitentiam agere* (July 1962), though less well known, are hardly unknown.

4 Carlen, ed., *The Papal Encyclicals*, vol. V, p. 77.

5 Maura Velati, ed., *Pater amabilis: agende del pontifice, 1958–1963*

(Bologna, 2007), p. x.

6 'Spiritual Retreat of 1927 in Slovenia', in *Il giornale dell'anima: soliloqui, note e diari spirituali*, ed. Alberto Melloni (Bologna, 2003), p. 305.
7 'Vatican II Documents Still Relevant', *The Tablet* (24 November 2012), p. 8.
8 Giovanni XXIII, *Lettere ai familiari*, ed. Loris Capovilla (Rome, 1968), vol. I, p. 8.
9 Vottorio Gorresio, *The New Mission of John XXIII*, trans. C. L. Markmann (New York, 1970), p. 64.
10 Roncalli's *Tener da conto: agendine di Bulgaria, 1925–1934* (Bologna, 2008) deal with his decade-long and unexpected appointment as apostolic delegate there.
11 Gorresio, *The New Mission of John XXIII*, pp. 71–3.
12 Angelo Roncalli, *La mia vita in Oriente: agende del delegato apostolico* (Bologna, 2008). It is a massive volume of almost 800 pages, edited by Valeria Martana, whose doctorate was in social and religious studies and who has a special interest in Eastern Christianity.
13 Roncalli, *La mia vita in Oriente*, vol. II: *1940–1944*.
14 In my studies under Hans Rosenberg at Brooklyn College in the 1950s he never referred to the Holocaust, but to the Final Solution.
15 See Roncalli's notes of 28 and 29 December in his *Anni di Francia: agenda di nunzio, 1945–1948* (Bologna, 2004), pp. 5–7.
16 *Acta Apostolicae Sedis*, L (1958), pp. 905–6.
17 Raymond F. Bulman, 'Vatican Council II', in *Encyclopedia of the Vatican and Papacy*, ed. Frank J. Coppa (Westport, CT, 1999), p. 429.
18 'Vatican II Documents Still Relevant', p. 23.
19 Gorresio, *The New Mission of John XXIII*, p. 268.
20 Bulman, 'Vatican Council II', p. 431.
21 'Vatican II Encouraged Good Liturgy', *The Tablet* (9 March 2013), p. 4.
22 Austin Flannery, ed., *Vatican Council II: The Conciliar and Post Conciliar Documents* (Grand Rapids, MI, 1992), vol. I, pp. 350–426, 441–51, 452–70.
23 Claudia Carlen, ed., *Papal Pronouncements: A Guide, 1740–1978* (Ann Arbor, MI, 1990), vol. I, pp. 329–31.
24 Ibid., vol. I, pp. 342, 344, 346.
25 Flannery, ed., *Vatican Council II*, vol. I, pp. 707–43.
26 Coppa, *The Papacy Confronts the Modern World*, p. 158.

XI: The Papacy of John Paul II and the Aftermath of the Council

1 James Corkery and Thomas Worcester, 'Conclusion', in *The Papacy since 1500* (Cambridge, 2010), p. 251.
2 Claudia Carlen, ed., *Papal Pronouncements: A Guide, 1740–1978* (Ann Arbor, MI, 1990), vol. II, p. 843.
3 Ibid., vol. II, pp. 845–8.

4 *The Tablet* [Brooklyn] (22 September 2012).

5 Carlen, ed., *Papal Pronouncements*, vol. II, p. 98.

6 Hebblethwaite, *The Year of Three Popes* (New York, 1979), pp. 154, 165, 176; Gordon Thomas and Max Morgan-Witts, *Pontiff* (New York, 1990), pp. 304, 324; Malachi Martin, *The Keys of this Blood: The Struggle for World Dominion between Pope John Paul II, Mikhail Gorbachev and the Capitalist West* (New York, 1990), pp. 60–61.

7 Mieczysław Maliński, *Pope John Paul II: The Life of Karol Wojtyła*, trans. P. S. Fall (New York, 1979), p. 23.

8 Daughters of St Paul, ed., *Messages of John Paul II* (Boston, MA, 1979), vol. II, pp. 15–16; 'The Pope: A See Change', *The Economist* (29 April 1995); Maliński, *Pope John Paul II*, pp. 82, 118; André Frossard, *'Be Not Afraid': Pope John Paul Speaks Out on his Life, his Beliefs and his Inspiring Vision for Humanity*, trans. J. R. Foster (New York, 1984), p. 28.

9 Daughters of St Paul, ed., *Messages of John Paul II*, vol. II, pp. 212–18.

10 Ibid., vol. II, pp. 274–81; Malinski, *Pope John Paul II*, p. 241.

11 Frossard, *'Be Not Afraid'*, p. 207.

12 'Pius XII's Contributions Hailed', *The Tablet* (5 April 1979).

13 An official schedule of the papal visit can be found in *US News and World Report* (8 October 1979).

14 Pope John Paul II, *Crossing the Threshold of Hope*, ed. Vittorio Messori (New York, 1994), p. 48.

15 Frossard, *'Be Not Afraid'*, p. 60.

16 At the end of 1993 the dire situation continued as the Vatican revealed it would have to ask dioceses across the world to increase their contributions to cope with the projected deficit in 1994 of more than $26 million. In 1994, however, under the careful supervision of the pope, the Vatican had a surplus of $412,000. 'Vatican Appeals for Funds', *New York Times* (7 November 1993); 'Vatican Paid All its Bills in 1994', *The Tablet* (1 July 1994).

17 Daniela Iacono, 'Censure of Hans Küng Discussed by Pope John', *The Tablet* (31 May 1980).

18 Gordon Thomas and Max Morgan-Witts, *Pontiff* (Garden City, NY, 1983), pp. 406–7.

19 Richard L. Camp, 'From Passive Subordination to Complementary Partnership: The Papal Conception of a Woman's Place in the Church and Society since 1878', *Catholic Historical Review*, LXXXVI/3 (July 1990), p. 523; Pope John Paul II, *Crossing the Threshold of Hope*, p. 131.

20 Carl Bernstein, 'The Holy Alliance', *Time* (24 February 1992), p. 28.

21 Ibid., pp. 34–5.

22 'The Pope: A See Change', p. 24.

23 Eduard Shevardnadze, *The Future Belongs to Freedom* (New York, 1991), pp. 36–7.

24 Leonard Silk, 'Beyond Parley', *New York Times* (14 November 1986).

25 Ibid., pp. 434–6; Bernstein, 'The Holy Alliance', p. 35; Richard N. Ostling, 'Cross Meets Kremlin', *Time* (4 December 1989).

26 Thomas Patrick Melady, *The Ambassador's Story: The United States and the Vatican in World Affairs* (Huntington, IN, 1994), p. 11.

27 Richard N. Ostling, 'Cross Meets Kremlin', *Time* (4 December 1989), pp. 74–6.

28 Michael Mandelbaum, 'Coup de Grâce: The End of the Soviet Union', *Foreign Affairs*, LXXI (Spring 1992), pp. 164–82; Shevardnadze, *The Future Belongs to Freedom*, pp. 25–7.

29 Melady, *The Ambassador's Story*, p. 18.

30 Ibid., p. 25.

31 Ibid., pp. 1558–60; 'The Pope: A See Change', p. 24.

32 'Excerpts from the Pope's Encyclical: *On Giving Capitalism a Human Face*', *New York Times* (3 May 1991).

33 Frossard, *'Be Not Afraid'*, pp. 142–3.

34 Alan Cowell, 'Pope Challenges Brazil Leaders on Behalf of the Poor', *New York Times* (15 October 1991); Cowell, 'Pope's Law: Less Politics', *New York Times* (16 October 1991); Cowell, 'Protect Children, Pope tells Brazil', *New York Times* (21 October 1991); Cowell, 'Pope Asks Amends of Brazil's Indians', *New York Times* (17 October 1991); Frossard, *'Be Not Afraid'*, pp. 152, 154.

35 Tim Golden, 'Mexico Ending Church Restraints after 70 Years of Official Hostility', *New York Times* (20 December 1991).

36 Stephen Kinzer, 'Pope Tells Croats He Supports Them', *New York Times* (18 August 1991).

37 Alan Cowell, 'Vatican Formally Recognizes Independence of Croatia and Slovenia', *New York Times* (14 January 1992).

38 Melady, *The Ambassador's Story*, pp. 95–6, 113–24.

39 'Pope Rips Xenophobia', *New York Newsday* (29 October 1992).

40 Paul Moses, 'Smooth Sailing on O'Connor Trip', *New York Newsday* (12 January 1992); Judith Harris, 'Shalom to Pope', *New York Newsday* (22 September 1993); 'Israel and Vatican Agree on Diplomatic Relations', *New York Times* (30 December 1993); Bob Keeler, 'Vatican Near Pact', *New York Newsday* (21 December 1993); Alan Cowell, 'Vatican Seeks Arab Favor; Plans Accord with Jordan', *New York Times* (31 December 1993).

41 Frossard, *'Be Not Afraid'*, p. 196.

42 Alan Cowell, 'Pope Visits Angola, Urging Amith after Long War', *New York Times* (5 June 1992); ibid. (21 February 1992); Agostino Bono, 'At Beatification: The Pope's Mind is on Africa', *The Tablet* (23 May 1992); 'Pope Scolds Sudan', *New York Newsday* (11 February 1993).

43 Laurie Hansen, 'Pope Tells Latin American Bishops: Put Church at Centre of All Life', *The Tablet* (24 October 1992); Ron Howard, 'Pope:

Spread Faith', *New York Newsday* (12 October 1992); Howard W. French, 'Dissent Shadows Pope on his Visit', *New York Times* (14 October 1992).

44   'French Bishop Removed for Challenging Vatican', *New York Times* (14 January 1995); 'The Pope: A See Change', p. 24; Ari L. Goldman, 'Censured Archbishop Quietly Departs for Seattle', *New York Times* (14 November 1986).

45   Pope John Paul II, *Crossing the Threshold of Hope*, pp. 172–3; Joe Nicholson, 'Pope Levels New Blast at "Evil" Birth Control', *New York Post* (23 September 1993); Peter Steinfels, 'Papal Encyclical says Church Must Enforce Basic Morality', *New York Times* (3 October 1993); Richard N. Ostling, 'A Refinement of Evil', *Time* (4 October 1993); Richard N. Ostling, 'Till Annulment Do Us Part', *Time* (16 August 1993).

46   'Turn Off Tube, Pope Warns', *New York Newsday* (25 January 1994).

47   'Pope Condemns European Resolution on Gay Marriages', *St Petersburg Times* (21 February 1994).

48   Alan Cowell, 'The Pope's Struggle against Marxism and its Successors', *New York Times* (26 September 1993).

49   Susan Page, 'Prez and Pope Pop Off', *New York Newsday* (3 June 1994).

50   Eugene Linden, 'Showdown in Cairo', *Time* (5 September 1994); 'The Pope: Why the Cairo Meeting Makes Him Mad as Hell', *Newsweek* (12 September 1994).

51   Barbara Brossette, 'Vatican Picks U.S. Women as Delegate to UN Parley', *New York Times* (25 August 1995).

52   'Pontiff's Letter Calls for Equality', *New York Newsday* (11 July 1995); 'Pope Opens Synod on Religious Life', *New York Times* (3 October 1994); 'The Pope: A See Change', p. 24; 'Pope: Nonmarital Sex is Wrong', *The Tablet* (9 July 1994).

53   Alan Cowell, 'Pope is Recovering Very Rapidly, Doctors Say', *New York Times* (1 May 1994); Beth McMurtie, 'Recovery Problems', *New York Newsday* (23 September 1994).

54   Bob Keeler, 'Pope Urges Peace in Rwanda, Opens Talks on Africa', *New York Newsday* (11 April 1994); Alan Cowell, 'Vatican Ponders Church Role in Africa', *New York Times* (1 May 1994).

55   Maliński, *Pope John Paul II*, p. 189.

56   Alan Cowell, 'Pope Appoints 30 Cardinals, 2 from U.S.', *New York Times* (31 October 1994).

57   'Pope Arrives in Manila Amid Bomb Threats', *New York Post* (13 January 1995); 'Chinese To See Pope', *Tampa Tribune* (9 January 1995).

58   Alan Cowell, 'Pope in Sydney: Defends Vatican's Ban on Ordaining Women', *New York Times* (20 January 1995).

59   Pope John Paul II, *Crossing the Threshold of Hope*, p. 86.

60   'Pope's Letter: A Sinister World Has Led to Crimes against Life', *New York Times* (31 March 1995).

61 'The Pope: A See Change'.

62 Carl Bernstein, 'The Holy Alliance', *Time* (24 February 1992), p. 35.

63 'The Pope: A See Change', p. 23.

64 Carl Eifert, 'Religion Prize Winner Michael Novak Says John Paul is among Best Popes', *The Tablet* (9 July 1994).

65 Janice C. Simpson, 'Watch Out: An Unrepentant Sinead O'Connor Blasts the Catholic Church', *Time* (9 November 1992); Kieran Crowley, 'Pope's Doc Calls him "Unbalanced"', *New York Post* (6 October 1994).

XII: Benedict XVI: Conflict and Conciliation with the Contemporary Age

1 John L. Allen, Jr, *Pope Benedict XVI: A Biography of Joseph Ratzinger* (New York, 2000), p. 67.

2 Francis X. Rocca, 'Benedict Assesses Legacy of Vatican II', *The Tablet* [Brooklyn] (20 October 2012), p. 32.

3 Ibid.

4 Frank J. Coppa, *Politics and the Papacy in the Modern World* (Westport, CT, 2008), pp. 209–10.

5 '*Dominus Iesus:* On the Unicity and Salvific Universality of Jesus Christ and the Church', *The Tablet* [Brooklyn] (30 September 2000), p. 3A.

6 Coppa, *Politics and the Papacy*, p. 208.

7 Press conference of Father Federico Lombardi, SJ, director of the Vatican Press Office, *Zenit* (20 February 2013).

8 Pope Benedict: 'Working Too Much is Never a Good Thing', *The Tablet* [Brooklyn] (26 August 2006), p. 7.

9 Allen, *Pope Benedict XVI*, p. 310

10 James Corkery and Thomas Worcester, 'Conclusion', in *The Papacy since 1500* (Cambridge, 2010), p. 251.

11 'Benedict Cites Legacy of Vatican II', *The Tablet* [Brooklyn] (23 February 2013), p. 7.

12 Carol Glatz, 'Pope calls for Strong Catholicism in America', *The Tablet* [Brooklyn] (12 December 2012), p. 10.

13 'Benedict XVI, Pope', *New Catholic Encyclopedia: Supplement 2012* (New York, 2000), vol. I, pp. 114–22.

14 Ibid.

15 Rocca, 'Benedict Assesses Legacy of Vatican II', p. 32.

16 Coppa, *Politics and the Papacy*, p. 211.

17 Father Federico Lombardi, SJ, 20 February 2013.

18 'Papal Resignation Stuns U.S. Church', *The Tablet* [Brooklyn] (16 February 2013), p. 1.

19 *New York Daily News* (12 February 2013), p. 1.

20 'Factoids about Popes' Ages and Nationalities', *The Tablet* [Brooklyn]

(2 March 2013), p. 5.

21 Cindy Wooden, 'Resigned Pope to Live in Monastery at the Vatican',
    The Tablet [Brooklyn] (16 February 2013), p. 13.

22 Denis Slattery and J. Lemire, 'No Gay in Hell! Pope-Blackmail Report
    Ripped', *New York Daily News* (24 February 2013), p. 7.

23 Laurie Goodstein, 'Pope Has Gained the Insight to Address Abuse, Aides
    Say', *New York Times* (23 April 2005), p. A1.

24 Rocca, 'Benedict Addresses Legacy of Vatican II', p. 32.

25 'Vatican: No Gay Seminary Teachers', *Newsday* (4 December 2005), p. A22.

26 Press conference of Federico Lombardi, SJ, 20 February 2013.

27 Jonathon Luxemoore, 'Pope Exhausted', *The Tablet* [Brooklyn]
    (23 February 2013), p. 3.

28 Rabbi Arthur Schneier, 'Rabbi to Miss his Pontiff Pal', *New York Daily
    News* (13 February 2013).

29 Cindy Wooden, 'Pope Seeks Prayers for an "Unusual Time"', *The Tablet*
    [Brooklyn] (23 February 2013), p. 1.

30 Frank J. Coppa, *The Modern Papacy since 1789* (London, 1998), pp. 64–5.

31 Francis X. Rocca, 'Pope will Serve Church through Prayer', *The Tablet*
    [Brooklyn] (2 March 2013), p. 1.

Conclusion: The Papacy Past and Present

1 Gordon Thomas and Max Morgan-Witts, *Pontiff* (New York, 1983),
   pp. 406–7.

2 Carl Bernstein, 'The Holy Alliance', *Time* (24 February 1992), p. 28.

3 Ibid.

4 'The Pope: A See Change', *The Economist* (29 April 1995), p. 24.

5 John Cornwell, 'Benedict's Noble Ploy', *New York Daily News* (10 March
   2013), p. 12.

6 Bergoglio was born in Argentina, the son of Italian immigrants from
   Piedmont.

SELECT BIBLIOGRAPHY

Primary Sources

Acta Apostolicae Sedis: commentarium officiale, vol. XXIII (1931) to vol. XL (1948) (Rome, 1931–48)

Acta Nuniature Polanae: Achilles Ratti, 1918–1921 (Rome, 1995)

Acta Pio IX: Pontificis Maximi: Pars prima acta exhibens quae ad Ecclesiam universam spectant, 1846–1854 (Rome, 1855)

Acta Romana Societatis Iesu, vol. VII (1932–4) and vol. IX (1938–40) (Rome, 1932–40)

Acta Sanctae Sedis [Compendium of Documents of Holy See], 1865–1908

Actes de Benoit XV: encycliques, motu proprio, brefs, allocutions, actes des dicastres (Paris, 1926–34)

Actes de Léon XIII: encycliques, motu proprio, brefs, allocutions, actes des dicastres (Paris, 1931–7)

Actes di S.S. Pie XI: encycliques, motu proprio, brefs, allocutions, actes des dicastres (Paris, 1932–6)

Actes et documents du Saint Siège relatifs à la seconde guerre mondiale, ed. P. Blet et al., 11 vols (Rome, 1965–81)

Advocates for the Doomed: The Diaries and Papers of James G. McDonald, ed. Richard Breitman et al. (Bloomington, IN, 2007)

Akten deutscher Bischöfe über die Lage der Kirche, 1933–1945, ed. Berhard Stasiewki (Mainz, 1968)

Akten Kardinal Michael von Faulhaber, 1917–1945, ed. Ludwig Volk (Mainz, 1978)

Alfieri, Dino, *Dictators Face to Face*, trans. David Moore (Westport, CT, 1978)

Althaus, Friedrich, ed., *The Roman Journals of Ferdinand Gregorovius, 1852–1874* (London, 1906)

Anglo-Vatican Relations, 1914–1939: Confidential Reports of the British Minister to the Holy See, ed. Thomas E. Hachey (Boston, MA, 1972)

Annuario Pontificio / Papal Yearbook / Annual Papal Directory [published under these various titles by the Libreria Editrice Vaticana]

Appeals for Peace of Pope Benedict XV and Pope Pius XI (Washington, DC, 1931)

Bertone, Domenico, ed., *Discorsi di Pio XI* (Turin, 1959)

Beyrens, Eugene, *Quatre ans à Rome* (Paris, 1934)

Blet, Pierre, *Pie XII et la Seconde Guerre Mondiale après les Archives du Vatican* (Paris, 1997)

——, and Angelo Martini, Burkhard Schneider, eds, *Records and Documents of the Holy See Relating to the Second World War, I: The Holy See and the War in Europe, March 1939–August 1940*, trans. Gerard Noel (Washington, DC, 1968)

Blet, Pierre, et al., eds, *The Holy See and the War in Europe, March 1939–August 1940* (London, 1965)

Braga, Carlo, *La riforma liturgica di Pio XII: documenti, vol. I: La 'memoria sulla riforma liturgica'* (Rome, 2003)

Bressan, Edoardo, '*L'Osservatore Romano* e le relazioni internazionali della Santa Sede, 1917–1922', in *Benedetto XV e la Pace, 1918*, ed. G. Rumi (Brescia, 1990), pp. 233–53

Carlen, Claudia, ed., *A Guide to the Encyclicals of Roman Pontiffs from Leo XIII to the Present Day, 1878–1937* (New York, 1939)

——, ed., *Papal Pronouncements: A Guide, 1740–1978*, 2 vols (Ann Arbor, MI, 1990) [vol. I: *Benedict XIV to Paul VI*; vol. II: *Paul VI to John Paul I*]

——, ed., *The Papal Encyclicals*, 5 vols (Ann Arbor, MI, 1981) [vol. I: *1740–1878*; vol. II: *1878–1903*; vol. III: *1903–1939*; vol. IV: *1938–1958*; vol. V: *1958–1981*]

Cavalleri, Ottavio, and Germano Gualdo, eds, *L'Archivio de Mons: Achille Ratti visitatore apostolico e nunzio a Varsavia, 1918–1921* (Vatican City, 1990)

Caveterra, Emilio, *Processo a Pio XII: intervista con P. Raimondo Spiazzi: opinioni di De Felice, Del Noce, Valsecchi: documenti per la storia* (Milan, 1979)

Charles-Roux, François, *Huit ans au Vatican* (Paris, 1947)

Cianfara, Camille M., *The War and the Vatican* (London, 1945)

Ciano, Galeazzo, *Diario* (Milan, 1950)

——, *L'Europa verso la catastrofe* (Verona, 1948)

——, *Hidden Diaries* (New York, 1953)

Civiltà Cattolica, La (1850–)

Colleción de enciclicas y otras cartas de los Papas Gregory XVI, León XIII, Pio X, Benedicto XV y Pio XI (Madrid, 1935)

Collins, Joseph B., ed., *Catechetical Documents of Pope Pius X* (New York, 1946)

Correspondence between President Roosevelt and Pope Pius XII (New York, 1947)

Correspondence between President Truman and Pope Pius XII (New York, 1952)

Crispolti, Filippo, *Pio IX, Leone XIII, Pio X, Benedetto XV: ricordi personali* (Milan, 1932)

Dalla Torre, Giuseppe, *Memorie* (Milan, 1965)

Di Nolfo, Ennio, *Vaticano e Stati Uniti, 1939–1952: dalle carte di Myron C. Taylor* (Milan, 1978)

Diritto e giustizia nel magistero pontificio: da Pio XII a Giovanni Paolo II,
ed. Unione Giuristi Cattolici Italiani (Rome, 1998)

Discorsi di Pio XI, ed. Domenico Bertetto (Turin, 1959)

Discorsi e radio messagi di Sua Santità Pio XII, 2 vols (Milan, 1941)

*Discorsi indirizzati dai sommi pontefici Pio XI, Pio XII, Giovanni XXIII, Paolo VI,
Giovanni Paolo II alla Pontificia Accademia delle Scienze dal 1936 al 1986*
(Vatican City, 1986)

*Discourses of the Popes from Pius XI to John Paul II to the Pontifical Academy
of Sciences, 1936–1986* (Vatican City, 1986)

Documents diplomatiques français (Paris, 1931–9)

Documents in the Political History of the European Continent, 1815–1939,
ed. G. A. Kertesz (Oxford, 1968)

Documentos inéditos para la historia del Generalisimo Franco (Madrid, 1991)

Documents on British Foreign Policy, 2nd ser., vol. v, no. 342 (London, 1956)

Dulles, Avery, and Leon Klenicki, eds, *The Holocaust: Never to be Forgotten:
Reflections on the Holy See's Document We Remember* (New York, 2001)

Enchiridion delle encicliche: ediz. bilingue, vol. VI: *Pio XII (1939–1958)*
(Bologna, 2003)

Federzoni, Luigi, *Diario di un ministro del fascismo*, ed. Adriana Macchi
(Florence, 1993)

Foundations for Peace: Letters of Pope Pius XII and President Roosevelt
(London, 1941)

Fremantle, Anne, ed., *The Papal Encyclicals in their Historical Context* (New
York, 1956)

Great Britain, Foreign Office, *British Documents on the Origins of the War,
1898–1914*, ed. George P. Gooch and Harold Temperly (London, 1926)

*Guide for Living: An Approved Selection of Letters and Addresses of His Holiness
Pope Pius XII* (New York, 1969)

Guide to the Documents of Pius XII, 1939–1949, ed. Sister Claudia Carlen
(Westminster, MD, 1951)

Hachey, Thomas E., ed., *Anglo-Vatican Relations, 1914–1939: Confidential
Reports of the British Minister to the Holy See* (Boston, MA, 1972)

Haffner, Paul, ed., *Discourses of the Popes from Pius XI to John Paul II to the
Pontifical Academy of Sciences* (Vatican City, 1986)

Herzl, Theodor, *Diaries*, trans. Marvin Lowental (New York, 1956)

Hilberg, Raul, *The Destruction of the European Jews* (Chicago, IL, 1961)

Hill, Leonidas, 'The Vatican Embassy of Ernst von Weizsacker, 1943–1945',
Journal of Modern History, XXXIX (1967), pp. 138–59

Hitler, Adolf, *Mein Kampf*, trans. Ralph Manheim (Boston, MA, 1943)

——, *Hitler's Secret Conversations* (New York, 1953)

Hürten, Heinz, 'Die Briefe Pius XII. an die deutschen Bischöfe zur Kriegszeit:
eine zentrale Quelle für seine Amtsauffassung?', *Annali dell'Istituto Storico
Italo-Germanico in Trento*, XXXI (2005), pp. 355–65

I concordati di Pio xii (1939–1958): Belgio, Germania, Portogallo, Spagna,
   Argentina, Bolivia, Colombia, Rep. Domenicana, Haiti, ed. Pio Ciprotti
   and Anna Talamanca (Milan, 1970)
I documenti diplomatic italiani [9th ser., 1939–43] (Rome, 1959)
I fogli di udienza del Cardinale Eugenio Pacelli segretario di stato, 1930, ed.
   Sergio Pagano, Marcel Chappin and Giovanni Coco (Vatican City, 2010)
Il Leone di Münster e Hitler: Clemens August Cardinale von Galen: la sua
   attività episcopale nel periodo della dittatura Nazionalsocialista in Germania,
   ed. Reinhard Lettmann and Heinrich Mussinghoff (Rome, 1996)
Il magistero mariano di Pio xii: edizione italiana di tutti i documenti mariani di
   Pio xii con introduzione, sintesi dottrinali e indici, ed. Domenico Bertetto
   (Rome, 1960)
Inter Arma Caritas: Uffizio informazioni vaticano per i prigionieri di guerra
   istituito da Pio xii, 1939–1947 (Vatican City, 2004)
I papi e l'Europa: documenti: Pio xii, Giovanni xxiii, Paolo vi, ed. Pietro Elle
   Di Ci (Rome, 1978)
Katholische Kirche in Dritten Reich: eine Aufsatzsammlung zum Verhältnis vom
   Papsttum, Episkopat und deutschen Katoliken zum Nationalsozialismus,
   1933–1945 (Mainz, 1976)
Kelp, Rosabelle, *Sixteen Encyclicals of Pope Pius xi* (Washington, DC, 1939)
Kennan, George, *Memoirs, 1925–1940* (Boston, MA, 1967)
Klemperer, Victor, *I Will Bear Witness: A Diary of the Nazi Years* (New York,
   1999)
——, *The Lesser Evil: The Diaries of Victor Klemperer, 1945–1959* (London, 2003)
La chiesa e il fascismo: documenti e interpretazioni, ed. Pietro Scoppola (Bari,
   1971)
La Pira, Giorgio, *Beatissimo padre: lettere a Pio xii,* ed. Andrea Riccardi and
   Isabella Piersanti (Milan, 2004)
Lehnert, Pascalina, *Pio xii: Il prilegio di servivlo* (Milan, 1984)
Lettres apostoliques de S.S. Pie x: encycliques, motu proprio, brefs, allocutions,
   actes des dicastres, 8 vols (Paris, 1930–36)
Lieber, Robert, sj, 'Pius as I Knew Him', *Catholic Mind,* lvii (1959),
   pp. 292–304
Lloyd George, David, *War Memoirs,* vol. iv (Boston, MA, 1937)
Löffler, Peter, *Bischof Clemens August Graf von Galen: Akten, Briefe und*
   Predigten, 1933–1946. Band i: 1933–1939, 2 vols (Mainz, 1988)
Luciani, Albino, *The Message of John Paul i* (Boston, MA, 1978)
Ludwig, Emil, *Talks with Mussolini* (Boston, MA, 1933)
Macmillan, Harold, *The Blast of War, 1939–1945* (New York, 1968)
Merry del Val, Cardinal Raphael, *Memories of Pope Pius x* (Westminster, MD,
   1999)
Miccoli, Giovanni, *Chiesa e società in Italia dal concilio Vaticano i (1870)*
   al pontificato di Giovanni xxiii: i documenti (Turin, 1973)

——, 'Santa Sede e Chiesa italiana di fronte alle Legge antiebriache del 1938',
    Studi storici, XXIX/4 (October–December 1988)

Montini, Giovanni Battista, 'Pius XII and the Jews', *The Tablet* [London]
    (29 June 1963)

Morgan, Thomas B., *A Reporter at the Papal Court: A Narrative of the Reign
    of Pope Pius XI* (New York, 1937)

——, *The Listening Post: Eighteen Years on Vatican Hill* (New York, 1944)

Napolitano, Matteo Luigi, 'Eugenio Pacelli: diplomatico nell'archivio di
    famiglia', *Incipit*, I/2 (July–August 2007), pp. 39–43

——, 'I documenti diplomatici come fonte per il dibattito storiografico su
    Pio XII', *Annali dell'Istituto Storico Italo-Germanico in Trento*, XXXI (2005),
    pp. 367–94

——, and Andrea Tornielli, *Il papa che salvò gli ebrei: dagli archivi segreti vaticani
    tutta la verità su Pio XII* (Casale Monferrato, 2004)

Official German Documents Relating to the World War (New York, 1923)

Osservatore Romano, L' (1861–)

Pacelli, Eugenio, *Discorsi e panegirici* (Milan, 1939)

——, *La personalità e la territorialità delle leggi, specialmente del Diritto
    Canonico* (Vatican City, 1912)

Pacelli, Francesco, *Diario della Conciliazione* (Vatican City, 1959)

Papers Relating to the Foreign Relations of the United States, 1931–1939
    (Washington, DC, 1931–9)

Passelecq, Georges, and Bernard Suchecky, *The Hidden Encyclical of Pius XI*,
    trans. Steven Rendall (New York, 1997)

*Patti lateranensi, convenzioni e accordi successivi fra il Vaticano e l'Italia fino
    al 31 dicembre 1945*, ed. Mario Belardo (Vatican City, 1972)

*The Persecution of the Catholic Church in the Third Reich: Facts and
    Documents* (London, 1940)

Picciotto Fargion, Liliana, *L'occupazione tedesca e gli ebrei di Roma: documenti
    e fatti* (Rome, 1979)

Pio X Pontificis Maximi Acto, or *Acta Pio X*, 5 vols (Rome, 1905–14)

Pio XII, ed. Andrea Riccardi (Rome and Bari, 1984)

Pio XII parla alla chiesa del silenzio [Documenti pontifici, 5], ed. Jean Pierre
    Dubois-Dumée and Alberto Giovannetti (Milan, 1958)

*Pio XII e l'umana sofferenza: edizione italiana del magistero di Pio XII sul
    dolore*, ed. Domenico Bertetto (Rome, 1961)

Pius XII, *Scritti e discorsi di S. Santità Pio XII nel 1958* (Siena, 1959)

——, *The Mind of Pius XII* (New York, 1955)

Pio XII, vescovo di Roma [Pontificia Opera per la Preservazione della Fede
    e la Costruzione di Nuove Chiese in Roma] (Rome, 1958)

Pius XII and Peace, 1939–1940 (Washington, DC, 1940)

*The Pope and the People: Select Letters and Addresses on Social Questions by
    Pope Leo XII, Pope Pius X, Pope Benedict XV and Pope Pius XI* (London, 1932)

The Pope Speaks: The Words of Pius XII (New York, 1940)

Principles for Peace: Selection from Papal Documents, Leo XIII to Pius XII,
    ed. Harry C. Koenig (Washington, DC, 1943)

'Provida Mater' e 'Primo feliciter' di Pio XII: validità ed attualità degli istituti
    secolari, ed. Nicola Giordano (Rome, 1997)

Records and Documents of the Holy See Relating to the Second World War:
    The Holy See and the War in Europe, ed. P. Blett et al., trans. Gerard Noel
    (Washington, DC, 1968)

Roncalli, Angelo, *La mia vita in Oriente: agendo del delegato apostolico*, vol. II:
    1940–1944 (Bologna, 2008)

——, *Scritti e discorsi, 1953–1958*, 4 vols (Rome, 1959–62)

Sale, Giovanni, *Hitler, la Santa Sede e gli ebrei: con documenti dell'Archivio
    Segreto Vaticano* (Milan, 2004)

Schaefer, Mary C., *A Papal Peace Mosaic, 1878–1936: Excerpts from the
    Messages of Popes Leo XIII, Pius X, Benedict XV and Pius XI* (Washington,
    DC, 1936)

Schneider, Burkhart, *Die Briefe Pius XII: an die deutschen Bischofe, 1939–1944*
    (Mainz, 1966)

Selected Documents of His Holiness Pope Pius XII, 1939–1958 (Washington,
    DC, n.d.)

Selected Papal Encyclicals and Letters, 1928–1931 (London, 1932)

Sonnino, Sidney, *Diario, 1914–1916* (Bari, 1972)

Tapia de Renedo, Benedicto, *Pio XII: ¿inocente o culpable? confrontacion de
    documentos secretos* (Madrid, 1972)

Tardini, Domenico, *Memories of Pius XII*, trans. Rosemary Goldie
    (Westminister, MD, 1961)

——, *Pio XII* (Vatican City, 1960)

Thierry, Jean Jacques, *Journal sans titre: sur les écrits de Pie XII* (Paris, 1970)

Tittmann, Harold H. III, ed., *Inside the Vatican of Pius XII: The Memoir of
    an American Diplomat during World War II* (New York, 2004)

*Tutte le encicliche e i principali documenti Pontifici emanati dal 1740: 250 anni
    di storia visti dalla Santa Sede*, vol. XI: *Pio XII, 1939–1958: parte prima,
    1939–1949*, ed. Ugo Bellocchi (Vatican City, 2004)

United States Department of State, *Papers Relating to the Foreign Relations
    of the United States: The World War* (Washington, DC, 1917–18)

Wartime Correspondence between President Roosevelt and Pope Pius XII,
    ed. Myron C. Taylor (New York, 1947)

Wiseman, Cardinal Nicholas Patrick, *Recollections of the Last Four Popes
    and of Rome in their Times* (New York, 1958)

Wynne, John J., ed., *The Great Encyclical Letters of Pope Leo XIII* (New York,
    1903)

Yzermans, Vincent A. ed., *All Things in Christ: Encyclicals and Selected
    Documents of Saint Pius X* (New York, 1954)

——, ed., *The Major Addresses of Pope Pius XII*, ed. V. Yzermans (St Paul, MN, 1961)

Zolli, Eugene, *Before the Dawn* (New York, 1954)

Secondary Sources

Aarons, Mark, and John Loftus, *Unholy Trinity: How the Vatican's Nazi Networks Betrayed Western Intelligence to the Soviets* (New York, 1991)

Alberigo, Giuseppe, 'Pio XII: uno sconosciuto', *Cristianesimo nella storia*, XXV (2004), pp. 987–94

Alcover Valle, Manuel, *Pio XII, el Papa de la paz* (Bilbao, 1959)

Allessandrini, Raffaele, 'Washington e Londra di fronte alla tragedia degli ebrei europei', *L'Osservatore Romano* (14 August 2009)

Alexander, Edgar, *Hitler and the Pope: Pius XII and the Jews* (New York, 1964)

——, 'Rolf Hochhuth: Equivocal Deputy', *America* (12 October 1963), pp. 416–18, 423

Alvarez, David, and Robert A. Graham, *Nothing Sacred: Nazi Espionage against the Vatican, 1939–1945* (London, 1997)

——, *Spies in the Vatican: Espionage and Intrigue from Napoleon to the Holocaust* (Lawrence, KS, 2002)

Anderson, Robin, *Between Two Wars: The Story of Pope Pius XI (Achille Ratti), 1922–1939* (Chicago, IL, 1977)

Andreotti, Giulio, *Pio XII* (Rome, 1965)

——, *Il Vaticano nella seconda guerra mondiale* (Milan, 1992)

Aradi, Zsolt, *Pius XI: The Pope and the Man* (Garden City, NY, 1958)

Arendt, Hannah, *Anti-Semitism* (New York, 1967)

Aretin, Karl Otmar von, *The Papacy and the Modern World*, trans. Roland Hill (New York, 1970)

Arlington, R. René, with Paul L. Murphy, *La popessa* (New York, 1983)

Aubert, Roger, et al., *The Church in a Secularized Society* (New York, 1978)

Balfour, R. E., 'The Action Française Movement', *Cambridge Historical Journal*, III/2 (1930), pp. 182–205

Bartlett, J. V., *The Popes: A Papal History* (Scottsdale, AZ, 1990)

Bayern, Konstantin von, *Papst Pius XII: ein Lebensbild* (Stein am Rhein, 1980)

Becker, Winfried, 'Diplomats and Missionaries: The Role played by German Embassies in Moscow and Rome in the Relations between Russia and the Vatican from 1921 to 1929', *Catholic Historical Review*, XCII/1 (January 2006), pp. 25–45

Bently, Eric, *The Storm over 'The Deputy'* (New York, 1964)

Berenbaum, Michael, *The World Must Know: The History of the Holocaust as Told in the United States Holocaust Memorial Museum* (Boston, MA, 1993)

——, ed., *Witness to the Holocaust* (New York, 1997)

Berliner, Abraham, *Storia degli ebrei di Roma* (Milan, 1992)

Bernabei, Domenico, *Orchestra nera: militari, civili, preti cattolici, pastori, una rete contro Hitler: che ruolo ebbe Pio XII?* (Turin, 1991)

Bertetto, D., *Pio XII e l'umana sofferenza* (Rome, 1960)

Besier, Gerhard, with Francesca Piombo, *The Holy See and Hitler's Germany*, trans. W. R. Ward (New York, 2007)

Besse, Jean Pierre, *Pie XII: le pape outragé, suivi de Bonne nuit, très saint Père: petite histoire anecdotique de ce livre* (Grez-en-Bouère, 1988)

Biffi, Monica, *Cesare Orsenigo, nunzio apostolico in Germania, 1930–1946* (Milan, 1997)

Binchy, D. A., *Church and State in Fascist Italy* (New York, 1941)

Bizzarri, Luigi, *Il principe di Dio: la vera storia di Pio XII* (Milan, 2004)

Borden, Sarah, *Edith Stein* (New York, 2003)

Bottum, Joseph, and David G. Dalin, eds, *The Pius War: Responses to the Critics of Pius XII* (New York, 2004)

Braham, Randolph, *The Politics of Genocide*, 2 vols (New York, 1981)

Brands, H. W., *The Devil We Knew: Americans and the Cold War* (New York, 1993)

Brechenmacher, Thomas, *Der Vatikan und die Juden* (Munich, 2005)

Brennan, Anthony, *Pope Benedict XV and the War* (London, 1917)

Bullock, Alan, *A Study in Tyranny* (New York, 1964)

Buonaiuti, Ernesto, *Pio XII* (Florence, 1958)

Burgellini, Piero, *Pius XII: The Angelic Shepherd* (New York, 1950)

Burton, Katherine, *The Great Mantle: The Life of Giuseppe Melchiore Sarto, Pope Pius X* (New York, 1950)

Callahan, William J., *The Catholic Church in Spain, 1875–1998* (Washington, DC, 2001)

Canepa, Andrew M., 'Pius X and the Jews: A Reappraisal', *Church History*, LXI/3 (1992), pp. 362–72

Carpi, Daniel, 'The Catholic Church and Italian Jewry under the Fascists', *Yad Vashem Studies,* IV (1960)

Carrillo, Elisa A., 'Italy, the Holy See and the United States, 1939–1945', in *Papal Diplomacy in the Modern Age*, ed. Peter Kent and John F. Pollard (Westport, CT, 1994), pp. 137–51

Castiglione, Luigi, *Pio XII e il nazismo* (Turin, 1965)

Casula, Carlo Felice, *Domenico Tardini (1888–1961): L'azione della Santa Sede nella crisi fra le due guerre* (Rome, 1988)

Chadwick, Owen, *A History of the Popes, 1830–1914* (Oxford, 1998)

——, *Britain and the Vatican during the Second World War* (Cambridge, 1986)

Charguéraud, Marc-André, *Les Papes, Hitler et la Shoah, 1932–1945* (Fribourg, 2002)

Chelini, Jean, *L'Eglise sous Pie XII* (Paris, 1983)

Chenaux, Philippe, *Pie XII: diplomate et pasteur* (Paris, 2003)

Clarke, Duncan L., and Eric Flohr, 'Christian Churches and the Palestinian

Question', *Journal of Palestine Studies*, xxi/4 (Summer 1992), pp. 67–79

Clonmore, Lord, *Pope Pius xi and World Peace* (New York, 1938)

Conway, John S., 'Myron C. Tayor's Mission to the Vatican', *Church History*, xliv/1 (March 1975), pp. 85–99

——, 'The Meeting between Pope Pius xii and Ribbentrop', *Historical Papers of the Canadian Historical Association* (1968), pp. 215–27

——, *The Nazi Persecution of the Churches, 1933–1945* (London, 1968)

——, 'The Silence of Pope Pius xii', *Review of Politics*, xxvii/1 (January 1965), pp. 105–31

——, 'The Vatican, Britain and Relations with Germany, 1938–1949', *Historical Journal*, xvi (1973), pp. 147–67

——, 'The Vatican, Germany and the Holocaust', in *Papal Diplomacy in the Modern Age*, ed. Peter Kent and John F. Pollard (Westport, CT, 1994), pp. 105–20

——, 'The Vatican and the Holocaust: A Reappraisal', *Miscellanea Historiae Ecclesiasticae*, ix (1984), pp. 475–89

Conway, Martin, *Catholic Politics in Europe, 1918–1945* (London, 1997)

Coppa, Frank J., 'Between Morality and Diplomacy: The Vatican's "Silence" during the Holocaust', *Journal of Church and State*, l (Summer 2008), pp. 541–68

——, ed., *Controversial Concordats: The Vatican's Relations with Napoleon, Mussolini and Hitler* (Washington, DC, 1999)

——, 'Pius xii: Between History and Controversy', *Journal of Modern Italian Studies*, vii (Summer 2002), pp. 261–6

——, 'Pius xii's Cautious Diplomacy', *The Tablet* [Brooklyn] (27 February 2010), p. 25

——, *Politics and the Papacy in the Modern World* (Westport, CT, 2008)

——, 'Pope Pius xi's "Encyclical" *Humani Generis Unitas* against Racism and Anti-Semitism and the "Silence" of Pope Pius xii', *Journal of Church and State*, xl/4 (Autumn 1998), pp. 775–95

——, 'Pope Pius xii and the Cold War: The Post-War Confrontation between Catholicism and Communism', in *Religion and the Cold War*, ed. Dianne Kirby (London, 2003), pp. 50–66

——, 'The Hidden Encyclical of Pius xi against Racism and Anti-Semitism Uncovered – Once Again!', *Catholic Historical Review*, lxxxiv/1 (January 1998), pp. 63–72

——, *The Modern Papacy since 1789* [Longman History of the Papacy] (London and New York, 1998)

——, *The Papacy, the Jews and the Holocaust* (Washington, DC, 2006)

——, 'The Vatican and the Dictators between Diplomacy and Morality', in *Catholics, the State and the European Radical Right*, ed. Richard J. Wolff and Jorg K. Hoensch (New York, 1987), pp. 199–223

Cornwell, John, *Hitler's Pope: The Secret History of Pius xii* (New York, 1999)

Coverdale, John F., *Italian Intervention in the Spanish Civil War* (Princeton, NJ, 1975)

Delzell, Charles, 'Pius XII, Italy and the Outbreak of War', *Journal of Contemporary History*, II/4 (October 1967), pp. 137–61

Dietrich, Donald J., 'Catholic Resistance in the Third Reich', *Holocaust and Genocide Studies*, III/2 (1988), pp. 171–86

Donadio, Rachel, 'At Rome Synagogue, Pope Tries to Sooth Tensions with Jews', *New York Times* (18 January 2010), p. A7

Doyle, Charles Hugo, *The Life of Pope Pius XII* (New York, 1945)

Duffy, Eamon, *Saints and Sinners: A History of the Popes* (New Haven, CT, 1997)

Esposito Rosario F., *Processo al Vicario: Pio XII e gli ebrei secondo la testimonianza della storia* (Turin, 1964)

Falconi, Carlo, *The Silence of Pius XII*, trans. Bernard Wall (Boston, MA, 1970)

Fattorini, Emma, *Germania e Santa Sede: La Nunziature di Pacelli tra la Grande Guerra e la Repubblica di Weimar* [Annali dell' Istituto storico italo-germanico] (Bologna, 1992)

——, *Pio XI, Hitler e Mussolini: la solitudine di un papa* (Turin, 2007)

——, 'Santa Sede e Germania alla vigilia della seconda guerra mondiale', *Dimensioni e problemi della ricerca storica*, I (1990), pp. 99–117

Favara, Fedele, *De iure naturali in doctrina Pii Papae XII* (Rome, 1966)

Feis, Herbert, *From Trust to Terror: The Onset of the Cold War, 1945–1950* (New York, 1970)

Fiorentino, Carlo M., *All'Ombra di Pietro: La Chiesa Cattolica e lo spionaggio fascista in Vaticano, 1929–1939* (Florence, 1999)

Fogarty, Gerald, SJ, 'The United States and the Vatican', in *Papal Diplomacy in the Modern Age*, ed. Peter Kent and John F. Pollard (Westport, CT, 1994), pp. 221–43

Fontenelle, René, and Mary Elizabeth Fowler, *His Holiness Pope Pius XI* (London, 1939)

Friedländer, Saul, *Nazi Germany and the Jews*, vol. I: *The Years of Persecution, 1933–1939* (New York, 1997)

Gallagher, Charles R., SJ, *Vatican Secret Diplomacy: Joseph P. Hurley and Pope Pius XII* (New Haven, CT, 2008)

Gallo, Patrick J., ed., *Pius XII, the Holocaust and the Revisionists* (Jefferson, NC, 2006)

Garzia, Italo, 'Pope Pius XII, Italy and the Second World War', in *Papal Diplomacy in the Modern Age*, ed. Peter Kent and John F. Pollard (Westport, CT, 1994), pp. 121–36

Gasbarri Carlo, *Quando il Vaticano confinava con il Terzo Reich* (Padua, 1984)

Gaspari, Antonio, *Gli ebrei salvato da Pio XII* (Rome, 2001)

Gilbert, Martin, *The Holocaust: A History of the Jews of Europe during the Second World War* (New York, 1987)

——, *The Righteous: The Unsung Heroes of the Holocaust* (New York, 2001)

Giordani, Igino, *Pio XII: un grande papa* (Turin, 1961)

——, *Roma città aperta* (Milan, 1962)

Goldhagen, Daniel Jonah, *A Moral Reckoning: The Role of the Catholic Church in the Holocaust and its Unfulfilled Duty of Repair* (New York, 2003)

——, 'What Would Jesus Have Done?', *New Republic* (January 2002), pp. 21–45

Godman, Peter, *Hitler and the Vatican: Inside the Secret Archives that Reveal the New Story of the Nazis and the Church* (New York, 2004)

Gotto, Klaus, and Konrad Repgen, *Die Katholiken und das Dritte Reich* (Mainz, 1990)

Graham, Robert A., and David Alvarez, *Nothing Sacred: Nazi Espionage against the Vatican, 1939–1945* (London, 1997)

——, *Vatican Diplomacy: A Study of Church and State on the International Plane* (Princeton, 1959)

Gurian, Waldemar, 'Hitler's Undeclared War on the Catholic Church', *Foreign Affairs*, VI (January 1938), pp. 260–71

Halecki, Oscar, *Eugenio Pacelli: Pope of Peace* (New York, 1951)

Hales, E.E.Y., *The Catholic Church in the Modern World* (Garden City, NY, 1958)

Handren, Walter J., *Pius XI* (Westminster, MD, 1955)

Harrigan, Wiliam M., 'Pius XII's Efforts to Effect a Détente in German–Vatican Relations, 1939–1940', *Catholic Historical Review*, XLIX (July 1963), pp. 173–91

Hatch, Alden, and Seamus Walshe, *Crown of Glory: The Life of Pope Pius XII* (New York, 1957)

Hearley, John, *Pope or Mussolini* (New York, 1929)

Hecht, Robert A., *An Unordinary Man: A Life of Father John LaFarge, SJ* (Lanham, MD, 1996)

Helmreich, Ernst C., *The German Churches under Hitler* (Detroit, MI, 1979)

Herber, Charles J., 'Eugenio Pacelli's Mission to Germany and the Papal Peace Proposals of 1917', *Catholic Historical Review*, XLV/1 (January 1979), pp. 20–48

Hilberg, Raul, *The Destruction of the European Jews* (Chicago, IL, 1961)

Hochhuth, Rolf, *The Deputy* (New York, 1964)

Holmes, J. Derek, *The Papacy in the Modern World, 1914–1978* (New York, 1981)

Hughes, John Jay, 'The Pope's Pact with Hitler: Betrayal or Self-defense?', *Journal of Church and State*, XVII (Winter 1975), pp. 63–80

Hughes, Philip, *Pope Pius the Eleventh* (New York, 1938)

Hürten, Heinz, *Pius XII und die Juden* (Cologne, 2000)

Innocenti, Ennio, *Presenza di Pio XII* (Rome, 1967)

Katz, Robert, *Death in Rome* (Cambidge, 1967)

——, *The Battle for Rome: The Germans, the Allies, the Partisans and the Pope* (New York, 2003)

Keeler, Bob, 'The Church and the Holocaust', *Newsday* (15 October 1997), pp. 5–6, 12

Kent, George O., 'Pope Pius XII and Germany: Some Aspects of German–
Vatican Relations, 1933–1943', *American Historical Review*, LXX
(October 1964), pp. 59–78

Kent, Peter C., 'A Tale of Two Popes: Pius XII and the Rome–Berlin Axis',
Journal of Contemporary History, XXIII/4 (October 1988), pp. 589–608

——, *The Pope and the Duce* (New York, 1981)

Kershner, Isabel, 'Unusual Partners Study Divisive Jerusalem', *New York Times*
(15 November 2009), p. 8

Kertzer, David I., *The Pope against the Jews* (New York, 2001)

Kirby, Dianne, *Religion in the Cold War* (New York, 2003)

Klein, Charles, *Pie XII face au Nazis* (Paris, 1975)

Kreutz, Anrej, 'The Vatican and the Palestinians: A Historical Overview',
in *Papal Diplomacy in the Modern Age*, ed. Peter Kent and John F. Pollard
(Westport, CT, 1994), pp. 167–79

Kurzman, Dan, *Hitler's Secret Plot to Seize the Vatican and Kidnap Pope Pius
XII* (New York, 2008)

Lannon, Frances, *Privilege, Persecution and Prophecy: The Catholic Church in
Spain* (Oxford, 1987)

Lapide, Pinchas E., *Roma e gli ebrei: l'azione del Vaticano a favore delle vittime
del Nazismo* (Milan, 1967)

Lapomarda, Vincent, *The Jesuits and the Third Reich* (Lewison, NY, 1989)

Lavi, Theodore, 'The Vatican's Endeavors on Behalf of Rumanian Jewry
during World War II', *Yad Vashem Studies*, V (1963), pp. 405–18

Lawler, Justus George, *Popes and Politics* (New York, 2002)

Lazarus, Joyce Block, *In the Shadow of Vichy: The Final Affair* (New York,
2008)

Levai, Jeno, *Hungarian Jewry and the Papacy* (London, 1967)

Lewy, Guenter, 'Pius XII, the Jews and the German Catholic Church',
Commentary, XXXVII (February 1964), pp. 23–33

——, *The Catholic Church and Nazi Germany* (New York, 1965)

Littell, Franklin H., '*Kirchenkampf* and Holocaust: The German Church
Struggle and Nazi Anti-Semitism in Retrospect', *Journal of Church and
State*, XIII/1 (Winter 1971), pp. 209–26

Low, Alfred D., *The Anschluss Movement, 1931–1938, and the Great Powers*
(Boulder, CO, 1985)

Lukacs, John, 'The Diplomacy of the Holy See during World War II', *Catholic
Historical Review*, LX (July 1974), pp. 271–8

McDermott, Thomas, *Keeper of the Keys: A Life of Pope Pius XII* (Milwaukee,
WI, 1946)

McInerny, Ralph, *The Defamation of Pope Pius XII* (South Bend, IN, 2001)

Manhattan, Avro, *The Vatican in World Politics* (New York, 1949)

Marchione, Sister Margherita, *Consensus and Controversy: Defending
Pope Pius XII* (New York, 2002)

——, *Crusade of Charity: Pius XII and POWs, 1939–1945* (New York, 2006)

——, *Did Pope Pius XII Help the Jews?* (Malwah, NJ, 2007)

——, *Man of Peace: Pope Pius XII* (Malwah, NJ, 2003)

——, *Pope Pius XII: Architect for Peace* (New York, 2000)

Marrus, Michael R., 'The History of the Holocaust: A Survey of Recent Literature', *Journal of Modern History*, LIX/1 (March 1987), pp. 114–60

Martini, Angelo, 'L'ultima battaglia di Pio XI', in *Studi sulla questione romano e la conciliazione*, ed. A. Martini (Rome, 1963), pp. 175–230

Mazzolari, Primo, *La Chiesa, il fascismo e la Guerra* (Florence, 1966)

Micklem, Nathaniel, *National Socialism and the Roman Catholic Church* (London, 1939)

Milkowski, Tadeusz, 'The Spanish Church and the Vatican during the Spanish Civil War', *Polish Foreign Affairs Digest*, III (2004), pp. 207–42

Mondin, Battista, *The Popes of the Modern Ages: From Pius IX to John Paul II* (Rome, 2004)

Morley, John F., *Vatican Diplomacy and the Jews During the Holocaust, 1939–1943* (New York, 1980)

Moro, Renato, *La Chiesa e lo sterminio degli ebrei* (Bologna, 2002)

Naughton, James, *Pius XII on World Problems* (New York, 1943)

Nichols, Peter, *The Politics of the Vatican* (New York, 1968)

Noel, Gerard, *Pius XII: The Hound of Hitler* (New York, 2008)

O'Carroll, Micheal, *Pius XII, Greatness Dishonoured: A Documented Study* (Dublin, 1980)

Olf, Lillian Browne, *Their Name is Pius: Portraits of Five Great Modern Popes* (Milwaukee, WI, 1941)

O'Shea, Paul, *A Cross too Heavy: Eugenio Pacelli and the Jews of Europe, 1917–1923* (Kenthurst, NSW, 2008)

Padellaro, Nazareno, *Portrait of Pius XII*, trans. Michael Derrick (New York, 1957)

Payne, Stanley, 'Fascist Italy and Spain, 1922–1945', *Mediterranean Historical Review*, XIII/1 (June–December 1998), pp. 99–115

——, *The Franco Regime, 1936–1975* (Madison, WI, 1987)

Persico, A. A., *Mezzo secolo di dibattito su Eugenio Pacelli* (Milan, 2008)

Peters, Walter H., *The Life of Benedict XV* (Milwaukee, WI, 1959)

Pfister, Pierre, *Pius XII: The Life and Work of a Great Pope* (New York, 1954)

Phayer, Michael, *Pius XII: The Holocaust and the Cold War* (Bloomington, IN, 2008)

——, *The Catholic Church and the Holocaust* (Bloomington, IN, 2000)

Pichon, Charles, *The Vatican and its Role in World Affairs*, trans. Jean Misrahi (Westport, CT, 1950)

Pollard, John F., *Money and the Rise of the Modern Papacy: Financing the Vatican, 1850–1950* (Cambridge, 2005)

——, *The Unknown Pope: Benedict XV (1914–1922) and the Pursuit of Peace* (London and New York, 1999)

Pope Pius XII and the Holocaust, ed. Carol Ann Rittner and John K. Roth (New York, 2002)

Portier, William L., *Isaac Hecker and the First Vatican Council* (New York, 1985)

Pulzer, P. G., *The Rise of Political Anti-Semitism in Germany and Austria* (New York, 1964)

Purdy, William Arthur, *The Church on the Move: The Characters and Politics of Pius XII and Johannes XXIII* (London, 1966)

Raguer Suñer, Hilario M., *Gunpowder and Incense: The Catholic Church and the Spanish Civil War* (London, 2007)

Randall, Alec, *The Pope, the Jews and the Nazis* (London, 1963)

Rhodes, Anthony, *The Vatican in the Age of Dictators, 1922–1945* (New York, 1973)

Riccardi, Andrea, *Il Vaticano e Mosca, 1940–1990* (Bari, 1992)

——, ed., *Pio XII* (Bari, 1985)

——, *L'inverno più lungo, 1943–1944* (Bari, 2008)

Rittner, Carol, and John K. Roth, eds, *Pope Pius XII and the Holocaust* (London, 2002)

Rocach, Livia, *The Catholic Church and the Question of Palestine* (London, 1987)

Royal, Robet, ed., *Jacques Maritain and the Jews* (Notre Dame, IN, 1994)

Rychlak, Ronald J., *Hitler, the War and the Pope* (Huntington, IN, 2000)

Sale, Giovanni, 'The First Anti-Jewish Measures and the Declaration of the Fascist Grand Council', *La Civiltà Cattolica* (20 September 2008)

Sánchez, José M., *Pius XII and the Holocaust: Understanding the Controversy* (Washington, DC, 2002)

——, 'The Popes and Nazi Germany: The View from Madrid', *Journal of Church and State*, XXXVIII (Spring 1996), pp. 365–76

——, *The Spanish Civil War as a Religious Tragedy* (Notre Dame, IN, 1987)

Smit, Jan Olav, *Angelic Shepherd: The Life of Pope Pius XII* (New York, 1950)

Spicer, Kevin P., *Hitler's Priests: Catholic Clergy and National Socialism* (De Kalb, IL, 2008)

Stehle, Hansjakob, *Eastern Politics of the Vatican* (Athens, OH, 1981)

Sullivan, Brian R., 'Fascist Italy's Military Involvement in the Spanish Civil War', *Journal of Military History*, LIX (October 1995), pp. 697–727

Tavard, George H., 'American Contributions to Vatican II's Documents on Ecumenism and Religious Liberty', *Chicago Studies*, XLII/1 (Spring 2003), pp. 17–30

Teeling, William, *Pope Pius XI and World Affairs* (New York, 1937)

Tinnenmann, Ethel Mary, SNJM, 'The Silence of Pius XII', *Journal of Church and State*, XXI/2 (Spring 1979), pp. 265–85

Tornielli, Andrea, *Pio XII: il papa degli ebrei* (Casale Monferrato, 2001)

Townsend, W., and L. Townsend, *The Biography of His Holiness Pope Pius XI* (London, 1930)

Trevelyan, Raleigh, *Rome '44: The Battle for the Eternal City* (London, 1981)

Veneruso, Danilo, *Pio XII e la seconda guerra mondiale* (Rome, 1969)

Vian, Giovanni Maria, 'Il silenzio di Pio XII: alle origini della leggenda nera', *Archivum Historiae Pontificiae*, XLII (2004), pp. 223–9

Villa, Luigi, *Pio XII, papa calunniato e scomodo: nel XX anniversario della sua morte, 1958–9 ottobre 1978* (Brescia, 1979)

Vitello, Paul, 'Wartime Pope Has a Huge Fan: A Jewish Knight', *New York Times* (8 March 2010), pp. 1, 3

Walker, Reginald, *Pius of Peace: A Study of the Pacific Work of His Holiness Pope Pius XII in the World War, 1939–1945* (Dublin, 1945)

Walsh, Henry H., *The Concordat of 1801: A Study of the Problem of Nationalism in the Relations of Church and State* (New York, 1967)

Whealey, Robert H., *Hitler and Spain: The Nazi Role in the Spanish Civil War* (Lexington, KY, 1989)

Wheeler Bennet, John W., *Il patto di Monaco: prologo della tragedia*, Italian trans. Giuseppina Panzieri (Milan, 1968)

Williams, Paul L., *The Vatican Exposed: Money, Murder and the Mafia* (Amherst, NY, 2003)

Williamson, Benedict, *The Story of Pope Pius XI* (New York, 1931)

Wills, Gary, *Papal Sin: Structures of Deceit* (New York, 2000)

Wistrich, Robert S., *Hitler and the Holocaust* (New York, 2001)

Wolf, Hubert, *Pope and Devil: The Vatican's Archives and the Third Reich*, trans. Kenneth Kronenberg (Boston, MA, 2010)

Wolff, Richard J., and Jörg K. Hoensch, eds, *Catholics, the State and the European Radical Right, 1919–1945* (Boulder, CO, 1987)

Wyman, David S., *The Abandonment of the Jews: America and the Holocaust, 1941–1945* (New York, 1984)

Zahn, Gordon C., *German Catholics and Hitler's War* (London and New York, 1963)

Zuccotti, Susan, *The Italians and the Holocaust: Persecution, Rescue and Survival* (New York, 1987)

——, *Under his Very Windows: The Vatican and the Holocaust in Italy* (New Haven, CT, 2000)

INDEX